# Land Subdivision Regulation in North Carolina

2015

Adam S. Lovelady

**UNC** | SCHOOL OF GOVERNMENT

The School of Government at the University of North Carolina at Chapel Hill works to improve the lives of North Carolinians by engaging in practical scholarship that helps public officials and citizens understand and improve state and local government. Established in 1931 as the Institute of Government, the School provides educational, advisory, and research services for state and local governments. The School of Government is also home to a nationally ranked graduate program in public administration and specialized centers focused on information technology and environmental finance.

As the largest university-based local government training, advisory, and research organization in the United States, the School of Government offers up to 200 courses, webinars, and specialized conferences for more than 12,000 public officials each year. In addition, faculty members annually publish approximately 50 books, manuals, reports, articles, bulletins, and other print and online content related to state and local government. Each day that the General Assembly is in session, the School produces the *Daily Bulletin Online*, which reports on the day's activities for members of the legislature and others who need to follow the course of legislation.

The Master of Public Administration Program is offered in two formats. The full-time, two-year residential program serves up to 60 students annually. In 2013 the School launched MPA@UNC, an online format designed for working professionals and others seeking flexibility while advancing their careers in public service. The School's MPA program consistently ranks among the best public administration graduate programs in the country, particularly in city management. With courses ranging from public policy analysis to ethics and management, the program educates leaders for local, state, and federal governments and nonprofit organizations.

Operating support for the School of Government's programs and activities comes from many sources, including state appropriations, local government membership dues, private contributions, publication sales, course fees, and service contracts. Visit www.sog.unc.edu or call 919.966.5381 for more information on the School's courses, publications, programs, and services.

Michael R. Smith, Dean
Thomas H. Thornburg, Senior Associate Dean
Frayda S. Bluestein, Associate Dean for Faculty Development
Bradley G. Volk, Associate Dean for Administration

FACULTY

| | | |
|---|---|---|
| Whitney Afonso | Cheryl Daniels Howell | LaToya B. Powell |
| Trey Allen | Jeffrey A. Hughes | William C. Rivenbark |
| Gregory S. Allison | Willow S. Jacobson | Dale J. Roenigk |
| David N. Ammons | Robert P. Joyce | John Rubin |
| Ann M. Anderson | Diane M. Juffras | Jessica Smith |
| Maureen Berner | Dona G. Lewandowski | Meredith Smith |
| Mark F. Botts | Adam Lovelady | Carl W. Stenberg III |
| Michael Crowell | James M. Markham | John B. Stephens |
| Leisha DeHart-Davis | Christopher B. McLaughlin | Charles Szypszak |
| Shea Riggsbee Denning | Kara A. Millonzi | Shannon H. Tufts |
| Sara DePasquale | Jill D. Moore | Vaughn Mamlin Upshaw |
| James C. Drennan | Jonathan Q. Morgan | Aimee N. Wall |
| Richard D. Ducker | Ricardo S. Morse | Jeffrey B. Welty |
| Joseph S. Ferrell | C. Tyler Mulligan | Richard B. Whisnant |
| Alyson A. Grine | Kimberly L. Nelson | |
| Norma Houston | David W. Owens | |

Printed in the United States of America

21 02 19 18 17   3 4 5 6 7

ISBN 978-1-56011-841-1

# Contents

Chapter 3

# Defining Subdivision................................................................................. 19

Chapter 4

# Nature of Subdivision Review.................................................................. 27

Chapter 5

# Typical Steps of Subdivision Review....................................................... 39

## Chapter 6

# Subdivision Design and Improvements

## Chapter 7

# Subdivision Design Concepts

## Chapter 8

# Exaction Authority and Limits

## Chapter 9

# Enforcement

Chapter 10

# Preface

This book is a resource for understanding the legal framework and practical applications of land subdivision regulation in North Carolina. The primary audience includes subdivision ordinance administrators, city and county planners, attorneys, and other public and private professionals involved in land subdivision throughout the state. Not intended as a pure legal reference, it nonetheless includes substantial citations and case summaries to assist with legal issues. Cases decided and legislation enacted are current as of September 30, 2015. For updates, check the School of Government's Planning and Development Regulation website at sog.unc.edu/resources/microsites/planning-and-development-regulation and the Coates' Canons NC Local Government Law Blog at canons.sog.unc.edu.

My work benefits from and builds upon the tradition of practical scholarship on land subdivision established by faculty members at the School of Government (formerly Institute of Government). Dating back at least to the 1950s, publications have included Warren Jake Wicker's *Subdivision Improvement Requirements and Assessment and Utility Extension Policies in Seventeen North Carolina Towns with Populations of 2,500 to 10,000* (1957), Robert E. Stipe's *An Introduction to Subdivision Regulations* (1965, 1968), Philip P. Green Jr.'s *Regulating the Subdivision of Land* (1968), Richard D. Ducker's *Subdivision Regulations in North Carolina: An Introduction* (1980), David M. Lawrence's *Property Interests in North Carolina City Streets* (1985), William A. Campbell's *Guidebook for North Carolina Property Mappers* (2001), and David W. Owens's *Land Use Law in North Carolina* (2011) as well as a variety of other resources and publications related to land subdivision.

This book benefits greatly from research support provided by Alex Hess and Frank Alford in the Knapp Library of the UNC School of Government; editing and layout support from Katrina Hunt, Daniel Soileau, Lisa Wright, and Leslie Watkins in the School's publications department; and review and critiques from my School of Government colleagues, especially Richard Ducker, Kara Millonzi, David Owens, and Chuck Szypszak. Last, but certainly not least, endless thanks go to Tracy, Carter, Ben, and Andrew for their patience, encouragement, and regular reminders to play.

Adam S. Lovelady
Fall 2015

Chapter 1

# Introduction

## Purposes of Subdivision Regulation

Think about a farm on the edge of town. Today it is pasture and trees, but it sits along a major thoroughfare and right in the path of growth. Soon bulldozers will begin to cut the hills and level the ground for a new development. When new homes sprout in the place of crops, the community faces inevitable questions: Is the infrastructure adequate? Does the neighborhood design align with existing development? What amenities will the neighborhood need? Who will pay for the improvements now and who will maintain the neighborhood into the future? Subdivision regulations address these questions by seeking to strike a balance between private interests and community interests.

Land subdivision is the process of dividing a tract of land into smaller parcels. Commonly a subdivision starts with raw land that is divided into streets and lots for residential development. But subdivisions are not limited to residential development; a subdivision may occur for the sale of downtown property, site planning for commercial development, or establishment of an industrial park. According to the statutory definition, a subdivision is a division of land related to sale *or* development (or both), and that sale or development may take place immediately or be set for some time in the future.

That process may be regulated at the local level for several important reasons: to protect public health, to establish clear parcels and property rights, to ensure adequate infrastructure, and to facilitate orderly growth.

## Public Health and Safety

The foundations of subdivision regulation are rooted in basic public health and safety. The North Carolina General Statutes (hereinafter G.S.) note that, among other things, subdivision regulation is "for the distribution of population and traffic in a manner that will avoid congestion and overcrowding and will create conditions that substantially promote public health, safety, and the general welfare."[1] Subdivision regulations address infrastructure and safety, hand-in-hand, through road standards and traffic safety, clean water supply, septic or sewer performance, and stormwater management and protection of sensitive natural areas.

---

1. G.S. 153A-331(a) (counties); G.S. 160A-372(a) (cities and towns).

## Land Records and Sales

Land subdivision regulation facilitates good property records for the benefit of community, the seller, and the purchaser. An essential element of subdivision regulation is the submission, approval, and legal recording of carefully executed survey maps, called plats, to delineate parcel boundaries, easements and rights-of-way, and specific improvements.[2] The plat supplements and clarifies a deed's description of the property.

In addition, creating easements and dedicating rights-of-way is substantially easier when one owner holds the property. Subdivision regulation ensures that those necessary easements and rights-of-way are established in conjunction with dividing the land.

An average purchaser may lack the expertise to evaluate such technical qualities as waterline size, the road construction standards, or the suitability for installing a septic system. Established standards for subdivision improvements provide a community baseline from which to inform and protect future purchasers. The subdivision review process both enables the purchaser to take ownership of a clearly bounded piece of property with general assurance of adequate infrastructure and services and certifies the property lines and title of the property for future sales.

## Provision of Adequate Infrastructure

Subdivision regulation is crafted to ensure that adequate infrastructure and services—water, sewer, roads, and others—accompany the division of land and that the developer or owner shares in the cost of such increased capacity. The subdivision review process includes inspection to make sure improvements are properly constructed and to avoid undue maintenance costs in the future.

## Orderly Growth

Subdivision has long-term and significant impacts on the community, and a primary purpose for subdivision regulation is to encourage good land-planning practices. As stated simply in the enabling statutes, a "subdivision control ordinance may provide for the orderly growth and development of the city."[3] A community may set forth lot characteristics, establish roadway design standards, and coordinate adjoining developments as it deems appropriate.

While serving other important purposes, in both the short and long term, subdivision regulation nonetheless impedes the free use and transfer of private property. Local governments must therefore ensure that these regulations are justified, effective, and equitable. Toward that end, local governments must work within the state and federal legal framework, apply regulations to achieve legitimate purposes, establish and share clear policies and procedures, and ensure competent, timely, and equitable review of applications.

---

2. G.S. 153A-331(b); G.S. 160A-372(b).
3. G.S. 153A-331(a); G.S. 160A-372(a).

## A Decision for Generations

Consider the following example. A developer purchased land in Wake County, North Carolina. The developer hired a surveyor to plat out a new community on the four hundred–acre tract. The plan for subdivision established a grid of public streets; larger thoroughfares were ninety-nine feet wide while regular streets were sixty-six feet wide. The design included four 4-acre parks and one 6-acre park, each reserved for the public. The plan envisioned mixed-use development over a long-term build-out. One-acre lots were to be sold for private development with the proceeds to fund public improvements.[4]

That developer was the State of North Carolina, and that subdivision brought the City of Raleigh into existence for the purpose of establishing it as the state's new capital in 1792. Comparing the original plan with contemporary images of Raleigh (shown on the next pages), one can see the lasting legacy of subdivision decisions. The street grid remains, most of the parks remain, and the subdivided blocks of land remain. Once streets and lots are developed, the pattern of development is set because only rarely are streets relocated, lots aggregated, and parcel lines redrawn. Buildings come and go, but land subdivision remains etched into the landscape for generations.

## History of Subdivision Regulation

Land planning and subdivision regulation have long effects and have long been in effect. Well before the streets of Raleigh were platted, early-eighteenth-century charters for colonial towns in North Carolina set standards for dividing property and setting off public rights-of-way. The 1715 charter for the town Bath called for laying out half-acre lots and convenient streets. The 1723 charter for Beaufort called for streets at least sixty-six feet wide.[5]

In modern times, commentators describe several periods of subdivision regulation, each emphasizing, in turn, property records; orderly growth through the establishment of subdivision regulation; provision of infrastructure; and control of growth.[6] To be sure, these periods of subdivision regulation are not separate and distinct. They fold, one into the other,

---

4. "Plan for Raleigh," North Carolina Digital Collections, http://digital.ncdcr.gov/cdm/ref/collection/p249901coll26/id/2802 (accessed July 5, 2015); Ken Peters, "City of Raleigh," *North Carolina History Project*, www.northcarolinahistory.org/encyclopedia/13/entry (accessed July 5, 2015).

5. Laws of North Carolina, 1715, ch. 52 (Colonial and State Records of North Carolina, vol. 23, p. 73), http://docsouth.unc.edu/csr/index.html/document/csr23-0001; Laws of North Carolina, 1723, ch. 15 (Colonial and State Records of North Carolina, vol. 25, pp. 206–07), http://docsouth.unc.edu/csr/index.html/document/csr25-0015; *see* Philip P. Green Jr., Regulating the Subdivision of Land at 2 (1968).

6. Robert H. Freilich & S. Mark White, with Kate F. Murray, 21st Century Land Development Code 5–8 (2008) (The first period of subdivision regulation, which took place during the early twentieth century, focused on land records, thereby allowing a developer to record plats and sell lots in reference to that plat. The second period began in the 1920s, when focus turned to the orderly growth of urban areas. In 1928, U.S. Department of Commerce published A Standard State Zoning Enabling Act, which sought authority for cities to enact subdivision regulation to address street arrangement, avoid congestion, and implement a master plan. The third period addressed the provision of facilities and infrastructure within a subdivision. Finally, in the most recent period, subdivision regulation has become a tool for growth management and control.)

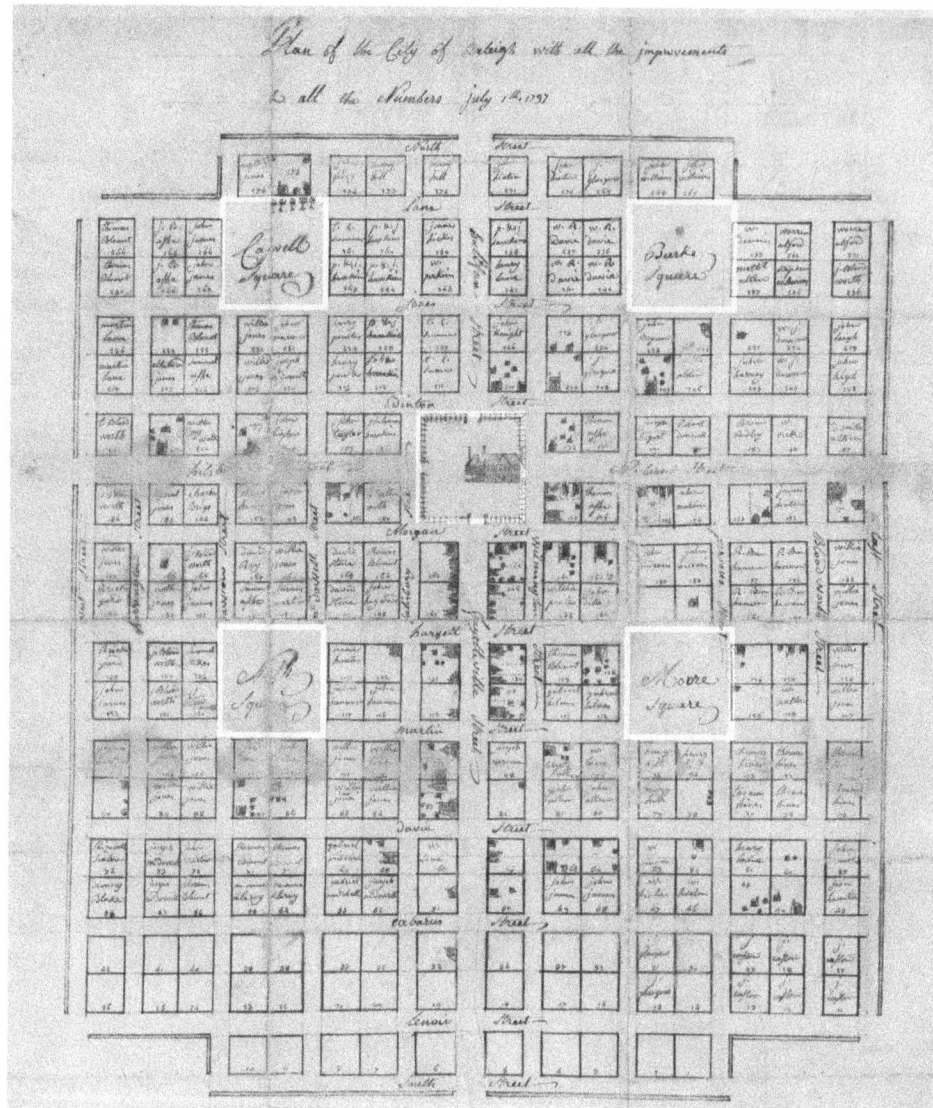

**Historic Plan for Raleigh.** The white squares added to the above illustration correspond to those added to the aerial photograph on the facing page.

so that today's subdivision regulations aim to achieve multiple governmental interests. The history of state subdivision regulation reflects similar interests.

Subdivision regulation in North Carolina dates back to 1929, when the General Assembly first granted that authority to municipalities.[7] The initial grant of power required that a map outlining the proposed streets and sidewalks of a subdivision be approved by the local government before that land could be subdivided. After the map was approved, it was required to become part of the records of the county. This initial authority applied to land within the municipal corporate limits and extended to lands within one mile of the corporate limit.

In 1955, the General Assembly granted municipalities more specific authority to regulate land subdivision. This legislation established the basic authority of contemporary subdivision regulation, including definition (and exemptions), plat approval and recordation, penalties

7. 1929 N.C. Sess. Laws ch. 186.

**Modern Raleigh from Google Earth.** The streets, blocks, and open spaces established more than two centuries ago remain the basic structure of modern-day downtown Raleigh. The impacts of subdivision decisions last for generations.

for enforcement, standards for subdivision development and improvements. The new law authorized adoption of a local subdivision ordinance with set standards for the

> orderly development of the municipality and its environs; for the coordination of streets within proposed subdivisions with existing or planned streets or with other public facilities; for the dedication or reservation of rights of way or easements for street and utility purposes; and for the distribution of population and traffic which shall avoid congestion and overcrowding, and which shall create conditions essential to public health, safety and general welfare.[8]

Many rural counties and the municipalities within those counties were exempted.

---

8. 1955 N.C. Sess. Laws ch. 1334; *see also,* Philip P. Green Jr., *Legislation of Interest to Municipal Officials,* POPULAR GOV'T, June 1955, at 15.

## Figure 1.1    Subdivision ordinances by county

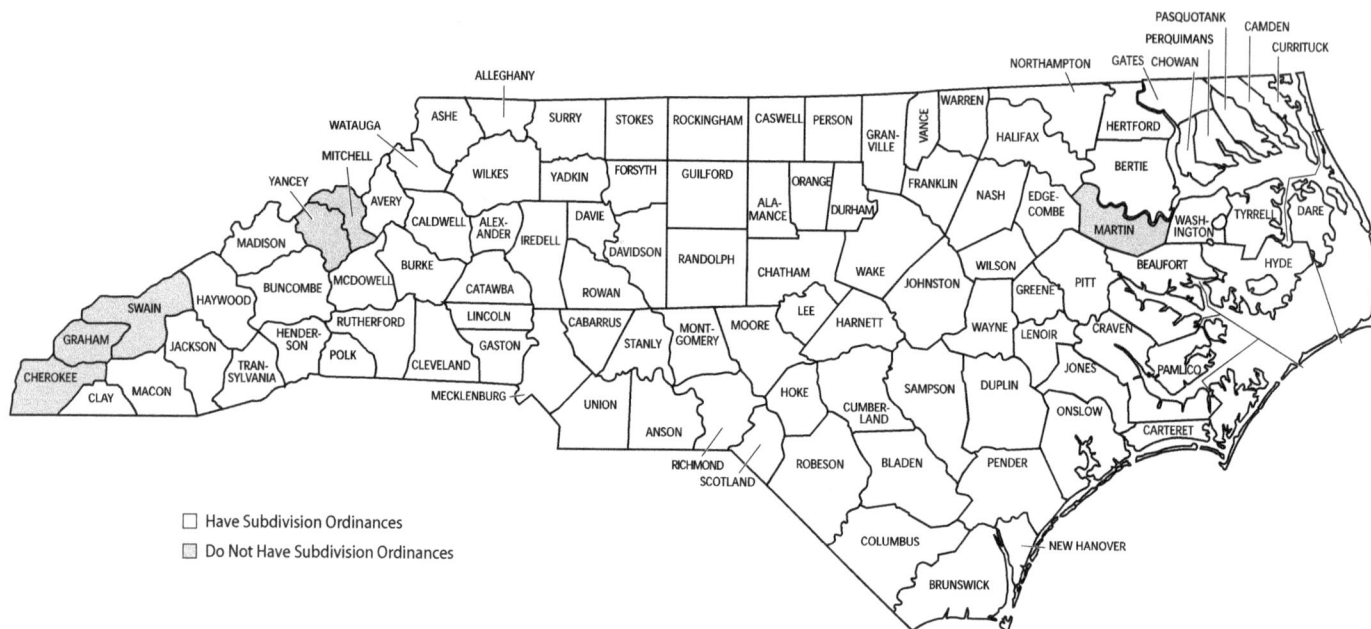

☐ Have Subdivision Ordinances
☐ Do Not Have Subdivision Ordinances

Counties gained the authority for subdivision regulation in 1959.[9] County authority closely followed that of existing municipal authority.

In 1961, legislation authorized cities to require "community service facilities," such as roads, water and sewer infrastructure, parks, and other improvements, and to require a developer to post a bond to ensure completion of required improvements.[10] By 1966, the vast majority of cities with populations above ten thousand had enacted subdivision regulation.[11] Subsequent legislation sought to tailor and clarify subdivision authority concerning approval and improvements, such as requiring park acquisition and school site reservation,[12] placing limits on required improvements within a municipality's extraterritorial jurisdiction,[13] and allowing developers to pay money for counties to use for park dedication and road construction.[14] In 2005 the General Assembly adopted a modernization amendment to the development regulation statutes. Changes to the subdivision enabling authority included clarification for the plat review process, performance guarantee options, definition of subdivision, and enforcement options.[15] A 2009 law clarified the nature of subdivision approval—administrative or quasi-judicial.[16]

---

9. 1959 N.C. Sess. Laws ch. 1007.

10. 1961 N.C. Sess. Laws ch. 1168.

11. N.C. Div. of Cmty. Planning, Training & Research Section, Local Development Policies: A Survey of Current Practices in North Carolina 6 (1967) (96 percent of responding cities with population above ten thousand had adopted subdivision standards).

12. 1971 N.C. Sess. Laws ch. 698; 1973 N.C. Sess. Laws ch. 426; 1985 N.C. Sess. Laws ch. 146.

13. 1983 N.C. Sess. Laws ch. 1080.

14. 1975 N.C. Sess. Laws ch. 231; 1985 N.C. Sess. Laws ch. 146; 1987 N.C. Sess. Laws ch. 747.

15. 2005 N.C. Sess. Laws ch. 426.

16. 2009 N.C. Sess. Laws ch. 421.

Today, most counties and municipalities have some subdivision regulation (see the break-down by county in Figure 1.1). In a 2005 survey, 88 percent of responding counties and 83 percent of responding municipalities indicated that they had adopted subdivision regulations; more than 97 percent of municipalities with populations over five thousand reported having done so.[17]

## Overview of the Contents of This Book

This book covers the law, policy, and practice of land subdivision regulation in North Carolina. Chapter 2 discusses the authority for regulation, the process for adopting and amending a subdivision ordinance, the boards involved in subdivision review, and the relation between subdivision ordinances and other public regulations and private agreements. Chapter 3 explores the statutory definition of subdivision and the divisions of land that are exempt from it. Chapter 4 outlines considerations for the subdivision approval process, and Chapter 5 walks through the typical steps of subdivision review.

Chapters 6 and 7 shift the focus to subdivision design and standards for improvements. Chapter 6 explores categories of standards, such as lots and blocks, transportation, utilities, and recreation facilities. Chapter 7 discusses different policy concepts related to subdivision regulation, including growth management and styles of development.

Chapter 8 reviews the legal limits for requiring dedication of property and improvements to the public, with a focus on the statutory and constitutional limits. Chapter 9 discusses enforcement matters related to subdivision regulation. Chapter 10 reviews procedures and standards for appeals and judicial review of subdivision decisions.

Finally, Appendix A provides a side-by-side comparison of the statutory authority for cities and counties to regulate land subdivision in North Carolina, while Appendix B presents case summaries of North Carolina court cases related to subdivision regulation and approval.

This book is intended primarily as a review of North Carolina law and a resource for practitioners in the state. It draws from the statutes and cases of North Carolina as well as ordinances from municipalities and counties across the state. The cited ordinances are offered as examples, not as models.[18]

Of course, it is not as though subdivision regulation ends at the state border. For that reason, the book draws lessons from publications providing a broader geographic scope, such as legal treatises, practitioner guides, and policy analysis. The inverse also may be true—the experience and policy considerations of North Carolina communities may apply to communities across the country. To be sure, though, state statutes and judicial interpretations will vary.

---

17. DAVID W. OWENS & NATHAN BRANSCOME, AN INVENTORY OF LOCAL GOVERNMENT LAND USE ORDINANCES IN NORTH CAROLINA (Special Series No. 21, May 2006), at 4.

18. The ordinances referenced are the adopted ordinances as of February 1, 2015, including, among others, the Statesville Unified Development Code, the Pasquotank County Subdivision Ordinance, the City of Concord Development Ordinance, Chatham County Subdivision Regulations, the City of Wilmington Land Development Code, the City of Wilson Unified Development Ordinance, the City of Boone Unified Development Ordinance, and the Buncombe County Land Development and Subdivision Ordinance.

Chapter 2

# Authority for the Subdivision Ordinance

## Governmental Function

The authority to control land subdivision arises from the general police powers to protect public health and safety and the general welfare.[1] As such, the exercise of subdivision control authority is governmental in nature: "The plain language of the statute and our case law thus indicate that subdivision control is a duty owed to the general public, not a specific individual."[2]

## Territory

"A city [or county] may by ordinance regulate the subdivision of land within its territorial jurisdiction."[3] For municipalities, that includes the municipal jurisdiction plus any extraterritorial jurisdiction.[4] A county may regulate subdivision in the territory outside of municipal jurisdiction. If desired, a county may limit subdivision regulation to areas with zoning regulation.[5]

## Content of the Ordinance

Cities and counties are authorized to address a variety of topics through the subdivision ordinance. Most of the statutory provisions on ordinance content are permissive ("the ordinance *may* provide . . . "). The one clear requirement is that the ordinance "shall contain provisions setting forth the procedures to be followed in granting or denying approval of a subdivision plat prior to its registration."[6] In addition, the statutes give a clear definition of "subdivision" and applicable exemptions[7] as well as appeals processes.[8]

---

1. As particularly authorized at Sections 153A-331 and 160A-372 of the North Carolina General Statutes (hereinafter G.S.).
2. Derwort v. Polk Cnty., 129 N.C. App. 789, 792 (1998).
3. G.S. 153A-330; G.S. 160A-371.
4. G.S. 160A-360.
5. G.S. 153A-330.
6. G.S. 153A-332; G.S. 160A-373.
7. G.S. 153A-335; G.S. 160A-376.
8. G.S. 153A-336; G.S. 160A-377.

The topics of the ordinances may include, among other things,

- definitions (discussed in Chapter 3),
- review procedures and approval standards (Chapters 4–6),
- plat preparation and recordation (Chapter 5),
- subdivision design and construction standards (Chapter 6),
- infrastructure provisions (Chapters 6 and 8),
- property dedication (Chapters 6 and 8),
- enforcement and performance guarantees (Chapter 9),
- appeals (Chapter 10).

Some of the statutory provisions of subdivision ordinances are plain and clear. Others, however, are ambiguous or may be ambiguous when applied to certain situations. Where there is lack of clarity in the statutory language, the General Assembly has directed that there be a broad reading of the statutory authority. G.S. 160A-4, and the county analog at G.S. 153A-4, state that the statutes "shall be broadly construed and grants of power shall be construed to include any powers that are reasonably expedient to the exercise of the power."

The North Carolina Supreme Court has interpreted this legislative direction of statutory construction to apply only when there is ambiguity.[9] But when the court does find ambiguity, it applies the direction for broad construction.[10]

## Notice

### Notice of Public Hearings

When adopting, amending, or repealing a subdivision ordinance, cities and counties must follow the public hearing and notice requirements of the respective chapters of the North Carolina General Statutes (hereinafter G.S.). The governing board must hold a public hearing prior to adoption. Notice of the public hearing must be published twice—once a week for two successive calendar weeks—in a newspaper of general circulation in the area. The first published notice must not be less than ten days nor more than twenty-five days before the date of the public hearing.[11] In contrast to the requirement for zoning ordinance amendments, there is no statutory requirement for planning board review of subdivision ordinance adoption or amendment. Even so, it is prudent policy to allow planning board review and comment on changes to the subdivision ordinance.

Notice requirements for quasi-judicial decisions and administrative decisions are discussed in Chapter 4, and appeals of subdivision ordinances and decisions are discussed in Chapter 10.

9. *See* Lanvale Props., L.L.C. v. Cnty. of Cabarrus, 366 N.C. 142 (2012); *see also,* Patmore v. Town of Chapel Hill, No. COA13-1049, 2014 WL 1365987 (N.C. Ct. App. April 1, 2014), distinguishing *Lanvale.*

10. *See* King v. Town of Chapel Hill, No. 281PA13, 2014 WL 2612603 (N.C. June 12, 2014), http://appellate.nccourts.org/opinions/?c=1&pdf=31737.

11. G.S. 153A-323; G.S. 160A-364.

## Notice of Subdivisions Near Military Bases

Adoption or modification of development ordinances affecting property near military bases requires both additional notice to the commander of the base and an opportunity for comment and analysis. The precise implication of this notice requirement for subdivision approvals is not clear. On one hand, the statutory requirement for commander notice addresses only adoption and modification of *an ordinance*, not, as with most subdivision decisions, *approvals made pursuant to the ordinance*. On the other hand, the statute specifically calls out the following actions:

- "Changes to proposed new major subdivision preliminary plats" or
- "An increase in the size of an approved subdivision by more than fifty percent (50%) of the subdivision's total land area including developed and undeveloped land."[12]

The notice requirement presumes a public hearing will take place, but a public hearing may not be necessary for these types of subdivision decisions. Thus, the applicability of this requirement is not clear.

If and when a specified change will affect property within five miles of a military base, the local government must provide written notice (certified mail or other means of actual notice) to the commander not less than ten days and not more than twenty-five days before the public hearing. The commander may comment on the compatibility of the change with military operations. If the commander does not respond within thirty days, the comment period is waived. The governing board must take any comments and analysis into consideration before making a final determination.[13]

## Fees and Fee Notice

Local governments may set reasonable fees to cover the cost of plat review administration. Such permit fees are reasonably necessary for the local government to execute its duties of development review.[14]

Municipalities must provide additional notice and comment to interested parties when the municipality is considering an imposition or increase of fees or charges related to subdivisions (unless the fee or charge is contained in a budget filed in accordance with G.S. 159-12). The fees subject to this additional notice and comment period may include plat review application fees, subdivision inspection fees, and recreation fees (or other development exactions), among others. Under G.S. 160A-4.1, at least seven days prior to the first meeting to consider the fees or charges, the municipality must provide at least two of the following:

1. notice of the meeting in a prominent location on a website managed or maintained by the city (a city that does not maintain its own website may request a county to post the notice to the county website);

---

12. G.S. 153A-323(b)(4) & (5); G.S. 160A-364(b)(4) & (5).
13. G.S. 153A-323; 160A-364.
14. Homebuilders Ass'n of Charlotte v. City of Charlotte, 336 N.C. 37 (1994).

2. notice of the meeting in a prominent physical location, including, but not limited to, any government building, library, or courthouse within the city;

3. notice of the meeting by electronic mail to a list of interested parties created by the city for the purpose of notification as required by this section;

4. notice of the meeting by facsimile to a list of interested parties created by the city for the purpose of notification as required by this section.

During consideration of subdivision fees or charges, the municipality must permit a period of public comment.

Under G.S. 160A-363, a municipality must repay a tax or fee plus 6 percent interest if that tax or fee is found to have been illegally exacted.

## Moratoria

Under G.S. 160A-381(e) and G.S. 153A-340(g), cities and counties may adopt temporary moratoria on "any development approval required by law." This includes zoning permits and building permits as well as subdivision plat approvals.

The statutory language states that local governments may not adopt a moratorium "for the purpose of developing and adopting new or amended plans or ordinances as to residential uses." This language clearly prohibits a moratorium imposed while new zoning rules are adopted for "residential uses." It is not clear, however, if this limitation applies to a moratorium imposed while new subdivision rules are adopted for land subdivision of lots intended for residential uses.

The statutes outline specific procedural requirements for adopting a moratorium. The duration of the moratorium must be reasonable in light of the conditions necessitating it, and the duration cannot extend past the time needed to adopt new rules. In cases of imminent and substantial threat to public health or safety, the governing board may adopt a moratorium without notice. For a moratorium of sixty days or shorter, the governing board must hold a public hearing and provide published newspaper notice at least seven days prior to the hearing. A moratorium for greater than sixty days (and any extension of shorter moratoria) requires a public hearing and the standard notice for land use regulations (two published notices in separate calendar weeks within the first ten to twenty-five days prior to the hearing).

The ordinance adopting a moratorium must, per G.S. 160A-381(e), include the following:

1. a clear statement of the problems or conditions necessitating the moratorium and what courses of action, alternative to a moratorium, were considered by the county and why those alternative courses of action were not deemed adequate;

2. a clear statement of the development approvals subject to the moratorium and how a moratorium on those approvals will address the problems or conditions leading to imposition of the moratorium;

3. An express date for termination of the moratorium and a statement setting forth why that duration is reasonably necessary to address the problems or conditions leading to imposition of the moratorium;

4. A clear statement of the actions, and the schedule for those actions, proposed to be taken by the county during the duration of the moratorium to address the problems or conditions leading to imposition of the moratorium.

Projects with certain prior approvals or application status are not subject to a development moratorium unless there is imminent threat to public health or safety. These include

- a valid building permit,
- a conditional use permit application or special use permit application that has been accepted,
- a site-specific or phased development plan approved pursuant to G.S. 153A-344.1 or G.S. 160A-385.1,
- a development for which substantial expenditures have already been made in good faith reliance on a prior valid administrative or quasi-judicial permit or approval,
- a preliminary or final subdivision plat that has been accepted for review prior to the call for public hearing to adopt the moratorium.

In addition, if a preliminary plat is accepted for review prior to the call for a public hearing, and if that preliminary plat is approved, final plat approval may proceed without being subject to the moratorium.

The statutes set requirements for any extension of a moratorium and allow that aggrieved parties may seek a court order enjoining enforcement of the moratorium.

## Relation to Other Laws

### Zoning

Subdivision ordinances typically reference and interrelate to other ordinance requirements. Indeed, the subdivision ordinance may stand alone or "may be adopted as part of a unified development ordinance" (UDO).[15] But the North Carolina Supreme Court has emphasized the distinction between zoning and subdivision.

> [T]he functional distinctions between zoning ordinances and subdivision ordinances remain intact even when they are adopted as part of a UDO. In enacting section 153A–322(d) [that authorizes UDOs], the General Assembly did not give counties the authority to eliminate the differentiation between zoning and subdivision ordinances. Rather, the General Assembly was providing counties with a means of compiling certain ordinances together to ensure the uniform use of "definitions and procedures."[16]

The distinction between zoning and subdivision carries over to enforcement. In *Town of Nags Head v. Tillett*,[17] the court found that the town lacked authority for enforcement under the subdivision ordinance but still had enforcement authority under the zoning ordinance

---

15. G.S. 153A-330; G.S. 160A-371.
16. Lanvale Props., L.L.C. v. Cnty. of Cabarrus, 366 N.C. 142, 159 (2012).
17. 314 N.C. 627 (1985).

Land subject to subdivision regulation generally is subject also to zoning regulation.

A larger discussion of subdivision enforcement is presented in Chapter 9.

and minimum lot size requirement.[18] In *Jones v. Davis*,[19] the court emphasized that the subdivision ordinance regulates the division of land, not the use of land.

So, under the court's interpretation of zoning and subdivision authority, local governments must recognize and respect the distinct regulatory and enforcement authority for zoning and subdivision. In practice, though, subdivision and zoning regulation are necessarily interconnected concepts of land development regulation. These topics overlap because of the structure of the ordinance, the topics covered, and the practice of land development. The zoning districts outlined in the zoning ordinance commonly regulate lot size, density, setbacks, buildable area, use restrictions, and other elements that necessarily impact the division of land. Moreover, the layout of a subdivision and related infrastructure may impact the land uses available for a particular property or development.

The local subdivision ordinance may clarify the overlaps and conflicts among various development standards. Some ordinances include specific language to resolve potential conflicts. Chatham County's subdivision ordinance, for example, states: "Wherever there is a discrepancy between minimum standards or dimensions noted herein and those contained in the zoning regulations or other agencies regulations the more stringent standards shall apply."[20]

---

18. *See also*, Tonter Invs., Inc. v. Pasquotank Cnty., 199 N.C. App. 579, *review denied*, 363 N.C. 663 (2009).

19. 163 N.C. App. 628 (2004), *aff'd*, 359 N.C. 314 (2005).

20. Chatham County Subdivision Regulations § 7.6 (1980; amended Dec. 15, 2014).

**Do Zoning Rules Apply to Exempt Subdivisions?**

Short answer: Yes. In one case, *Tonter Investments, Inc. v. Pasquotank County*,[†] the landowner attempted to complete an exempt subdivision under the ten-acre exemption. The county zoning ordinance prohibited residential development for a portion of the property and for the remainder of the property required frontage on public road and public water supply within one thousand feet. The landowner challenged the zoning amendments as an attempt to inappropriately regulate subdivision. The North Carolina Court of Appeals found that the zoning amendments were within the zoning powers granted by the General Assembly and that the statutory exemptions from subdivision regulation do not provide exemptions from all development regulation.

Subsequently, G.S. 153A-340(j) was amended to limit the ability of a county to regulate residential structures on lots greater than ten acres. Even so, the underlying legal principle from *Tonter* remains: Even if a local government cannot enforce the subdivision ordinance, the zoning ordinance—and zoning enforcement—may still apply to the development.

[†]199 N.C. App. 579 (2009).

The City of Wilson's subdivision regulations clearly point to the related development regulations that may apply, including

- parks and open spaces;
- tree protection, landscaping, and buffers;
- parking and driveways;
- lighting,
- signs,
- erosion, flood, stormwater, and watershed standards.[21]

Developing according to an approved subdivision plan may in fact limit development, even if zoning would have allowed for greater development. In *River Birch Associates v. City of Raleigh*,[22] the developer obtained approval and substantially completed a development with open space greater than the minimum required by zoning. The developer later sought approval to develop the excess open space. The court found that once the developer substantially undertook development according to the subdivision plat and site plan, the developer assented to the conditions and the city may hold the developer to those conditions.

In *ExperienceOne Homes*,[23] the conditional use zoning approval was conditioned on the development being consistent with the submitted site plan and subdivision plat. As such, the zoning and subdivision rules were tied together. When the developer sought to change the development (from townhomes to single family homes) that amendment implicated the overlapping standards of zoning and subdivision.

## Environment

Beyond zoning, a variety of other local, state, and federal regulatory provisions interconnect with land development and subdivision regulation. Health department rules address septic fields and well-water safety. Subdivision layout may be affected by laws concerning streams and wetlands, floodway protection, steep slopes, or mountain ridge protection.

---

21. Wilson Unified Development Ordinance § 6.2.5 (2013).
22. 326 N.C. 100 (1990).
23. ExperienceOne Homes, L.L.C. v. Town of Morrisville, 727 S.E.2d 26 (N.C. Ct. App.) (unpublished), *review denied*, 366 N.C. 247 (2012).

Local tree protection ordinances apply to land development that converts land from forestland to non-forest use.

Local governments are authorized to require deed restrictions and protective covenants for stormwater management and financial arrangements for adequate maintenance and replacement.[24]

Forestry and subdivision regulation are specifically addressed in the state statutes. Under G.S. 153A-452 and G.S. 160A-458.5, a local government may not adopt rules or ordinances that regulate forestry activity on forestland taxed at its present-use value or forestry activity conducted in accordance with a forest management plan. Tree-cutting *related to development*, though, is still subject to zoning, subdivision, and other development regulation. Under that statute, "development" is defined as the conversion of land from forestland to non-forest use. If an exempt timber harvest occurs, a city or county may withhold approval of a building permit, site plan, or subdivision plan for the site for three years after the timber harvest (five years if the harvest was a willful violation).

*Stormwater, forestry, and environmental considerations are discussed in greater detail in Chapter 6.*

## Transportation

Whether adjacent to a state road or a municipal street, a developing subdivision likely will require a driveway permit. Under G.S. 136-18 the North Carolina Department of Transportation (NCDOT) "may establish policies and adopt rules about the size, location, direction of traffic flow, and the construction of driveway connections into any street or highway which is a part of the State Highway System." Similarly, under G.S. 160A-307, a "city may by ordinance regulate the size, location, direction of traffic flow, and manner of construction of driveway connections into any street or alley." The authority in these statutes extends to requiring a developer to construct or reimburse the costs of construction for certain road improvements in connection with the driveway permit.

*Transportation network standards are discussed more fully in Chapter 6.*

24. G.S. 153A-454; G.S. 160A-459.

## Relation to Private Agreements

Aspects of subdivision regulation necessarily overlap with private contracts for real property, deed covenants and restrictions, and other private land agreements. This does not mean, however, that every neighbor dispute is a public dispute.

A discussion of private enforcement actions is presented in Chapter 9.

### Real Estate Contracts

The first and most direct relationship between subdivision regulation and private land agreements is the timing of sale. Under subdivision regulations, a property owner cannot subdivide land (or sell those lots) until the owner has met the applicable ordinance standards, obtained approval, and recorded a final plat.

The General Statutes, at Sections 160A-375 and 153A-334, authorize an owner or agent to enter into contracts to sell or lease land by reference to an approved preliminary plat if they meet certain requirements; the owner cannot close on the sale until final plat approval. In order to enter into these contracts based on preliminary plat approval, the statutes set specific disclosure standards and require an opportunity to terminate the contract if the final plat differs materially from the preliminary plat. Special provisions are allowed for selling lots to professional builders of residential or commercial buildings.

### Street Disclosures

A local subdivision ordinance may call for clear disclosures of whether streets and other improvements will be publicly or privately maintained (by the property owners).[25]

This disclosure also is required by state statute for residential subdivisions outside of municipal corporate limits and for those affecting state highways within municipalities. Prior to any conveyance or any agreement to convey land in those subdivisions, the developer and seller must prepare and sign a subdivision streets disclosure statement. The developer must provide the disclosure statement to the prospective buyer, and the buyer must sign an acknowledgement of receipt. This statement must disclose the status (public or private) of the street upon which the lot fronts. If the street is proposed as public, the seller must certify that the street design is approved by the Division of Highways and that it will be constructed to DOT standards for acceptance into the highway system. If the street is proposed as private, the seller must specify what parties are responsible for construction and maintenance and must state that the streets will not be constructed to standards allowing them to be included in the state highway maintenance program.[26]

### North Carolina Planned Community Act

The North Carolina Planned Community Act (Chapter 47F of the General Statutes) applies to residential subdivisions comprising more than twenty lots. The act outlines, among other things, the organization of the homeowners association and its obligations for the upkeep of common areas. The act does not modify local subdivision rules but does state that a zoning or subdivision ordinance may not impose "any requirement upon a planned community

---

25. *See, e.g.,* Wilmington Land Development Code § 18-378; Boone Unified Development Ordinance § 5.04.04.
26. G.S. 136-102.6(f).

The rights and responsibilities of property owners associations are discussed in Chapter 9.

which it would not impose upon a substantially similar development under a different form of ownership or administration."[27]

## North Carolina Condominium Act

Condominium ownership is structured so that individual owners own portions of the real estate (units within a building, for example) and that the remaining rights in the real estate (the common areas and the underlying dirt) are owned collectively by all of the individual owners. Chapter 47C of the North Carolina General Statutes outlines applicable procedures and rights related to the creation of condominiums in North Carolina.

Under G.S. 47C-1-106, a local zoning or subdivision ordinance may not prohibit the condominium form of ownership. A local ordinance cannot require recordation of a declaration prior to the timing required by the condominium act. Also, a local ordinance cannot impose requirements on a condominium that would not be imposed on a similar development under a different form of ownership.

More discussion of the definition of "subdivision" is presented in Chapter 3.

"Otherwise, no provision of [the Condominium Act] invalidates or modifies any provision of any zoning, subdivision, or building code or other real estate use law, ordinance, or regulation." With these provisions, multi-building condominium projects may be subject to subdivision ordinance regulations in the same way that a multi-building office park or apartment complex is. As discussed more in the next chapter, "land subdivision" is defined broadly to include more than merely divisions for sale. In the case of a condominium, for example, the division of air rights, that is, the division of legal rights to empty space above a parcel of land, may not be considered as a division of land subject to the subdivision ordinance. When the condominium project is developed, however, the division of the project site into multiple building sites may be subject to the subdivision ordinance.

---

27. G.S. 47F-1-106.

# Chapter 3

# Defining Subdivision

## Definition

The definition of land subdivision in North Carolina plainly includes the everyday concept of subdivision—the tract of land divided into lots for sale—but the statutory definition goes further. It includes language that broadens the definition to include certain actions related to site development and building. The statutes also outline specific exemptions from subdivision regulation (discussed in the next section).

As set forth in the General Statutes, "subdivision" is defined as

> all divisions of a tract or parcel of land into two or more lots, building sites, or other divisions when any one or more of those divisions is created for the purpose of sale or building development (whether immediate or future) and shall include all divisions of land involving the dedication of a new street or a change in existing streets[.][1]

## Even One Lot

If a landowner has fifty acres and decides to carve out one of those acres as a new parcel to sell or develop, that act is a subdivision subject to local regulation. In 2005, the enabling legislation was amended to clarify that a division is a subdivision if "any one or more of those divisions is created for the purpose of sale or building development." In other words, a landowner can trigger subdivision regulation just by carving off one small lot.

## Building Sites and Other Divisions

Subdivision regulations can apply to building sites and leased premises as well as lots for sale. As outlined above, the statute clearly includes divisions of "land into two or more lots, *building sites, or other divisions* . . . for the purpose of sale *or building development.*" The statute does not give additional clarification, and case law has not provided guidance for the scope of this provision. Even so, the implication is noteworthy: If a tract is clearly divided into sites for building development, it qualifies as a subdivision. A commercial site plan of less than the total tract may qualify. Reservation of out-parcels for future development may qualify. And, a long-term ground-lease of a clearly defined site that is part of a tract also may qualify.

---

1. Section 160A-376(a) of the North Carolina General Statutes (hereinafter G.S.); the county complement is G.S. 153A-335(a).

The definition of subdivision comprises more than just lots for sale—it also includes divisions of land into building sites for the purpose of building development, such as leased mobile home lots and multi-building commercial or apartment developments.

The platting of a mobile home park—even a park where the lots are leased to renters who place their own mobile homes there—is considered a subdivision under the applicable definition. When this question came before the N.C. Court of Appeals, it found that the phrase "'for the purpose of sale or building development' includes construction on subdivision lots, which are leased to third parties who place their own improvements on the property."[2]

The development of a multi-building apartment complex or office park also may be subject to subdivision regulation. To the extent that the development is a division of land into building sites for the purpose of building development, it would qualify as a subdivision.

The City of Charlotte, through its subdivision ordinance definition, clarifies the implications of the statutory definition. Under that ordinance, subdivision is defined as

> all divisions of a tract or parcel of land into two or more lots, building sites, or other divisions for the purpose, whether immediate or future, of sale, or building development of any type, *including both residential and nonresidential multiple building site and multi-site projects even if there is no division of the underlying land* into separate parcels which is to be recorded with the register of deeds and also includes all divisions of land involving the dedication of a new street or a new street right-of-way or a change in existing streets[.][3]

## Now or in the Future

The timing of sale or building development is irrelevant of purposes of defining a subdivision. The statute clearly states that the sale or building development related to the subdivision may be immediate or in the future.

---

2. Jones v. Davis, 163 N.C. App. 628 (2004), *aff'd*, 359 N.C. 314 (2005).
3. City of Charlotte Subdivision Ordinance § 20-6 (emphasis added).

## Settlement of an Estate

The division of land for the purpose of settling the estate of a decedent is not treated as a subdivision of land. In the case of *Williamson v. Avant*,[4] the North Carolina Court of Appeals determined that a conveyance made for the purpose of dividing up the estate of a decedent among his heirs was not a "division of land for immediate or future sale or development within the meaning of [the statute]." Other court-ordered surveys similarly fall outside the definition of subdivision.[5] Before such a plat can be recorded, the surveyor and local government must certify that the land division is not a regulated subdivision.[6]

The *Williamson* case begs another question: Aside from the estate of a decedent, could multiple owners of a single tract of land avoid subdivision regulation by voluntarily partitioning that land among themselves? Or, could multiple owners of a holding company dissolve the company and partition the property among themselves without meeting subdivision requirements? N.C. courts have not addressed these questions, but such actions would be suspect if the clear intent of the parties was to subvert the applicable subdivision requirements.

## Merger

Merger, or reversion to acreage, is the combination of two or more parcels to create one larger parcel. This action is not a division of land and does not fall within the definition of subdivision as long as the parcels are combined into one parcel with no change to streets. As with court-ordered surveys, before a merger plat can be recorded, the surveyor and the local government must certify that the land division is not a regulated subdivision.[7] If parcels are merged and then re-divided into multiple parcels, the recombination exemption may apply.

## Family Subdivisions

If a family is settling the estate of a deceased relative, the division of property does not fall within the statutory definition of subdivision. However, if a living parent wants to divide a tract of land among his or her children—a so-called family subdivision—that action would fall within the statutory definition. The General Statutes do not call out family subdivisions for any special treatment. Under the statutes, a family subdivision may qualify independently for one of the exemptions discussed below, and a local ordinance can provide expedited review for family subdivisions.[8]

Some jurisdictions have received local authorization to exempt family subdivisions.[9] Macon County, for example, received local legislation in 2009 (S.L. 2009-33) to exclude family subdivisions from the definition of subdivision with the following provisions:

> A "family subdivision" is the division of land into two or more parcels or
> lots for the purpose of conveying the resulting parcels or lots to a grantee

---

4. 21 N.C. App. 211 (1974), *cert. denied*, 285 N.C. 596 (1974).

5. G.S. 47-30(f)(11)(d).

6. G.S. 47-30(f)(11).

7. G.S. 47-30(f)(11).

8. G.S. 160A-376(b).

9. See, for example, Henderson County (S.L. 1989-863), exempting intrafamily subdivisions; and Harnett County and its municipalities ( S.L. 1997-246; S.L. 2001-50), exempting one-time divisions of land by any method of transfer among members of an immediate family.

or grantees who are in any degree of lineal kinship to the grantor, or to a grantee or grantees who are within four degrees of collateral kinship to the grantor. The exemption provided by the ordinance shall only apply if the deed of conveyance notes that it is a family subdivision as defined by this section. Degrees of kinship shall be computed in accordance with G.S. 104A-1.

The City of Wilson's ordinance exempts family subdivisions. But when the descendants who receive property "develop or build upon their respective property, the property must conform in all respects to the regulations of the City of Wilson."[10]

## Major and Minor Subdivisions

An ordinance may set different review procedures for different classes of subdivision.[11] Subdivision ordinances commonly provide for different review procedures based on the size of the subdivision: detailed review for major subdivisions and expedited review for minor subdivisions. An ordinance could also have other specified classes of subdivision review for such projects as development agreements, planned unit developments, or conditional rezonings.

Minor subdivisions are defined by the local ordinance, so the definition varies by community. A minor subdivision generally is defined to be relatively small (less than six lots, for example) and involves some or all of the following characteristics:

1. no need for new public streets to access a public street,
2. no need for new off-site easements or improvements,
3. a subdivision design and layout that conforms to all requirements of the applicable development code, and
4. no need for utility improvements.[12]

Approval of minor subdivisions is often assigned to a staff administrator, such as the planning director or subdivision administrator, with recommendation from the technical review committee.[13]

In addition to minor subdivisions, the Buncombe County Subdivision Ordinance has a category called "special subdivisions" for subdivisions where three or fewer lots will result. Special subdivisions must be reviewed by planning staff within two days of submission, and staff must affix to the plat a stamp indicating that the driveway is "approved as a special subdivision, the access is considered a private driveway."[14]

Family subdivisions, a special class of divisions related to minor subdivisions, are discussed above.

Separate classes of subdivisions can create an opportunity for circumventing the ordinance process and infrastructure standards. Imagine a subdivision ordinance that defines minor subdivisions as divisions creating three or fewer new lots. Major subdivisions, defined as anything else, require full subdivision review and approval by the planning board as well as more stringent infrastructure standards. Minor subdivisions, however, require only final plat

---

10. Wilson Unified Development Ordinance § 6.2.2.B.
11. G.S. 153A-330; G.S. 160A-371.
12. Statesville Unified Development Code § 2.02; Concord Development Ordinance § 5.1.1.B; Chatham County Subdivision Regulation § 4.B.
13. Concord Development Ordinance § 5.1.1.
14. Buncombe County Subdivision Ordinance § 70-37.

approval through staff review. So, a landowner who has ten acres and plans to divide them into ten, one-acre lots would trigger major subdivision review and infrastructure. However, phasing in the divisions—three this year, three next year, three the next—could qualify the lots as minor subdivisions and thereby subvert the intent of the ordinance.

To avoid this game, an ordinance could set a certain date to define parent tracts and then limit the number of minor subdivisions that may flow from the parent tract before its division triggers major subdivision review. Alternatively, an ordinance could set a waiting period before division into another minor subdivision can proceed from the same tract. In the case of family subdivisions, Pasquotank County prohibits further minor subdivision on the property for ten years.[15]

## Exempt Subdivisions

The statute provides four exemptions from the definition of subdivision. These exemptions do not provide an open door for any and every land division an owner may desire. Rather, they authorize specific land divisions to avoid certain regulatory obligations. Even if a land division qualifies for the exemption, local administrative certification is required if the landowner desires to record a plat. Certification of exemption on the face of the plat is needed from the surveyor and local government.[16] Also, exemption from subdivision regulations does not create an exemption from all development regulations.[17]

In addition to the general exemptions outlined in the statutes, some local governments have local legislation that alters or adds to these exemptions.[18]

---

**If It's Exempt, It's Exempt**

In *Three Guys Real Estate v. Harnett County*,[†] a property owner sought to divide a 231-acre tract into twenty-three lots of ten acres each with no dedicated right-of-way. The county planning department refused to certify that the plat was exempt. The trial court found that the private access easements were essentially open for public use and that the proposed division would circumvent the subdivision ordinance's standards for public health and safety. The state supreme court, however, found the division of land to be clearly exempt: The private access easements were not dedicated public rights-of-way, and the general standard for public health and safety could not overcome the specific statutory language creating the exemption from subdivision regulation.

[†]345 N.C. 468, 470 (1997).

---

15. Pasquotank County Subdivision Ordinance § 303.

16. G.S. 47-30(f)(11).

17. Tonter Invs., Inc. v. Pasquotank Cnty., 199 N.C. App. 579, *review denied*, 363 N.C. 663 (2009).

18. See, for example, Montgomery County (S.L. 1995-337), exempting some intrafamily transfers, some lots over five acres, and some subdivisions with less than ten lots of an acre each; Jones County (S.L. 1999-125), defining subdivision as division into five or more lots and exempting lots over five acres with no street right-of-way dedications; Richmond County (S.L. 2000-11), exempting divisions into parcels greater than five acres with no street right-of-way dedications.

## Public Right-of-Way Exemption

*The public acquisition by purchase of strips of land for the widening or opening of streets or for public transportation system corridors.*[19]

The public right-of-way exemption is fairly straightforward. Public bodies, including municipalities, NCDOT, transit authorities, and others, may acquire and plat rights-of-way for widening or establishing streets or other transportation corridors without triggering local subdivision regulation.

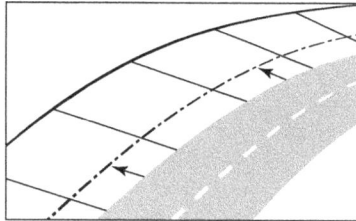

This provision is both narrow and broad. Note that this exemption applies to "acquisition by purchase." Under a plain reading, this exemption does not apply to land taken by eminent domain or to property offered for dedication by a private owner. On the other hand, the exemption may be used for "streets or for public transportation system corridors"—a fairly broad category of rights-of-way.

## Ten-Acre Exemption

*The division of land into parcels greater than 10 acres where no street right-of-way dedication is involved.*[20]

The basic requirement for the ten-acre exemption is clear: if lots are larger than ten acres and there is no street right-of-way dedication, then subdivision regulation is not required by statute. If a division includes some lots that are larger than ten acres but also some lots that are smaller than ten acres, that division does create a subdivision under the statute. However, a landowner could follow a two-step division and avoid some subdivision regulation. For example, a landowner could first divide a 100-acre tract into eight 10.1-acre tracts and one 19.2-acre tract. Such a division would not create a subdivision. Were the landowner to then divide the 19.2-acre tract into smaller lots, this step would create a subdivision that must meet the ordinance requirements.

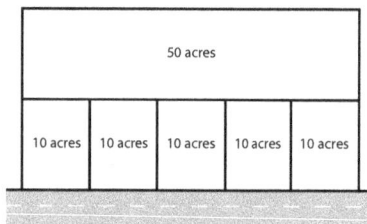

As noted above, in addition to the ten-acre threshold, the statute requires that there be no street right-of-way dedication. This element raises the question of what constitutes a street right-of-way dedication. Dedication implies a grant of property interest to the public through the municipality, NCDOT, or other public agency. Private drives or private driveway easements for lot owners or a homeowners association are not dedications to the public that would trigger regulation of the division into lots larger than ten acres.

Some commentators note that exempting large parcels from subdivision regulation "negates many of the theories behind the need for subdivision regulation," such as ensuring adequate

---

19. G.S. 160A-376(a)(3); the wording of the county statute is slightly different.
20. G.S. 160A-376(a)(2); the wording of the county statute is slightly different.

infrastructure, guiding future growth, and providing clear property records. Rather than exemption, they argue, such divisions should be subject to review as minor subdivisions.[21]

## Recombination Exemption

*The combination or recombination of portions of previously subdivided and recorded lots where the total number of lots is not increased and the resultant lots are equal to or exceed the standards of the municipality [or county]* as shown in its subdivision regulations.[22]

Recombination is similar to, but distinct from, lot merger. A lot merger is not a division of land, so merger falls outside of the definition of subdivision. The recombination exemption applies to an action that would otherwise be a subdivision. The exemption applies to boundary line adjustments and similar reconfigurations of existing lots. For example, suppose there are two neighboring lots, each 100 feet wide. Under the recombination exemption, the neighbors could adjust the common boundary by twenty feet—resulting in one 80-foot lot and one 120-foot lot. The existing lots must have been recorded, though there is no requirement that they be platted. The recombination must not result in a greater number of lots.

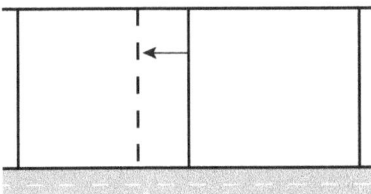

For both the recombination exemption and the two-into-three exemption discussed below, the resultant lots must equal or exceed the applicable standards of the sub-division ordinance, such as lot size, width, shape, and access. It is unclear to what extent standards beyond basic lot standards would apply.

## Two-into-Three Exemption

*The division of a tract in single ownership whose entire area is no greater than two acres into not more than three lots, where no street right-of-way dedication is involved and where the resultant lots are equal to or exceed the standards of the municipality [or county],* as shown in its subdivision regulations.[23]

The basic idea of the two-into-three exemption is that a two-acre parcel may be divided into three compliant lots. The language of the exemption, though, requires some careful review. The exemption applies to division of a *tract in single ownership* that is no greater than two acres. The other exemption provisions use the terms "lot" and "parcel," so "tract" would seem to mean something else. "Tract" likely means contiguous land, such that the owner may have a total of only two contiguous acres in order to benefit from the exemption. As with the recombination exemption, lots created under the two-into-three exemption must meet or exceed the subdivision standards.

---

21. ROBERT H. FREILICH & S. MARK WHITE, WITH KATE F. MURRAY, 21ST CENTURY LAND DEVELOPMENT CODE 168 (2008).
22. G.S. 160A-376(a)(1); the wording of the county statute is slightly different.
23. G.S. 160A-376(a)(4); the wording of the county statute is slightly different.

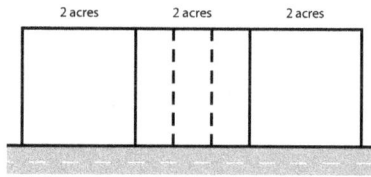

2 acres      2 acres      2 acres

The two-into-three exemption could create the curious situation of ever smaller exempt divisions. For example, suppose one ten-acre parent tract is divided into five, two-acre lots and sold to individual owners. The initial division of the ten acres would be subject to subdivision regulation. Under the two-into-three exemption, though, the individual landowners could then divide each of their parcels into three new lots as long as no right-of-way was dedicated and the new lots met local standards. Potentially, each of the resulting .66-acre lots could then be divided in thirds to create a total of nine, .22-acre lots. In this scenario, the ten-acre parent tract could undergo multiple two-into-three divisions. And, after the initial division of the ten acres, the resulting lots would fall outside the definition of subdivision.

As with the recombination exemption, the two-into-three exemption requires that the resultant lots meet or exceed the standards of the ordinance. And the applicable ordinance very likely sets a minimum lot size that will limit such a situation.

Chapter 4

# Nature of Subdivision Review

When a local government establishes a subdivision ordinance—and when courts review the actions pursuant to that ordinance—a variety of legal and policy issues are considered. These include the following:

- Is the review of a subdivision plat based on objective administrative standards, or is it based on quasi-judicial standards with some room for judgment and discretion?
- What board, committee, or staff person reviews the plats?
- What types of conditions may be imposed on plat approvals?
- Is there any allowance for variances or modifications?
- What vested rights are created by subdivision plat approval?

This chapter considers those questions and offers examples from case law, statutory requirements, and local ordinances.

## Nature of Standards: Administrative or Quasi-Judicial?

Governing board adoption of both the overall ordinance for subdivision regulation and an amendment to that ordinance is a legislative decision similar to a zoning ordinance amendment or rezoning. Legislative decisions are those through which a governing board sets broad policy for its jurisdiction. Elected officials have broad discretion to make such decisions based on public opinion, political views, and their determination of what is reasonable and in the public interest.

Decisions about specific subdivision plats are different. They are not legislative decisions because they are not decisions related to broad public policy. Subdivision plat review is based on standards set forth in the ordinance. Under Sections 153A-330 and 160A-371 of the North Carolina General Statutes (hereinafter G.S.), "Decisions on approval or denial of preliminary or final plats may be made only on the basis of standards explicitly set forth in the subdivision or unified development ordinance." In other words, preliminary and final plat review decisions are either administrative or quasi-judicial, the former based on clear, objective standards, the latter based on objective standards but also on standards requiring some level of judgment and discretion by the decision-making board. The procedural rules that apply depend on the nature of the decision, not the decision-maker (see Table 4.1). If a decision is based on objective standards set by the ordinance (no discretion), it is an administrative/ministerial decision, even if the decision is made by a city council.[1]

These procedures are in contrast to those for adopting or amending a subdivision ordinance, discussed in Chapter 2.

---

1. Guilford Fin. Servs., L.L.C. v. City of Brevard, 356 N.C. 655 (2003).

### Table 4.1   Procedural Rules as Determined by the Nature of the Action

| Action | Nature of the Action |
| --- | --- |
| Adoption or amendment of the subdivision ordinance | Legislative |
| Recommendation on adoption or amendment of the ordinance | Advisory |
| Plat review with subjective standards | Quasi-Judicial |
| Plat review with objective standards | Administrative |

Once procedures and standards are established by the ordinance, the local government is obligated to follow those standards. So, for example, if the ordinance requires certain findings to support a decision, the decision-maker cannot disregard that step.[2] If the ordinance prohibits subdivision names that duplicate existing subdivision names, the county commission cannot disregard that element of the ordinance by allowing a nearly identical name.[3]

In addition to following the standards that are in place, the decision-making board cannot add new standards beyond what the ordinance calls for. This means, for example, that if the ordinance does not include standards concerning the impact on property values, the board cannot base its denial on property values.[4]

It is worth noting that in some limited circumstances a legislative decision may be part of the subdivision approval process—when, for example, subdivision standards are incorporated into a form of conditional rezoning. In that case, the subsequent review of the preliminary and final plat must be based on standards set forth by the conditional rezoning.

## Administrative Subdivision Review

*Nature of Standards.* An administrative decision is one based on specific, objective standards set forth in an ordinance (for example, a minimum lot size of half an acre). It is black-and-white, so to speak—the project either meets the standards or it does not. Because an administrative decision is governed by the literal provisions of the ordinance, the decision-maker can decide an administrative approval based simply on the application, and no evidentiary hearing is needed. If an applicant clearly meets the standards of the ordinance,

---

2. Dellinger v. City of Charlotte, 114 N.C. App. 146 (1994) (The ordinance required a finding that the required dedication (1) will not result in deprivation of reasonable use of the original tract and (2) is either reasonably related to traffic from the development or the impact of the dedication is mitigated by provisions in the ordinance. Because planning staff failed to follow ordinance procedures, no evidence was provided enabling the planning commission to affirm the staff decision.).

3. Springdale Estates Ass'n v. Wake Cnty., 47 N.C. App. 462 (1980) (Court ruled that the county commission disregarded the county's own ordinance provision against duplicative names of subdivisions when it allowed "Springdale Gardens" and "Springdale Woods" despite the existing "Springdale Estates" subdivision.).

4. Knight v. Town of Knightdale, 164 N.C. App. 766, 766 (2004) (Council based its decision on impacts to neighboring property values, not physical impacts. Under the ordinance, the town had no authority to consider the site plan's effect on surrounding property values, so the court reversed the town decision and required that permits be issued.).

**A Right to the Permit**

A developer submitted a preliminary subdivision plat, watershed development plan, and erosion and sedimentation plan, all of which the planning staff approved.[†] Nearby homeowners challenged the decision as arbitrary and capricious. The court applied the whole-record test and found that the city followed the appropriate review process to find that the project met the applicable standards. Moreover, the court stated that ministerial decisions are governed by the literal provisions of the ordinance and may be made without a hearing at all. In the subdivision statutes, there is no requirement for either a hearing or notice to nearby property owners. If an applicant meets the ministerial standards, he or she has a right to the permit.

[†]Nazziola v. Landcraft Properties, Inc., 143 N.C. App. 564 (2001).

the applicant has a right to the permit and, if necessary, may seek a court order to require the decision-maker to grant the permit.[5]

*Notice.* Local ordinance provisions may address notice of administrative decisions. In contrast to the procedures required for quasi-judicial decisions, there is no statutory or constitutional requirement for notice *in advance* of an administrative decision.[6] To the extent that the provisions of G.S. 160A-388 apply to a local subdivision ordinance,[7] particular procedures for notice *after* an administrative decision are required. Under that statute, the administrator must provide notice of the decision to the applicant and the owner of the property (if different). The applicant, then, may choose to post a sign on the property to notify neighbors of the decision.

> Special notice required for subdivisions near military bases is discussed in Chapter 2. Appeals of staff decisions are discussed more fully in Chapter 10.

## Quasi-Judicial Subdivision Review

*Nature of Standards.* In contrast to administrative decisions, a quasi-judicial decision is based on standards that require some level of judgment and discretion. According to the statute, a decision is quasi-judicial "if the board is authorized to decide whether to approve or deny the plat based not only upon whether the application complies with the specific requirements set forth in the ordinance, but also on whether the application complies with one or more generally stated standards requiring a discretionary decision to be made" by the decision-making board.[8] In other words, there are some shades of grey in the standards. For instance, a quasi-judicial standard for a subdivision might be that "the project does not unduly overburden adjacent roads and utilities." Such a standard requires a judgment by the decision-maker.

Note that discretionary standards cannot be so vague that they permit complete discretion. "Whenever the ordinance includes criteria for decision that require application of judgment, those criteria must provide adequate guiding standards for the entity charged

---

5. Nazziola v. Landcraft Props., Inc., 143 N.C. App. 564 (2001); *see also*, Sanco of Wilmington Serv. Corp. v. New Hanover Cnty., 166 N.C. App. 471 (2004).

6. Coventry Woods Neighborhood Ass'n, Inc. v. City of Charlotte, 202 N.C. App. 247 (2010).

7. Section 160A-388 of the North Carolina General Statutes (hereinafter G.S.) outlines certain requirement for subdivision decisions if the subdivision regulations are part of a unified development ordinance or if a stand-alone subdivision ordinance calls for appeals pursuant to G.S. 160A-388.

8. G.S. 153A-336(c); G.S. 160A-377(c).

## Quasi-Judicial Standards and Evidence

In *Blue Ridge Co., L.L.C. v. Town of Pineville*,[†] the landowner met the objective technical and engineering standards, but the town, based on subjective standards for traffic and school crowding, denied the subdivision request. The subjective standards called for consistency with adopted plans and policies and conformity with the existing community. For school capacity, the court did not find a clearly adopted school crowding policy, neither did the ordinance require a school impact study. So, the court found that denial based on school impact was not supported by the evidence. For traffic, an engineer provided expert testimony concerning the modesty of traffic impacts, and the opponents rebutted with general perceptions, which were not enough to overcome the expert testimony. Moreover, the court found the conformity standard for the "most advantageous development" to be vague. Finally, the court considered consistency with the adopted land use plan and found that the town lacked sufficient evidence to deny the subdivision on those grounds. The court listed the goals for residential development that substantively matched aspects of the landowner's proposal.

[†]188 N.C. App. 466, 473 (2008).

with plat approval."[9] Thus, for example, a standard stating that the subdivision in question be the "most advantageous development" is overly vague.[10]

*Notice.* Under both zoning-enabling statutes and case law, certain procedural rules apply to quasi-judicial zoning decisions[11] and appear to apply to quasi-judicial subdivision decisions as well. The board must hold an evidentiary hearing; must provide mailed notice to the applicant, the owner, the owners of abutting property, and any other persons entitled to notice; and must post a sign on the property. Mailed and posted notice must be provided between ten and twenty-five days prior to the hearing.

*Special notice required for subdivisions near military bases is discussed in Chapter 2.*

*Evidentiary hearing.* The applicant and any opponents have an opportunity to present evidence at the evidentiary hearing and to make their case for approval or denial. Under the statutes specifying appeals of quasi-judicial decisions, the decision-making board must follow certain procedural requirements. The board must

- determine contested facts within a reasonable time;
- base decisions on competent, material, and substantial evidence in the record; and
- issue and deliver a written decision, signed by the chair, to reflect the board's determination of contested facts and applicable standards.

Even with discretionary standards, the board must follow the ordinance and rely on evidence in the record to make its decision. If, for example, a standard calls for "consistency with adopted plans" but there are no clearly adopted school-capacity plans and no evidence in the record of school impacts, a board cannot base its denial on generalized notions of school overcrowding.[12] The burden is on the applicant to show compliance, but if the applicant makes a prima facie showing of compliance with the subdivision standards and opponents present no evidence to overcome that evidence, the applicant is entitled to the subdivision plat.[13]

---

9. G.S. 153A-330; G.S. 160A-371.

10. Blue Ridge Co., L.L.C. v. Town of Pineville, 188 N.C. App. 466, 473 (2008).

11. G.S. 153A-345.1; G.S. 160A-388.

12. *Blue Ridge*, 188 N.C. App. at 473.

13. Guilford Fin. Servs., L.L.C. v. City of Brevard, 356 N.C. 655 (2003), *per curiam, adopting dissent in* 150 N.C. App. 1 (2002); William Brewster Co., Inc. v. Town of Huntersville, 161 N.C. App. 132 (2003).

## Decision-Makers

After the adoption of a subdivision ordinance, no subdivision plat of land within its jurisdiction may be filed or recorded until that plat is submitted to and approved by the board or agency specified by the ordinance. A typical subdivision approval process includes several steps taken by several decision-makers. Final decisions on preliminary and final plats may be made by the governing board (with or without the recommendation of a designated body); a technical review committee; or a designated planning board, body, or staff person.[14]

While statutes leave room for communities to structure review in a few different ways, but some legal and practical considerations are worth noting. When staff is the decision-maker for a subdivision plat review, the standards *must* be administrative (i.e., not quasi-judicial).

As a corollary, it is not recommended for governing boards to handle administrative subdivision plat reviews. While such review is technically allowed, it results in the governing board handling ministerial tasks without any room for policy choices or discretion. Policy choices are to be made when the subdivision ordinance is first adopted or amended and not when an individual plat is reviewed. If discretion is desired, that must be established through quasi-judicial standards, not through administrative review of preliminary plats.

Examples of how some North Carolina communities have assigned decision-making in the subdivision review process are presented in Table 4.2. In each case, the application may require advisory review by staff and/or the planning board before final approval.

## Technical Review Committee

Most communities have a technical review committee serving as either a decision-making board or an advisory committee for the decision-maker. Departments that may be involved in technical subdivision review include

- planning or development services,
- engineering or public works,
- water authority,
- transportation (municipal or NCDOT),
- parks and recreation,
- city or county attorney,
- public health or environmental health,
- fire department,
- public safety/E-911,
- mapping/GIS,
- stormwater or environmental services,
- schools,
- Division of Coastal Management as to the locations of any areas of environmental concern,
- tax, finance, and/or budgeting.

---

14. G.S. 153A-332; G.S. 160A-373.

**Table 4.2 Examples of Assignments of Decision-Making in North Carolina**

| Decision Assignments | City of Statesville | City of Concord | Pasquotank County | Chatham County |
|---|---|---|---|---|
| Minor Subdivision | Planning Director | Subdivision Administrator with TRC | Board of Commissioners | Subdivision Administrator |
| Sketch Plan Review (Major) | City Council | N/A | Board of Commissioners | TRC |
| Preliminary Plat Review (Major) | TRC | Planning & Zoning Commission | Board of Commissioners | Board of Commissioners |
| Construction Plan Review (Major) | City Engineer | Director of Engineering | N/A | TRC; (Commissioners if substantial changes) |
| Final Plat Review (Major) | TRC | Planning & Zoning Commission | Board of Commissioners | TRC |
| Acceptance of Dedications* | City Council | City Council | Board of Commissioners | Chair or Manager on behalf of the Board of Commissioners |

*Other public bodies, such as the North Carolina Department of Transportation or a local water authority, also may accept dedications.

The county enabling statutes require that the following agencies be given an opportunity to review and make recommendations on certain aspects of plats prior to approval:

- district highway engineer as to proposed state streets, highways, and related drainage systems;
- county health director or local public utility, as appropriate, as to proposed water or sewerage systems;
- any other agency or official designated by the board of commissioners.[15]

## Approval and Conditions

The timing and process of subdivision approval assume a level of conditional approval. As the applicant moves through the process—from sketch plan to preliminary plat to final plat—each stage represents a form of conditional approval. Preliminary plat approval is not a guarantee of final plat approval; the developer must actually meet the standards imposed (e.g., regarding road design, open space provisions, infrastructure). Nonetheless, preliminary plat approval gives a developer some assurance that the subdivision as proposed meets the standards of the ordinance even as those standards remain to be met. Final plat approval also may be conditioned on certain actions and enforced by performance guarantees.

15. G.S. 153A-332.

## Conditions for Objective Standards (Administrative Decisions)

Within this approval framework, a preliminary plat may be approved with conditions. Consider a preliminary plat that fails to meet an open space requirement. The review board could deny the plat and require redesign and resubmission, costing the applicant time and money. Alternatively, the review board could approve the preliminary plat on the condition that the required change will be incorporated into the actual development and the final plat. Conditions imposed as part of an administrative subdivision decision must be based on clear, objective standards set forth in the ordinance (e.g., 15 percent open space, the extension of public water to each lot, or provision of a sidewalk).

## Conditions for Subjective Standards (Quasi-Judicial Decisions)

For quasi-judicial subdivision decisions, a review board can require the applicant to meet the objective standards of an administrative decision and also impose conditions related to conformance with applicable subjective standards. Other quasi-judicial decisions, such as special use permits, variances, and certificates of appropriateness, have express statutory authority to impose conditions on approvals. While there is no express authority for imposing conditions on quasi-judicial subdivision decisions, imposing conditions is an implied characteristic of quasi-judicial decision-making and may be "reasonably necessary or expedient to carry [the subdivision statutes] into execution and effect."[16]

## Variances and Modifications

In limited cases, the strict application of an ordinance is disproportionately onerous on a particular property and creates an unnecessary hardship for the owner. In such cases, the owner may seek a variance from the local board of adjustment. If a subdivision ordinance allows for variances it must follow the procedures and standards for variances set forth in the zoning statutes.[17] An as alternative, some ordinances allow for minor modifications, discussed below.

Under G.S. 160A-388(d), the applicant for a variance must show that an unnecessary hardship will result from a strict letter application of the subdivision ordinance. The applicant bears the burden of showing all of the following:

1. Unnecessary hardship would result from the strict application of the ordinance. It shall not be necessary to demonstrate that, in the absence of the variance, no reasonable use can be made of the property.
2. The hardship results from conditions that are peculiar to the property, such as location, size, or topography. Hardships resulting from personal circumstances, as well as hardships resulting from conditions that are common to the neighborhood or the general public, may not be the basis for granting a variance.

---

16. G.S. 160A-4.

17. G.S. 160A-388; under prior law, courts interpreted the zoning variance authority as not applying to subdivision ordinances. Hemphill Nolan v. Town of Weddington, 153 N.C. App. 144 (2002).

3. The hardship did not result from actions taken by the applicant or the property owner. The act of purchasing property with knowledge that circumstances exist that may justify the granting of a variance shall not be regarded as a self-created hardship.
4. The requested variance is consistent with the spirit, purpose, and intent of the ordinance, such that public safety is secured and substantial justice is achieved.

A four-fifths vote is needed to grant a variance. As part of granting a variance, the board of adjustment may impose appropriate conditions reasonably related to it.

*Administrative modification.* Rarely does a construction project go exactly according to plan. Designs are slightly off, site issues are revealed, and projects get delayed. This is a practical reality of construction. Some subdivision ordinances recognize this reality and allow administrative approval of minor modifications to the approved plans. To be clear, minor modifications are not expressly authorized in the General Statutes, but such actions may reasonably be necessary and expedient to implementing the subdivision ordinance.[18]

Because it is an administrative decision, a minor modification must be based on objective standards. Once the procedures and standards for allowing minor modifications are clearly set forth in the subdivision ordinance, the local government must follow them.

In Concord, for example, after the planning and zoning commission has approved a preliminary plat, the subdivision administrator is authorized to approve certain amendments, including

1. changes in the location, size, or configuration of not more than 10 percent of the number of approved lots, provided that all lots comply with the applicable zoning district and the total number of lots is not increased;
2. changes in the location, size, or configuration of open space equivalent to not more than 10 percent of the approved gross open space acreage, provided that the percentage of the subdivision gross land area in open space is not reduced; or
3. changes in the location or configuration of proposed streets equivalent to not more than 10 percent of the approved total street length, provided that the number of external access points is not decreased and the minimum street connectivity ratios are maintained.[19]

In Concord, changes to infrastructure and utility design must be approved through the construction plan approval process.

Like most ordinances, Wilmington's land development code includes various highly technical standards. However, it also includes a specific provision allowing the flexibility to use alternatives to specified standards. "The city engineer shall approve any such alternate, provided he finds the proposed design is satisfactory and complies with the minimum requirements as specified [in the technical standards] and that the material, method, or work offered is, for the purpose intended, at least the equivalent of the minimum requirements as specified [in the technical standards]."[20]

---

18. G.S. 160A-4; G.S. 153A-4.
19. Concord Development Ordinance § 5.2.7.
20. Wilmington Land Development Code § 18-399.

**A Major Change Can't Be a Minor Modification**

A developer proposed to develop two hundred townhomes on property that was rezoned to residential multi-family conditional use.[†] Conditions included, among other things, that the development would arise consistent with the submitted site plan and subdivision plat. After an economic downturn, the developer wanted to amend the conditions to instead build single-family homes. Single-family homes required flexible design option approval to alter lot size, setback, and other dimensions. The developer sought administrative approval of the changes, but the town required governing board approval. The governing board denied the requested change, and the developer challenged the necessity and effect of the governing board review. The court found that the proposed changes were not a "minor amendment" and that the town followed its ordinance procedures.

[†]ExperienceOne Homes, L.L.C. v. Town of Morrisville, 727 S.E.2d 26 (N.C. Ct. App.) (unpublished), *review denied*, 366 N.C. 247 (2012).

## Vested Rights

In the case of amendments to the subdivision ordinance or related standards, a property owner who has submitted an application or obtained approval may have rights to proceed under the prior rules. In North Carolina, a special allowance is given so that an applicant can choose which standards apply when a subdivision ordinance is changed after an application is submitted. Also, N.C. courts recognize common law vested rights in certain circumstances, and the General Statutes allow for statutory vested rights against changes to the zoning ordinance. Valid building permits create statutory vested rights not to be impacted by changes to the zoning ordinance but not to the subdivision ordinance.[21] These options for vested rights are discussed below.

## Permit Choice

If an applicant submits an application for a permit and prior to the permit decision the applicable ordinance or rules are changed, the applicant may choose review under the new or the old rules.[22] The statutory provision applies to development permits, including subdivision approvals.

Consider the following. A property owner submits a preliminary plat to divide a four-acre parcel into four, one-acre lots with no right-of-way. At the time the plat is formally submitted and accepted, it qualifies as a minor subdivision. One week after the plat is submitted, but before it is reviewed and approved, the governing board changes the definition of minor subdivision to be a division resulting in three or fewer lots. Under the new rules, the plat would no longer qualify as a minor subdivision. In such a situation, the permit choice provisions of G.S. 143-750 would allow the owner to select review under either the old rules (minor subdivision review) or the new rules (major subdivision review).

---

21. G.S. 153A-344; G.S. 160A-385(b).
22. G.S. 153A-320.1; G.S. 160A-360.1, both referencing G.S. 143-750.

## Common Law Vested Rights

After a subdivision is approved, an owner may have a common law vested right to complete the project as it was approved, despite subsequent changes to the subdivision ordinance. North Carolina courts have found common law vested rights when the owner can show that he or she

- obtained a valid governmental approval,
- made a substantial expenditure in reliance on the approval,
- acted in good faith, and
- will suffer harm if required to comply with the new rules.

Most case law concerning common law vested rights in North Carolina arises from zoning rules.[23] Even so, subdivision approvals and regulations have been involved in common law vested right disputes.

An attempt to rush a subdivision plat approval may not be sufficient to secure vested rights. In *Koontz v. Davidson County Board of Adjustment*,[24] the developer entered a contract to purchase property for development as a mobile home community. Neighbors proposed an amendment to the county zoning ordinance that would exclude mobile homes from the area. The developer, aware of the proposed zoning amendment, moved forward with development actions in advance of the public hearing for the amendment. The developer obtained subdivision plat approval, recorded the plat, obtained zoning and building permits, and constructed a street and landscaping.

Shortly thereafter, the county commission adopted the zoning ordinance amendment prohibiting mobile homes in the area. The board of adjustment and superior court found that the developer had vested rights. The N.C. Court of Appeals, however, found that the developer had knowledge of the proposed zoning amendment and that their development efforts and expenditures were made after learning about it. "Despite this knowledge, developers actively sought and heeded advice on how to avoid or prevent the ordinance from halting their proposed development and unilaterally proceeded with their development activities. Therefore, developers did not exercise good faith reliance on a valid permit, as a matter of law, and thus they do not have a vested right to avoid the enacted zoning changes."[25]

## Statutory Vested Rights

The General Statutes recognize certain statutory vested rights that protect owners from changes to the *zoning* ordinance. Although the statute specifically calls out changes to the zoning ordinance and *not* the subdivision ordinance,[26] a subdivision plat approval may itself be sufficient to establish a vested right against changes to the zoning ordinance. This is because statutory vested rights may be established by approval of a site-specific development plan or phased development plan.[27] The statute clearly identifies "subdivision plat" as a possible

---

23. See Chapter 19 of DAVID W. OWENS, LAND USE LAW IN NORTH CAROLINA (2nd ed., 2011).

24. 130 N.C. App. 479, 480 (1998).

25. *Id.*

26. To be sure, an owner may still establish a common law vested right against changes to the subdivision ordinance. Common law vested rights are discussed in the previous section.

27. G.S. 153A-344.1; G.S. 160A-385.1.

site-specific development plan. Sketch plans are expressly excluded from creating statutory vested rights.

In order for a specific plan or a phased plan to qualify for the vested right, the approval process must include notice to the public and a public hearing. A document that serves to create vested rights should be identified as such.

Lawmakers have determined that approval of a specific plan or a phased plan gives the owner the "right to undertake and complete the development and use of said property under the terms and conditions of the site specific development plan or the phased development plan."[28] These vested rights for specific plans and phased plans last at least two years from the approval. Vested rights may last longer—up to five years—if desired by the local government based on relevant factors, such as the size of the development, market conditions, and level of investment.

Even having vested rights in approved plans, the owner must still comply with the conditions set for those plans, and a city may revoke an approval (and thus vested rights) for the owner's failure to do so.

Statutory vested rights are not absolute. General ordinances may apply to a project with statutory vested rights. For example, an overlay zoning that imposes additional requirements but does not affect the allowable type or intensity of use may still apply. Also, ordinances of general application—like plumbing or electric codes—may still apply. And, a local government may still adopt ordinances to address nonconforming situations.

In addition, statutory vested rights may be limited or revoked in the case of

- a serious threat to public health, safety, and welfare;
- compensation to the owner for costs incurred after development approval;
- misrepresentation by the owner;
- enactment of state or federal law that prevents the development as approved.

In addition to site-specific and phased development plans, an owner may have vested rights to develop under prior rules through a development agreement.[29] A development agreement is a formal contract between the landowner and the local government concerning the terms of a development project approval. It sets forth the nature and phasing of the buildings, public improvements and investments, and private improvements and investments. And—most important for this discussion—development agreements create long-term vested rights applicable to the development at the time of the agreement, including in subdivision ordinances.

It is worth noting that a development agreement is a useful, but particular, tool. Plans must be reasonably detailed, and the planning and legal costs for the developer and local government can be substantial.

---

28. *Id.*
29. G.S. 153A-349.7; G.S. 160A-400.26.

## Phased Plans

Large-scale subdivisions typically take years to build-out, which makes phased approvals both necessary and appropriate. In some scenarios, an overall concept plan or a preliminary plat may be approved at the outset with final plats to be approved in phases as infrastructure is completed.

Statesville's Unified Development Code allows such phasing and requires the phases to be related but distinct. Phasing must "ensure the provision of adequate community facilities and services for proposed and future development," and "each development project shall be designed so that the project is capable of functioning effectively and independently at completion of each phase."[30]

In some older cases N.C. courts have been reluctant to view a large development as a single unit merely because plats of smaller areas include a key map or context map of the overall project.[31] Also, mere proximity does not make two developments one. "The fact that the corporation owned both the townsite and farms and developed the two as contiguous subdivisions does not of itself make them one composite subdivision as a matter of law."[32]

By contrast, modern vested rights law has viewed phased developments as singular units for vested rights purposes. The statutory vested rights protect specifically defined "phased development plans" from zoning changes. In addition, in *Town of Midland v. Wayne*, the state supreme court treated a multi-phase, multi-owner development as having unity of ownership and vested rights for the total project.[33]

---

30. Statesville Unified Development Code § 8.01.

31. *See* Stephens Co. v. Myers Park Homes Co., 181 N.C. 335 (1921); Janicki v. Lorek, 255 N.C. 53 (1961).

32. *Janicki*, 255 N.C. at 62.

33. No. 458PA13, 2015 WL 3747169 (N.C. June 11, 2015).

# Chapter 5

# Typical Steps of Subdivision Review

A subdivision ordinance usually requires a multi-step approval process including sketch plan, preliminary plat, final plat, and dedication of property.[1] Sketch plan review is an initial review of the general concepts of the development and the ordinance requirements that apply. Preliminary plat review is a review of the proposed subdivision for compliance with all applicable standards. Some jurisdictions require construction plan review in conjunction with or following preliminary plat review. Final plat review confirms that the subdivision was constructed as approved in the preliminary plat. The final plat is recorded with the register of deeds, and then property may be sold from the subdivision. In addition to final plat approval, the government body must take action to formally accept property that is offered by the developer for dedication to the public.

| Sketch Plan Review | Preliminary Plat Review (and Construction Plan) | Improvements Inspection or Performance Guarantee | Final Plat Approval and Recording | Acceptance of Any Dedicated Lands |
| --- | --- | --- | --- | --- |

## Sketch Plan

Even before sketch plan submission and review, some communities offer an optional pre-application conference at which the developer and staff "discuss the nature of a proposed application, submittal requirements, and review procedures and standards."[2]

Sketch plan review (also called concept plan review) is an initial review of the development concept and provides an opportunity for the local government to better understand the project and for the developer to better understand the local requirements. Sketch plan review is authorized, but not required, by statute. Local ordinances may require sketch plan review in certain circumstances. Pasquotank County, for example, requires sketch plan review for subdivisions greater than ten acres and for subdivisions of waterfront property.[3]

Working together, the developer and public staff can identify potential issues of the concept before substantial investment by the developer in design and site plan preparations. Typically, sketch plan review is an advisory opinion and does not create vested rights in the project. At this stage the local government unit is primarily concerned with the location of the proposed subdivision, the general pattern of streets and lots, and the provision of community facilities or public facilities.

---

1. Sections 153A-330 and 160A-371 of the North Carolina General Statutes (hereinafter G.S.).
2. Statesville Unified Development Code § 2.01.A.
3. Pasquotank County Subdivision Ordinance § 304.

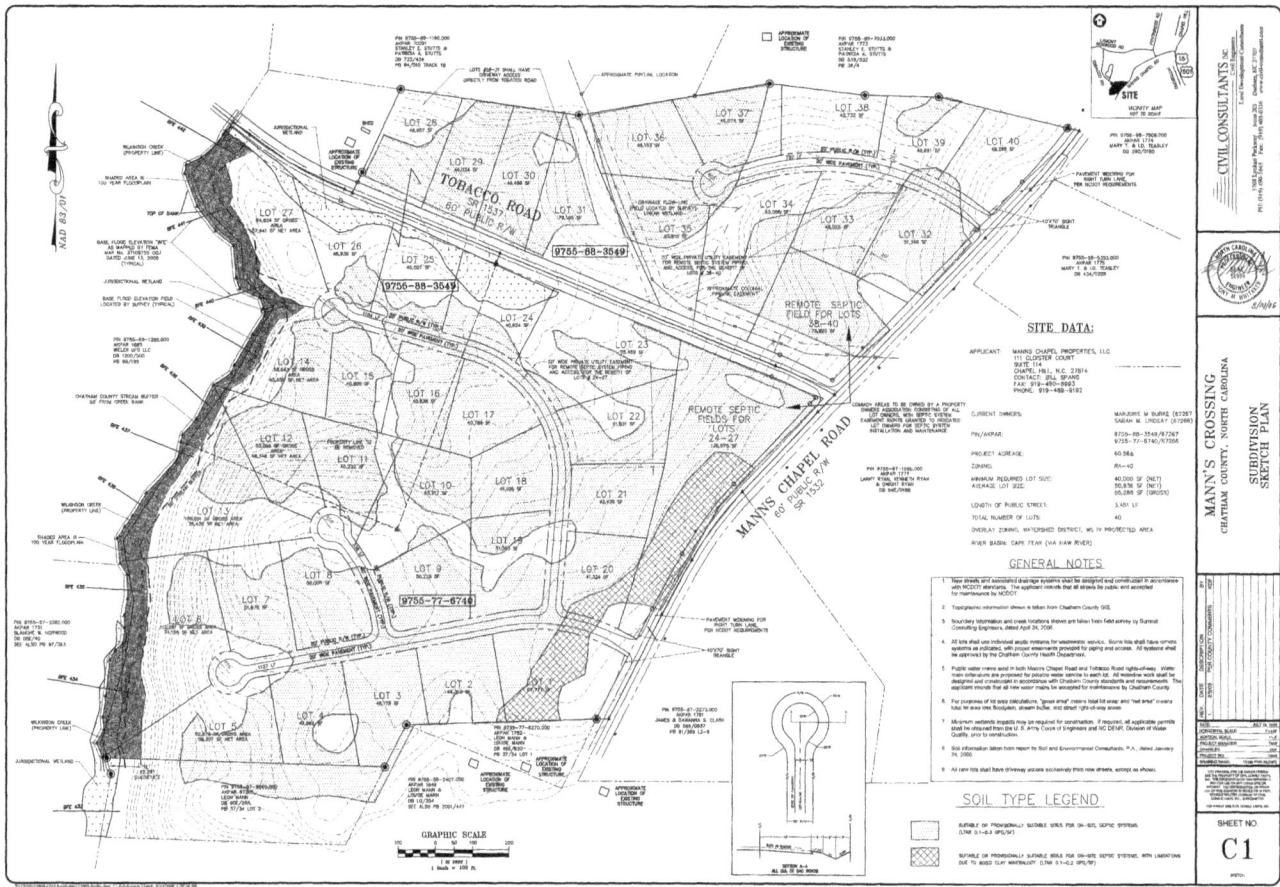

Sketch plan of Mann's Crossing. Reprinted with permission from Civil Consultants, Inc., copyright 2006.

The sketch plan must show sufficient detail to enable review of the proposal. Thus, the ordinance may require the sketch plan to contain such information as tract boundary; existing rights-of-way, improvements, and easements; proposed rights-of-way, improvements, and easements; layout of lots and streets; environmental characteristics; vicinity map; and site data, such as total acreage, lot sizes, acreage in open space; and other relevant information. Review topics may include

a. consistency with the goals and objectives of the comprehensive plan;

b. consistency with applicable zoning of the property;

c. consistency of public improvements within the development and surrounding area;

d. availability and adequacy of required public utilities and services necessary to serve the project, including but not limited to, sanitary and storm sewers, water, electrical, police, fire, roads, and pedestrian accessibility;

e. capacity or safety of the street network influenced by the use;

f. adverse environmental impacts generated by the project.[4]

In some cases, a community meeting may be required as part of the sketch plan review process.[5]

---

4. Statesville Unified Development Code § 2.03.
5. Chatham County Subdivision Regulations § 5.2.B.

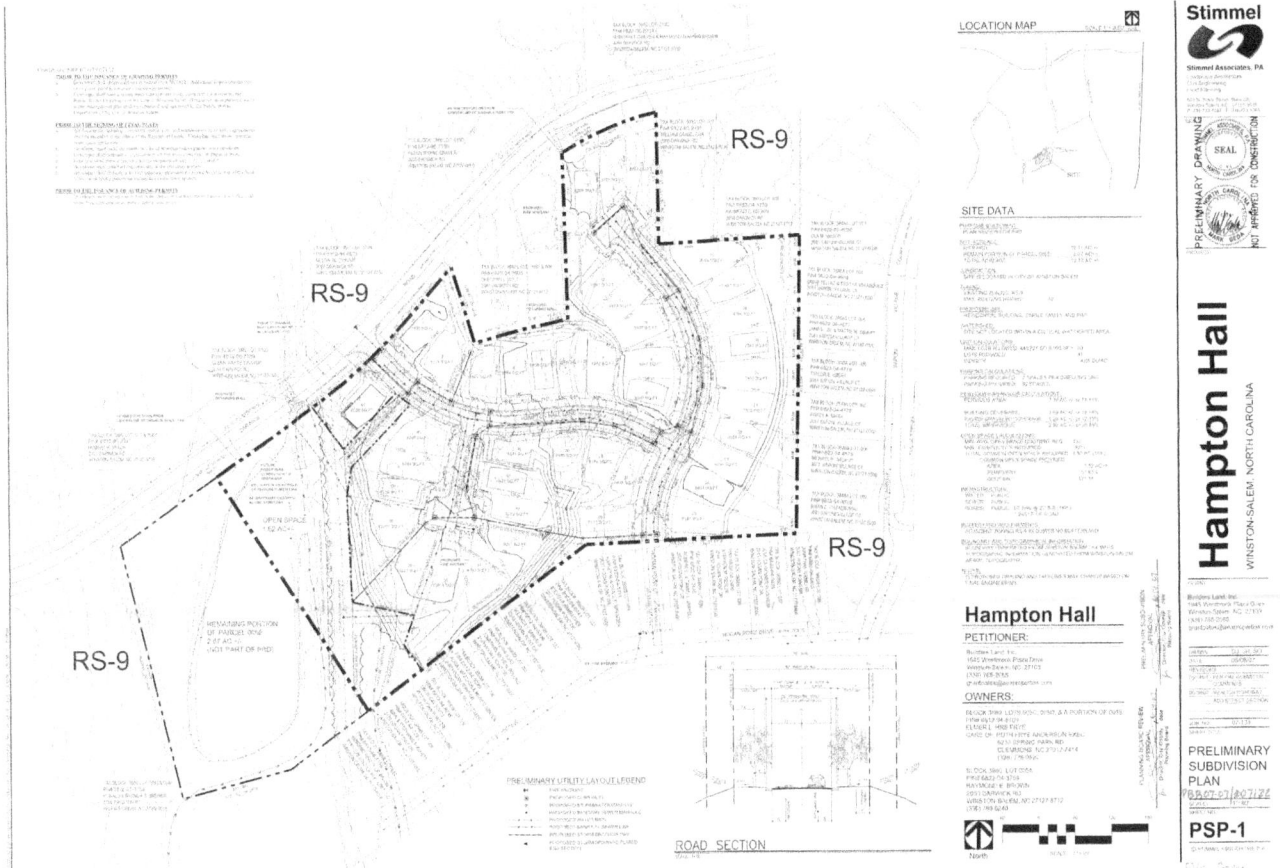

Preliminary plat for Hampton Hall. Reprinted with permission from Stimmel Associates, copyright 2007.

## Preliminary Plat Review

### Nature of Review

Preliminary plat review is a substantial review of the subdivision layout and improvement standards. While this step is commonly called preliminary plat review, the term "preliminary" is misleading. ("First plat" or "initial plat" are more accurate.) The preliminary plat sets the nature, design, and scope of the development. Approval allows the developer to move forward with improvements and, sometimes, to contract to sell property. As noted by the North Carolina Supreme Court,

> The appellation "preliminary" is a beguiling one, for the preliminary plat is hardly a rough introductory document. Unlike a sketch plan, which is used as a vehicle for informal discussion between developers and city planners, the preliminary plan is a formal document that constitutes the most critical step in the subdivision approval process.[6]

Most of the information included and reviewed as part of the preliminary plat is highly technical. As such, most communities have a technical review committee review preliminary plats. In some jurisdictions the technical review committee is the decision-maker; in

---

6. River Birch Assocs. v. City of Raleigh, 326 N.C. 100, 111–12 (1990).

other jurisdictions the technical review committee reviews and comments on the proposed subdivision in advance of planning board or governing board action. The statutes granting subdivision authority to counties requires technical review of subdivision plats by

1. the district highway engineer as to proposed state streets, state highways, and related drainage systems;
2. the county health director or local public utility, as appropriate, as to proposed water or sewerage systems;
3. any other agency or official designated by the board of commissioners.[7]

*A list of departments commonly represented on the technical review committee is presented in Chapter 4.* Preliminary plat approval may expire. Subdivision ordinances allow an approved preliminary plat to remain valid for a set amount of time (commonly one to two years). The developer must obtain final plat approval for the subdivision (or some phase of the subdivision) or obtain a permit extension from the decision-maker.

## Criteria

Preliminary plat review may include the following objective criteria, among others:

- provision of all required information;
- consistency with the sketch plan, if applicable;
- conformance with all standards and regulations, including, among other things,
  ○ lot and land layout,
  ○ street connectivity,
  ○ adequate and safe access,
  ○ adequate drainage to minimize flood damage;
- offer of required dedications;
- infrastructure capacity;
- adequate drainage to reduce exposure to flood hazards.[8]

In some communities, preliminary plat review is quasi-judicial in nature. In addition to the objective criteria, those communities have subjective criteria, thereby requiring the decision-maker to exercise judgment and discretion. Such criteria may, for example, include that the subdivision, if completed as proposed,

- will not materially endanger the public health or safety,
- will not substantially injure the value of adjoining or abutting property,
- will be in harmony with the area in which it is to be located,
- will be in general conformity with the comprehensive plan and all other relevant plans officially adopted by the governing board.[9]

These quasi-judicial standards are common to zoning conditional use permits and special use permits. Indeed, some communities require an applicant to obtain a special use permit as part of the subdivision approval process.[10]

---

7. G.S. 153A-332.
8. Statesville Unified Development Code § 2.03.D.
9. Boone Unified Development Ordinance § 6.02.01.
10. Aberdeen Unified Development Ordinance § 152-76.

Other communities tie their quasi-judicial standards more directly to the statutory purposes of subdivision. Clayton's standards, for example, include plan consistency as well as

> (c) The subdivision will not be detrimental to the use or orderly development of other properties in the surrounding area and will not violate the character of existing standards for development of properties in the surrounding area.

> (d) The subdivision design will provide for the distribution of traffic in a manner that will avoid or mitigate congestion within the immediate area, will provide for the unified and orderly use of or extension of public infrastructure, and will not materially endanger the environment, public health, safety, or the general welfare.[11]

*The nature of standards—either administrative or quasi-judicial—and their related procedural requirements are discussed in greater detail in Chapter 4.*

## Information on the Preliminary Plat

The local subdivision ordinance will specify what information must be provided on the preliminary plat. In short, the applicant must provide information to show that the proposed development meets all applicable standards. The required information may include the following:

- Basic plat information:
  - title, date, north point, and graphic scale;
  - name of owner, surveyor, or land planner;
  - scale;
  - size.
- Current conditions:
  - vicinity map;
  - boundaries of tract shown with bearings and distances;
  - existing and platted property lines;
  - names of adjoining property owners or subdivisions;
  - streets and street names, railroads, transmission lines, sewers, water mains, existing fire hydrant location nearest to site, and public easements;
  - buildings;
  - water courses, bridges, culverts, and drain pipes;
  - wooded areas, marshes, and any other conditions affecting the site;
  - zoning classification on the land to be subdivided and on adjoining land;
  - topography contour lines, including flood plain.
- Proposed conditions:
  - proposed lot lines, lot and block numbers, and approximate dimensions;
  - proposed streets, street names, rights-of-way, roadway widths, and approximate grades;
  - proposed utility layouts (sewer, water, gas, electricity) showing connections to existing systems or plans for individual water supply, sewage disposal, storm drainage, etc.;

---

11. Clayton Unified Development Ordinance § 155.706(I)(10).

- other proposed right-of-way or easements; locations, widths, and purposes;
- proposed minimum building setback lines;
- proposed parks, school sites, or other public open spaces, if any;
- landscape plan.
- Site data:
  - acreage in total tract,
  - acreage in parks or other land usage,
  - total number of lots,
  - lineal feet in streets.

In addition, the subdivision ordinance may require supplemental submissions at the time of preliminary plat submission. Depending on the ordinance and the proposed development, these may include the following submissions, among others:

- environmental impact statement (discussed more fully below),
- stormwater management plan,
- open space provision and maintenance plan,
- letter from the appropriate electric utility company certifying that the utilities will be installed underground.

## Environmental Impact Statement

In some cases, an environmental impact statement may be required in conjunction with preliminary plat review.

Under the North Carolina State Environmental Policy Act, a local government may by ordinance require a detailed environmental impact statement (EIS) for a "major development project," including a subdivision. Major development projects are defined to include, without limitation, "shopping centers, subdivisions and other housing developments, and industrial and commercial projects, but shall not include any projects of less than ten contiguous acres in extent."[12] The ordinance must include minimum criteria for determining whether an EIS is required.[13] A local EIS may not be required if a comparable review is required by state or federal law. In addition, a local EIS may not be required for certain classes of development outlined at Section 113A-12 of the North Carolina General Statutes (hereinafter G.S.), including certain types of utility construction, driveway connections, and redevelopment projects.

As outlined at G.S. 113A-4, a detailed environmental impact statement includes the following:

a. the environmental impact of the proposed action;
b. any significant adverse environmental effects that cannot be avoided should the proposal be implemented;
c. mitigation measures proposed to minimize the impact;
d. alternatives to the proposed action;

---

12. G.S. 113A-9(5).
13. A court may strike down the local environmental impact assessment requirement if minimum criteria are not in place. Marriott v. Chatham Cnty., 187 N.C. App. 491 (2007).

e. the relationship between the short-term uses of the environment involved in the proposed action and the maintenance and enhancement of long-term productivity; and

f. any irreversible and irretrievable environmental changes that would result from the proposed action should it be implemented.

Pasquotank County requires an EIS for developments exceeding ten acres and when the board deems it necessary "due to the nature of the land to be subdivided, or peculiarities in the proposed layout."[14] In Chatham County, an EIS is required for subdivisions greater than fifty lots. Smaller subdivisions submit a general document of environmental information.[15]

Chatham County's ordinance requires that the Environmental Impact Assessment (EIA) include the following information, as applicable:

- proposed project description and need, including location, site plan, adjacent development, land disturbance, public benefits, and utilities;
- alternatives analysis, including comparison of reasonable alternatives for site selection, layout, infrastructure, and other factors;
- existing environment, including geography, soils and farmlands, land use, wetlands, public and scenic lands, historic and archeological resources, air quality, noise levels, light levels, water resources, habitats and ecology, and hazardous materials.[16]

## Contracts Relying on Preliminary Plat Approval

The General Statutes authorize an owner or agent to enter into contracts to sell or lease land by reference to an approved preliminary plat if the owner or agent meets certain requirements (the owner cannot close on the sale until final plat approval). As outlined at G.S. 160A-375 and G.S. 153A-334, contracts signed in advance of final plat approval must

- incorporate as an attachment the preliminary plat,
- obligate the owner to deliver the recorded plat to the buyer prior to closing;
- plainly and conspicuously notify the prospective buyer that
  - no final plat has been approved at the time of the contract,
  - no governmental body will incur any obligation to the prospective buyer or lessee with respect to approval of the final subdivision plat,
  - changes between preliminary plat and final plat are possible,
  - the contract or lease may be terminated without breach by either party if the final plat materially differs from the preliminary plat;
- stipulate that closing shall not be any earlier than
  - five days after delivery of the final recorded plat, if there are no material changes from preliminary plat;
  - fifteen days after delivery of the final recorded plat, if there are material changes from preliminary plat (during the fifteen days a buyer may terminate the contract and receive all prepaid funds).

---

14. Pasquotank County Subdivision Ordinance § 305.1.
15. Chatham County Subdivision Regulations § 5.2.C.
16. Chatham County Subdivision Regulations § 6.2.B.

If the person buying or leasing land is a residential or commercial builder, the parties may enter into contracts for the sale or lease of land prior to final plat recordation provided that no conveyance will occur and no lease contract will be effective until after the final plat is recorded.

## Construction Plan

The use and role of construction plans vary by jurisdiction. Generally, the construction plan constitutes the detailed plans and specifications for all improvements required for the subdivision. The details may include, among other things, layout, street profile, electric utility information; easements and rights-of-way; and calculations such as street length, pipe length, stormwater flow, and pavement design. Due to their very technical nature, construction plans typically are approved by the technical review committee or the city engineer. The construction plan may establish the costs of improvements for performance guarantees.

Statesville requires submission prior to preliminary plat approval,[17] but in Chatham County the construction plan is used to ensure compliance with the preliminary plan.[18] In Wilmington, the construction plan follows preliminary plat approval; construction plan approval is overseen by the city engineer and done in conjunction with sedimentation and erosion control permitting.[19]

## Improvements Inspection or Performance Guarantee

With preliminary plat approval, the developer can move forward to lay out lots and construct improvements. An ordinance may require that before final plat approval the developer must complete the improvements to the standard of the city or county. Alternatively, if the local government allows, the developer may provide a performance guarantee and financial assurance that the improvements will be completed as required. Either way—whether the improvements are constructed or a financial assurance is issued—the local government must inspect and confirm that the construction or assurance meets the applicable standards. Some ordinances call for as-built drawings of improvements, with engineer certification, prior to final inspection.

To be sure, inspection and approval do not constitute acceptance of any improvements offered for dedication to the public. The public body must act to accept them.

Inspection may be required at the following steps, among others:

1. completion of site grading and installation of erosion control measures,
2. start and completion of each phase of underground utility construction,
3. preparation of subgrade prior to installation of aggregate base,
4. installation of concrete curb and gutter,

---

17. Statesville Unified Development Code § 2.03.E.
18. Chatham County Subdivision Regulations § 5.2.C.
19. Wilmington Land Development Code § 18-364.

5. compaction of aggregate base prior to installing pavement,

6. completion of final surfacing.[20]

Chapter 6 offers additional discussion of technical standards. For more on performance guarantees see Chapter 9.

# Final Plat Review

## Generally

"Final plat approval is, essentially, a ministerial check and statement made by the city affirming that what the developer has done is in conformity with city standards."[21] Final plat review determines if the development complies with the preliminary plat. Because it is ministerial in nature, final plat review commonly is assigned to a staff person or the technical review committee.

Even if approval is ministerial, the final plat, once approved and recorded, stands as a significant legal document. To ensure compliance with applicable regulations, to protect the interests of lot purchasers, and to clarify rights and obligations of the owners and the public, strict standards apply to the creation and certification of final plats. These standards and certifications arise from both local ordinance requirements as well as statutory requirements. Required certifications are discussed below.

The approval of a final plat does not constitute acceptance by the public body of any dedication of property to the public.[22] The public body must take formal action to accept the dedicated property. (The process and limitations of dedication are discussed more fully in the next section.)

If approved, the final plat may be recorded with the register of deeds. Generally final plat approval follows construction of improvements that are substantially in conformance with the approved preliminary plat. Or, alternatively, the ordinance may allow final plat approval in conjunction with a performance guarantee to ensure completion of the improvements.

The subdivision ordinance may place a time limit, requiring the owner to record the plat within a certain number of days (ninety days, for example). The developer may begin conveying newly created lots after the final plat is approved and recorded.

Once a developer relies on and benefits from a preliminary plat approval, "a city may refuse to consider a subsequent stage of the overall project that fails to take into account the prior development as proposed and undertaken in the prior stages of development."[23]

## Certifications Required by Statute

### Surveyor Certification

The person supervising a survey or plat is to provide certification stating the origin of the information shown, including recorded deed or plat references. In addition, the plat must indicate the ratio of precision before any adjustments and identify any lines not actually surveyed (and the source of information for such lines). Where a plat consists of more than

---

20. Concord Development Ordinance § 5.7.3; Statesville Unified Development Code § 2.03.E.8.b.

21. River Birch Assocs. v. City of Raleigh, 326 N.C. 100, 112 (1990).

22. G.S. 153A-333; G.S. 160A-374.

23. *River Birch*, 326 N.C. at 115.

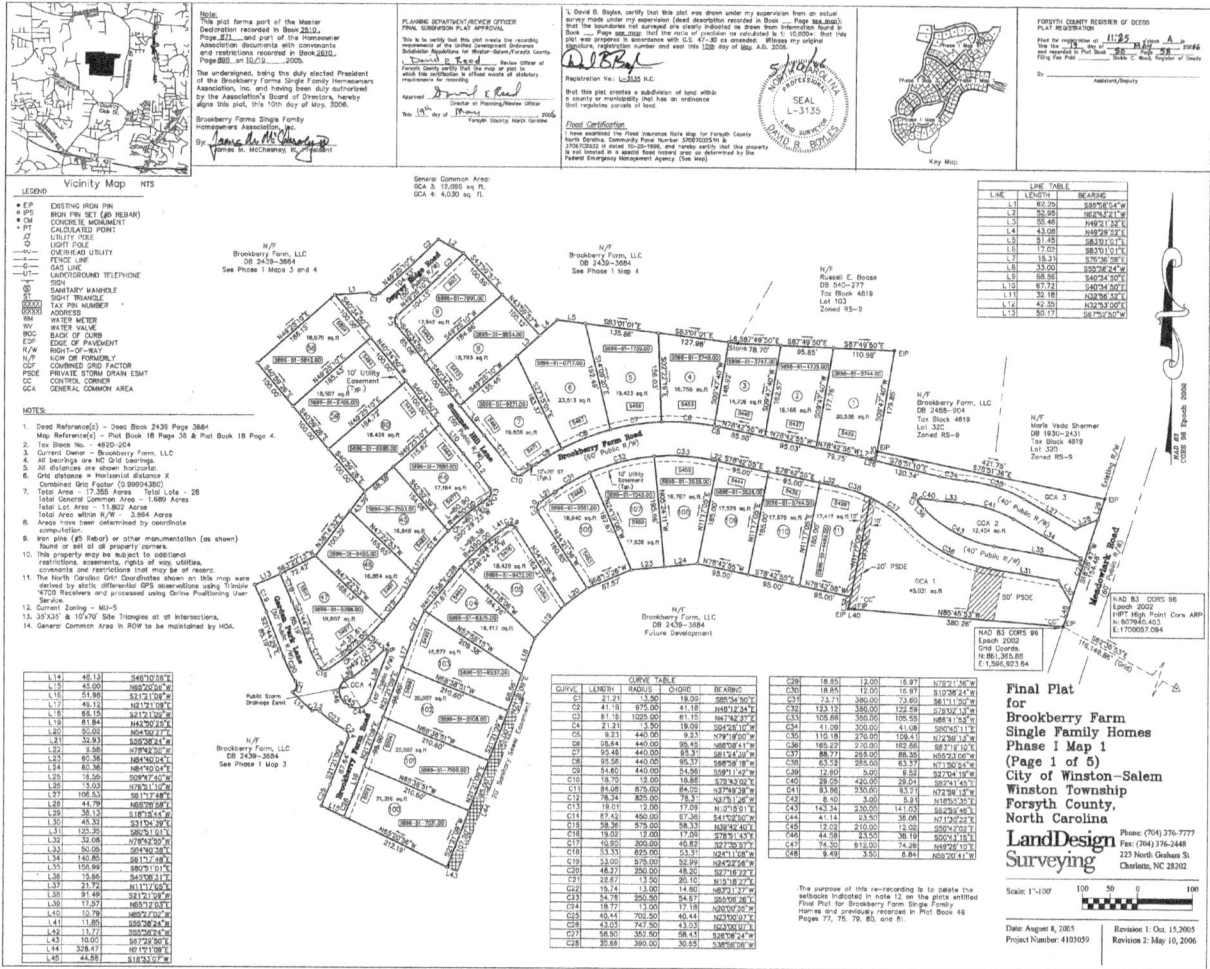

Final plat for Brookberry Farm. Reprinted with permission from LandDesign, copyright 2006.

one sheet, only one sheet must contain the certification, but all other sheets must be signed and sealed.[24]

The certificate must be substantially in the following form:

"I, _____, certify that this plat was drawn under my supervision from an actual survey made under my supervision (deed description recorded in Book ____, page ____, etc.) (other); that the boundaries not surveyed are clearly indicated as drawn from information found in Book ____, page ____; that the ratio of precision as calculated is 1: ____; that this plat was prepared in accordance with G.S. 47-30 as amended. Witness my original signature, registration number and seal this ____ day of ____, A.D., ____.

Seal or Stamp

_____
Surveyor
Registration Number"

_____

24. G.S. 47-30(d).

The surveyor also must certify whether the plat is subject to local subdivision regulation and one of the following statements concerning the status of subdivision regulation:[25]

a. that the survey creates a subdivision of land within the area of a county or municipality that has an ordinance that regulates parcels of land;

b. that the survey is located in a portion of a county or municipality that is unregulated as to an ordinance that regulates parcels of land;

c. any one of the following:

    1. that the survey is of an existing parcel or parcels of land and does not create a new street or change an existing street;

    2. that the survey is of an existing building or other structure, or natural feature, such as a watercourse; or

    3. that the survey is a control survey;

d. that the survey is of another category, such as the recombination of existing parcels, a court-ordered survey, or other exemption to the definition of subdivision;

e. that the information available to the surveyor is such that the surveyor is unable to make a determination to the best of the surveyor's professional ability as to provisions contained in (a) through (d) above.

### Subdivision Regulation Certification

If land is subject to subdivision jurisdiction of a municipality or county, a plat review officer cannot certify the plat for recordation until it is properly approved by the local government. Such certification typically is provided by a subdivision officer in the planning department. The local ordinance may require certifications from other related departments.

If a surveyor certifies that the plat is not subject to subdivision regulation (certification "b" or "c" above), then the plat may be presented for recording without subdivision officer review. If, however, the plat is certified as a subdivision or exempt subdivision (certification "a," "d," or "e," above), the appropriate local government subdivision review officer must certify "approval" or "no approval required" on the face of the plat before it may be recorded.[26] That could be accomplished by use of a certificate or a plat stamp to indicate exempt subdivision.

### Street Standards and Department of Transportation Approval

For residential subdivisions outside of municipal corporate limits and those affecting state highways within municipalities, certain standards and approvals apply to streets. When an owner divides land into two or more lots, building sites, or other divisions for sale or building development for residential purposes, and the division includes a new street or change to an existing street, the owner must record a map or plat with the register of deeds prior to any

---

25. G.S. 47-30(f)(11).

26. G.S. 153A-332; G.S. 160A-373, each referencing G.S. 47-30(f)(11), which states that "the plat shall have, in addition to said surveyor's certificate, a certification of approval, or no approval required, as may be required by local ordinance from the appropriate government authority before the plat is presented for recordation." The precise interpretation of this provision is challenging: it includes the mandatory "shall have" and the permissive "as may be required." Arguably an exempt plat must obtain a certificate of subdivision exemption regardless of the ordinance, but for clarity's sake, the subdivision ordinance should clearly state this requirement.

conveyance.[27] The right-of-way must be particularly delineated on the plat and designated as public or private. The plat review officer may not certify a plat for recording unless new streets or changes to existing streets are designated as either public or private.[28]

For a street proposed as public, the developer must design and build it to the applicable minimum standards.[29] The developer must obtain a certificate of approval from the Division of Highways within NCDOT that proposed public streets are designed in accordance with the minimum standards for acceptance into the state highway system.[30]

The subdivision ordinance of a municipality may require similar certification on the plat from the city transportation official that the roads comply with applicable standards.

### Plat Review Officer Certification

In each county, the board of commissioners designates by resolution a plat review officer. The statute authorizes more than one review officer, so a county could designate additional individuals to serve as the review officer for a municipality or certain areas of the county. In order to maintain uniform plat review, however, it may be prudent to designate only one plat review officer. The officer must be experienced in mapping or land records management and, "if reasonably feasible, be certified as a property mapper pursuant to G.S. 147-54.4." The resolution designating the officer is recorded in the register of deeds.[31]

The plat review officer must sign off on nearly all plats presented for recording, even those that are not subdivisions under the statutory definition. A few exceptions apply. No officer review is required for: (1) land not subject to municipal or county subdivision regulation, or a survey of existing parcels, buildings, or natural features, or a control survey; (2) municipal boundary plats, highway right-of-way plans, or roadway corridor maps; or (3) a map recorded as an attachment to a recorded instrument.[32]

The plat review officer must expeditiously review those maps and plats prior to recording and certify if the map or plat meets all statutory requirements. If a map or plat is required to be submitted to the plat review officer, the register of deeds cannot accept the map or plat unless it has certification from the officer. The certification must be substantially the same as follows:[33]

> State of North Carolina
> County of
> I, _____, Review Officer of _____ County, certify that the map or plat to which this certification is affixed meets all statutory requirements for recording.
>
> _____
> Review Officer
> Date _____

---

27. G.S. 136-102.6(a).
28. G.S. 136-102.6(d).
29. G.S. 136-102.6(c).
30. G.S. 136-102.6(c) & (d).
31. G.S. 47-30.2(a).
32. G.S. 47-30.2(c).
33. G.S. 47-30.2(b).

### Riparian Buffer Boundaries

Pursuant to G.S. 143-214.23.A, if a riparian buffer is included within a lot, the subdivision ordinance shall require the riparian buffer to be shown on the recorded plat. There is no requirement, however, for the buffer area to be surveyed.

## Certifications Required by Ordinance

The local ordinance may require, among other things, "that plats show sufficient data to determine readily and reproduce accurately on the ground the location, bearing, and length of every street and alley line, lot line, easement boundary line, and other property boundaries, including the radius and other data for curved property lines, to an appropriate accuracy and in conformance with good surveying practice."[34]

In addition, the local subdivision ordinance may require certifications for final plat approval, including ownership and dedication, approval and acceptance of dedication, and others. The examples presented below are taken from the Town of Clayton Unified Development Code.[35]

### Ownership and Offer of Dedication

CERTIFICATE OF OWNERSHIP AND DEDICATION

I HEREBY CERTIFY THAT I AM THE OWNER OF THE PROPERTY SHOWN AND DESCRIBED HEREON, WHICH IS LOCATED IN THE SUBDIVISION JURISDICTION OF THE TOWN OF CLAYTON AND THAT I HEREBY ADOPT THIS SUBDIVISION PLAN WITH MY FREE CONSENT, ESTABLISH MINIMUM SETBACK LINES, AND DEDICATE ALL STREETS, ALLEYS, PARKS AND OTHER SITES AND EASEMENTS TO PUBLIC OR PRIVATE USE AS NOTED.

_____      _____

DATE                 OWNER

### Approval and Acceptance of Dedication by Governing Board

TOWN OF CLAYTON TOWN MANAGER CERTIFICATION FOR A FINAL PLAT

I HEREBY CERTIFY THAT THE TOWN OF CLAYTON, NC HAS APPROVED THIS PLAT FOR RECORDING IN THE OFFICE OF THE JOHNSTON COUNTY REGISTER OF DEEDS, AND ACCEPTS THE DEDICATION OF STREETS, EASEMENTS, RIGHTS-OF-WAY, AND PUBLIC LANDS SHOWN THEREON, BUT ASSUMES NO RESPONSIBILITY TO OPEN OR MAINTAIN THE SAME UNTIL, IN THE OPINION OF THE CLAYTON TOWN COUNCIL, IT IS IN THE PUBLIC INTEREST TO DO SO.

_____      _____

DATE                 TOWN MANAGER

---

34. G.S. 160A-372(b); *see also* G.S. 153A-331(b).
35. Section 155-706.

### Other Certifications

Depending on the local ordinance, other certifications may be required. These could include

- certificate of road maintenance obligation;
- certificate of streets, water, and sewer system approval and other improvements by the director of engineering;
- certificate of electric distribution system approval by the director of electrical systems;
- adequate soils certification or approval of sewage system from the health director;
- approval of draining improvements;
- certificate of fee payment by the finance director.

Other notations also may be required. In Boone, for example, final plats with private streets must include the following notation: "Further subdivision of any lot shown on this plat as served by a private road may be prohibited by the Town of Boone Unified Development Ordinance."[36]

The following discussion considers specific certifications required by statute for final plat approval and recording.

## Final Plat Characteristics

### Dimensions

Each county may choose from the following possibilities the required dimensions for plats to be recorded: (1) 18 inches by 24 inches, (2) a combination of 18 inches by 24 inches and 21 inches by 30 inches; (3) a combination of 18 inches by 24 inches and 24 inches by 36 inches; or (4) a combination of all three sizes. Plats must have a minimum one and one-half inch margin on the left side and a minimum one-half inch margin on the other sides.[37] Electronic documents are discussed more below.

### Reproducibility

Plats must be reproducible such that the public can obtain legible copies. A direct or photographic copy of each plat must be placed in the plat book or plat file. If the register makes a security copy of the plat, the original may be returned. Plats presented for recording must be either in original ink on polyester film (mylar) or a reproduced drawing that is transparent and archival as defined by the American National Standards Institute.[38] The plat review officer is not responsible for reviewing the archival quality of the plat[39] but must ensure that the quality of plat is reproducible (especially font size, boldness of lines, general legibility, and the like).

### Title Information

Each plat must include specified title information: "property designation, name of owner (the name of owner shall be shown for indexing purposes only and is not to be construed as title certification), location to include township, county and state, the date or dates the

---

36. Boone Unified Development Ordinance § 5.04.03.
37. G.S. 47-30(a).
38. G.S. 47-30(b).
39. G.S. 47-30(g).

survey was made; scale or scale ratio in words or figures and bar graph; name and address of surveyor or firm preparing the plat."[40]

### Additional Information

A recordable plat must include, among other things, a north arrow; course and distances of each property line; names of adjacent landowners or lot, block, parcel, subdivision designations; visible and apparent rights-of-way, watercourses, utilities, roadways, and other improvements when they cross or form a boundary line; a vicinity map; and, when applicable, accurate survey references, accurate curve data, accurately plotted street lines and widths, control corners and monuments.[41] The plat review officer is not responsible for reviewing these elements.[42]

Surveyors must use an accurate method of calculating acreage and ratio of precision. Only in certain limited circumstances may a surveyor use aerial photos or other sources to determine inaccessible acreage. Those methods must be disclosed on the plat.[43] The plat review officer is not responsible for reviewing the method of calculation.[44]

Chapter 39 of the General Statutes concerns conveyances of land; Article 5A establishes rules for control corners in real estate developments. Pursuant to those rules, when a developer divides a parcel into lots and streets, and offers for sale any lot or lots, the developer must designate one or more "control corners" for the development and must designate two or more monuments for streets. These locations must be marked with a permanent monument.[45]

The control corners and permanent markers must be affixed at the time of recording the plat and prior to the first sale of a lot.[46] The developer must file with the county register of deeds a plat showing the location of the control corners and permanent markers.[47] Subsequent sales of lots within the development may reference the established control corners. Reference to such control corners is prima facie evidence in court of the correct method of determining the boundary.[48]

## Electronic Documents

In order for a plat defined as an electronic document under G.S. 47-16.2(3) to meet the requirements for plat size, reproducible form, and necessary certification, the following conditions must be met:

1. The register of deeds has authorized the submitter to electronically register the electronic document.
2. The plat is submitted by a U.S. federal or a state governmental unit or instrumentality or a trusted submitter. For purposes of this subsection, "a trusted submitter" means a person or entity that has entered into a memorandum of understanding

---

40. G.S. 47-30(c).
41. G.S. 47-30(f).
42. G.S. 47-30(g).
43. G.S. 47-30(e).
44. G.S. 47-30(g).
45. G.S. 39-32.1.
46. G.S. 39-32.2.
47. G.S. 39-32.3.
48. G.S. 39-32.4.

regarding electronic recording with the register of deeds in the county in which the electronic document is to be submitted.

3. Evidence of required certifications appear[s] on the digitized image of the document as it will appear on the public record.

4. With respect to a plat submitted by a trusted submitter, the digitized image of the document as it will appear on the public record contains the submitter's name in the following completed statement on the first page of the document image: "Submitted electronically by _____ (submitter's name) in compliance with North Carolina statutes governing recordable documents and the terms of the submitter agreement with the _____ (insert county name) County Register of Deeds.["]

5. Except as otherwise provided in this subsection, the digitized image of the plat conforms to all other applicable laws and rules that prescribe recordation.[49]

## Offers and Acceptance of Dedications

Under the common law and statutory provisions, dedication of property requires two actions: an *offer* by the private owner to dedicate property for public use and *acceptance* of the offer by the public body.

### Offer of Dedication

#### Express

The offer of dedication typically is made by identifying areas on the plat as public. In counties, NCDOT rules require that streets on subdivision plats be designated as public or private, and designation as public is presumed to be an offer.[50] Municipal subdivision ordinances also may require that an express offer of dedication of public spaces be shown on the plat. (Relevant language from the Clayton ordinance is noted in the section on certifications, above.)

#### Implied

North Carolina common law has recognized offers of dedication in several circumstances short of an express offer. While such offers are less common in contemporary subdivisions, they continue to resolve disputes over rights in older streets and subdivisions. The typical situation is that a developer platted a subdivision showing lots and streets and then sold one or more lots in reference to the plat. "[W]hen sales are made in reference to a map showing streets and alleys, the sale is an offer of dedication of these streets and alleys to the municipality."[51] For this implied offer of dedication, case law emphasizes that there must be the sale of a lot in reference to the plat or some other manifestation of intent to

---

49. G.S. 47-30(o).

50. G.S. 136-102.6(b).

51. Osborne v. Town of N. Wilkesboro, 280 N.C. 696, 699 (1972); *see also,* Steadman v. Town of Pinetops, 251 N.C. 509, 516 (1960); Home Real Estate Loan & Ins. Co. v. Town of Carolina Beach, 216 N.C. 778 (1940).

make the offer absolute.[52] In modern times that intent likely is manifest by an express offer of dedication upon the face of the plat, so the sale of a lot may be unnecessary to make an unconditional offer of dedication.[53]

Courts have been willing to infer an offer of dedication from an owner's intent. "An easement by dedication can occur in express terms or it may be implied from conduct on the part of the owner. . . . The intention to dedicate must clearly appear, though such intention may be shown by deed, by words, or by acts."[54]

### Revocation

"A dedication of a road is a revocable offer until it is accepted on the part of the public in some recognized legal manner and by a proper public authority."[55] So, a developer may plat a subdivision with offers to dedicate a right-of-way to the public, but before the local government formally accepts the offer, the developer may revoke the offer and maintain the right-of-way as private.

Revoking an offer of dedication raises two practical issues for the developer, though. First, revoking an offer to dedicate may undermine subdivision approval. If the subdivision ordinance requires dedication of property and plat approval is conditioned on that dedication, then withdrawal of the offer to dedicate may revoke plat approval. And second, lot purchasers may still have rights in the offered right-of-way that are distinct from rights of the general public.

## Acceptance

### Express

Before an offered property becomes public, the relevant public body must affirmatively accept the offer of dedication. A "dedication is never complete until acceptance; neither burdens nor benefits with attendant duties may be imposed upon the public, unless in some proper way it has consented to assume them."[56] The mere act of approving the final plat is not sufficient. Under the subdivision statutes, "approval of a plat shall not be deemed to constitute or effect the acceptance by the city or public of the dedication of any street or other ground, public utility line, or other public facility shown on the plat."[57]

In other words, the city, county, or other public body must take some action to accept the dedication. Explicit acceptance may occur by "a formal ratification, resolution, or order by proper officials, the adoption of an ordinance, a town council's vote of approval, or the signing of a written instrument by proper authorities."[58] While mere approval of the final

---

52. State Highway Comm'n v. Thornton, 271 N.C. 227 (1967).

53. *See* David M. Lawrence, Property Interests in North Carolina City Streets § 1.08 (1985).

54. Kraft v. Town of Mt. Olive, 183 N.C. App. 415, 418 (2007) (quotation and citation omitted).

55. *Kraft*, 183 N.C. App. at 420 (quotations omitted) (citing Bumgarner v. Reneau, 105 N.C. App. 362, 366, *modified and aff'd*, 332 N.C. 624 (1992) (citation omitted)).

56. Irwin v. City of Charlotte, 193 N.C. 109 (1927).

57. G.S. 160A-374; *see also* G.S. 153A-333.

58. *Kraft*, 183 N.C. App. at 420.

plat is insufficient, a certification by an authorized official on the final plat will suffice. (Relevant language from the Clayton ordinance is noted in the section on certifications above.)

Acceptance may be conditioned on certain standards and obligations. For example, prior to acceptance of a dedication, Wilmington requires that

- lands and facilities are properly offered for dedication through plat, deed, or easement;
- lands and facilities have been inspected and meet all standards; and
- the subdivider requested acceptance by the city;
- the subdivider provided valuation of all lands and facilities.

In addition, acceptance of improvements is conditioned on

- an eighteen-month guarantee of materials and workmanship;
- developer and related parties are not relieved of obligations under the ordinance, policy, or contract;
- all rights are assigned to the city;
- certification by the subdivider of unencumbered title to the lands and improvements;
- no obligation for the city to provide facilities or utilities.[59]

### Implied

Courts also have found implicit acceptance of an offer of dedication. In older cases, the courts found it sufficient that if municipalities "improve the streets and open them to public use, acceptance is conclusively presumed."[60] More recently, courts have applied a clearer test for implied acceptance. "An implicit dedication occurs when: (1) the dedicated property is used by the general public; and (2) coupled with control of the road by public authorities for a period of twenty years or more. To be clear, it is not enough for the public to use the alley for twenty years, but the public authorities must assert control over [the dedicated property]."[61]

It is a fact-specific inquiry to determine if municipal action is sufficient to imply acceptance. Installation of publicly franchised utilities and a general resolution accepting historically dedicated streets in the city may be insufficient.[62] On the other hand, having opened and maintained a street for two to three years many years ago may be sufficient to imply acceptance.[63]

### What Public Body Accepts?

"A 'proper public authority' is a governing body having jurisdiction over the location of the dedicated property, such as . . . an incorporated town . . . or any public body having the power to exercise eminent domain over the dedicated property."[64] Water and sewer easements may

---

59. Wilmington Land Development Code § 18-351.
60. Osborne v. Town of N. Wilkesboro, 280 N.C. 696, 699 (1972); *see also,* Steadman v. Town of Pinetops, 251 N.C. 509, 516 (1960).
61. Waterway Drive Prop. Owners' Ass'n, Inc. v. Town of Cedar Point, ___ N.C. App. ___, 737 S.E.2d 126, 133 (2012) (citing *Kraft,* 183 N.C. App. at 420–21); *see also* Bumgarner v. Reneau, 105 N.C. App. 362, 367, *aff'd as modified,* 332 N.C. 624 (1992).
62. *Waterway,* ___ N.C. App. ___, 737 S.E.2d at 133; *see also Bumgarner,* 105 N.C. App. at 367.
63. *Steadman,* 251 N.C. at 509.
64. *Kraft,* 183 N.C. App. at 420.

be granted to a water authority, for example, and in a county subdivision, streets may be dedicated to the Division of Highways pursuant to G.S. 136-102.6.

A municipality may "accept any dedication made to the public of lands or facilities for streets, parks, public utility lines, or other public purposes, when the lands or facilities are located within its subdivision-regulation jurisdiction."[65] Acceptance of dedicated lands or facilities outside of a municipal boundary but within its extraterritorial jurisdiction does not create any duty for the municipality to open, operate, repair, or maintain streets or infrastructure in such dedicated lands (except for water systems in limited circumstances[66]).

## Abandoned and Withdrawn Dedication

Under certain circumstances a dedication that has not been opened and used may be withdrawn by private parties.

If property dedicated for a street is not actually opened and used by the public within fifteen years of dedication, the dedication is presumed abandoned and certain property owners may withdraw the dedication.[67] The dedicator or an individual claiming rights under the dedicator must record with the register of deeds a declaration withdrawing the dedicated property. There are limitations, however. Where dedicated property is necessary "to afford convenient ingress or egress to any lot or parcel of land sold and conveyed by the dedicator," the dedication may not be abandoned and withdrawn. In addition, property dedicated to be part of a future street shown on an adopted street plan pursuant to G.S. 136-66.2 may not be abandoned and withdrawn.

The right to withdraw is not generally enjoyed by lot purchasers. The statute authorizes withdrawal by "the dedicator or some one or more of those claiming under him." Those claiming rights under the dedicator will depend on the rights conveyed to lot purchasers and the organizational structure of the developer and/or homeowners association. In one case, the court of appeals found that because the dedicator was an individual and retained fee interest in the streets, the individual lot owners had only an easement and could not withdraw the dedication of the underlying fee interest.[68] By contrast, if the dedicator had been a corporation that became defunct, the lot owners might then have had more rights under G.S. 136.96.[69]

If a dedicator or successor withdraws a dedication of property, a municipality may preserve public and private utility easements.[70] Prior to the recording of a map, plat, or declaration of withdrawal, the city must hold a public hearing and declare its intent to retain the easements. The city must provide certified or registered mail notice to the withdrawing party at least

---

65. G.S. 160A-374.

66. For subdivisions outside of a municipal boundary (in county jurisdiction or municipal extraterritorial jurisdiction), if the ordinance requires dedication of water systems or facilities as a condition of subdivision approval, then the municipality, county, or other public water system must have agreed to begin operation and maintenance of the water system within one year of the issuance of the first certificate of occupancy for a housing unit in the subdivision. G.S. 160A-374.

67. G.S. 136-96.

68. Town of Atl. Beach v. Tradewinds Campground, Inc., 97 N.C. App. 655 (1990); *see also* Russell v. Coggin, 232 N.C. 674, 675 (1950).

69. Steadman v. Town of Pinetops, 251 N.C. 509 (1960) (The original dedicator was a corporation no longer in existence, so the owner had rights to withdraw under G.S. 136-96.)

70. G.S. 160A-299(g).

five days prior to the public hearing. After the public hearing, the city council must "approve a 'declaration of retention of utility easements' specifically describing such easements."[71] The declaration of retention, then, must be recorded with the withdrawal and shown on any map or plat of withdrawal.

For a very limited set of subdivisions (older county subdivisions bordering the Atlantic Ocean), G.S. 136-96.2 provides a procedure for withdrawing dedication of streets that were never accepted and maintained by NCDOT.

---

71. *Id.*

Chapter 6

# Subdivision Design and Improvements

The General Statutes authorizing subdivision regulation for municipalities and counties authorize a variety of design and improvement standards for subdivision approval.[1] A subdivision ordinance may provide for "the orderly growth of the city [or county]" as well as "the distribution of population and traffic in a manner that will avoid congestion and overcrowding and will create conditions that substantially promote public health, safety, and the general welfare." The ordinance may require, among other things, "coordination of transportation networks and utilities within proposed subdivisions with existing or planned streets and highways and with other public facilities"; "construction of community service facilities in accordance with municipal [or county] plans, policies, and standards"; and "dedication or reservation of recreation areas serving residents of the immediate neighborhood" and the "reservation of school sites in accordance with comprehensive land use plans." In addition, a subdivision ordinance may require dedication of certain property and improvements to the public or fees in lieu of those improvements. (These types of improvements are shown in Figure 6.1.)

Through this matrix of authority, municipalities and counties address such issues as site and context, lot and block size, street design and connectivity, infrastructure standards, and recreation and open space. Related and overlapping authorities may trigger additional design considerations for sensitive areas such as steep slopes or wetlands.

The standards for a particular community depend on the details of that community's ordinance as well as its policy choices. Different communities make different policy choices. Moreover, policies shift based on context—even within a single jurisdiction, the lot size and infrastructure requirements in a downtown area are quite different from those in a rural conservation area. This discussion provides examples of common issues and policy approaches to illustrate the concept but not to prescribe policy recommendations.

This chapter discusses exactions as they relate to subdivision standards. Other chapters further explore the legal limits of exactions and the practical procedures for dedicating property to the public.

Authority for and the limits of exactions are discussed in greater detail in Chapter 8, whereas the process for dedication of property is explored in Chapter 5.

## Site and Context

The design of a subdivision and the size of its lots are constrained by natural features. Federal and state regulations limit potential development and impacts to streams, wetlands, and flood plains, and a subdivision ordinance may incorporate such requirements. For instance, an easement or drainage right-of-way may be required for an existing watercourse. A subdivision

---

1. Sections 160A-372 and 153A-331 of the North Carolina General Statutes (hereinafter G.S.).

ordinance may call for minimizing impacts to steep slopes, trees, and other natural habitats and require the placement of a riparian buffer between streams, lakes, and rivers and an adjacent development.

A subdivision design could accommodate riparian buffer within individual lots or may be maintained within common area owned by the developer or a property owners association. Either way, the area of the riparian must be credited toward the lots for applicable dimensional standards, such as residential density standards, tree conservation area, open space or conservation area, setbacks, perimeter buffers, and lot area. If riparian buffer is designated as a privately owned common area (e.g., owned by a property owners association), "the local government shall attribute to each lot abutting the riparian buffer area a proportionate share based on the area of all lots abutting the riparian buffer area for purposes of development-related regulatory requirements based on property size."[2]

For developments relying on septic sewerage, lots must have soils sufficient to accommodate that need.

Taking into account flood plains, wetlands, and other protected areas, the ordinance should require subdivision lots to be designed to ensure adequate buildable area.

Local ordinances may require subdivision design and development that protect existing trees on the property. While bona fide forestry activities are exempt from local tree ordinances,[3] tree cutting related to any development that converts land from forestland to a non-forest use is not. A city or county may withhold approval for subdivisions, site plans, and building permits for three years after an exempt harvest that results in the removal of virtually all trees that

**Figure 6.1 Layers of subdivision design elements**

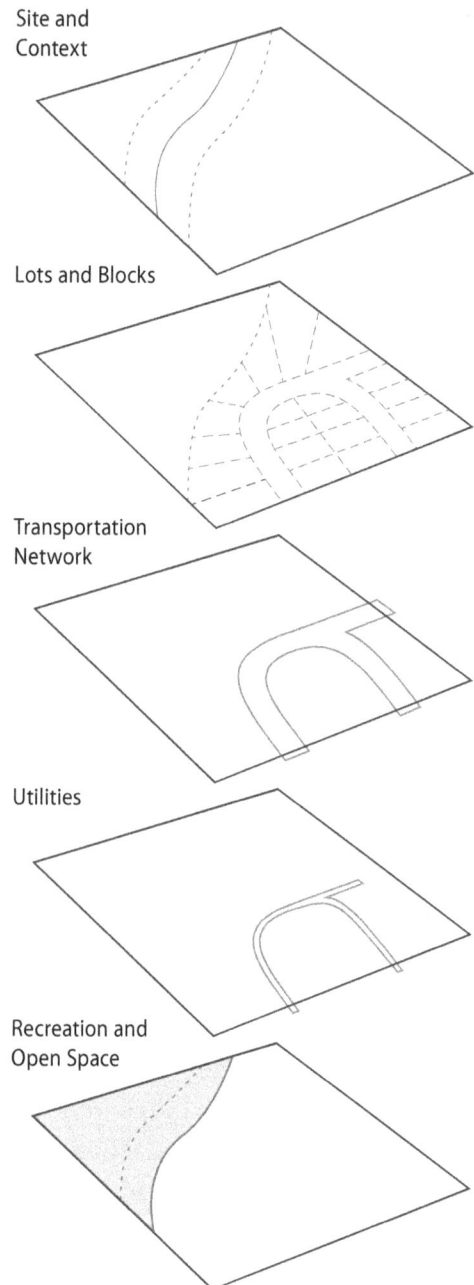

Site and Context

Lots and Blocks

Transportation Network

Utilities

Recreation and Open Space

---

2. G.S. 143-214.23A.

3. Bona fide forestry activities are protected so long as the property is used for forestry—if the land is taxed at present-use value or subject to a forest management plan. G.S. 153A-452(b); G.S. 169A-458.5(b).

had been protected under an existing development ordinance (five years if the harvest was a willful violation).[4] Thus, an applicant must design the subdivision to comply with applicable tree protections and, in fact, protect those trees or risk a delay in subdivision approval.

## Lots and Blocks

Subdivision ordinances require dimensional standards for the size of lots and blocks. Lot size may be regulated for area (acreage or square feet), width, depth, or a combination of dimensional standards. The lot size typically is particular to the zoning district, so the subdivision ordinance may reference the lot standards set forth in the zoning ordinance.

### Size

Lot restrictions should ensure sufficient buildable area for the intended development of the lot, taking into account size of the development, required setbacks, natural features, and other development limitations. This requirement ties directly to other ordinance provisions for site and context discussed above: any applicable steep slopes ordinance, flood damage prevention ordinance, watershed protection ordinance, tree protection ordinance, and others. And, as noted above, any area of riparian buffer must be credited toward the lots for applicable dimensional standards, such as lot size. In addition, lot size minimums may be scaled based on the infrastructure—the ordinance may require larger lots for development without public water and sewer.

Some ordinances build in exceptions or modifications to the basic lot size requirements. Development approved through a development agreement, conditional rezoning, or planned unit development may allow for adjustments to the lot standards. Ordinances authorizing clustered developments—where development is limited to a smaller footprint and additional open space is preserved—may eliminate the lot size minimums in favor of a net density standard. If corner lots are subject to front setbacks on two sides, an ordinance may increase the lot size to provide sufficient buildable area.

For more on cluster development and adjusting lot sizes see Chapter 7.

Representative examples of lot size requirements include those in the Statesville Unified Development Code (Table 6.1) and in Chatham County's subdivision ordinance, which ties lot dimensions to infrastructure serving the property, including roads, water, and sewer (Table 6.2).[5]

### Frontage

In order to ensure proper access to newly created lots, an ordinance may specify the minimum linear feet of frontage on the public right-of-way.[6] Alternatively, some ordinances allow a lot to be accessed by a private street or easement.

---

4. G.S. 153A-452(c)(1); G.S. 160A-458.5(c)(1).
5. Statesville Unified Development Code § 6.02; Chatham County Subdivision Regulations § 7.4.C, Table 1.
6. Pasquotank County Subdivision Ordinance § IV.12 ("minimum road or street frontage of fifty feet (50')").

**Table 6.1    Lot Dimension Requirements under Statesville Unified Development Code**

| Zone | Minimum Lot Size (square feet) | | Minimum Lot Width |
|------|------|------|------|
| R-A | 20,000 | | 100 |
| R-20 | 20,000 | | 100 |
| R-15, R-15M | 15,000 | | 90 |
| R-10, R-10M | 10,000 | | 75 |
| R-8, R-8M, R-8MF | 8,000 | | 70 |
| R-5, R5-M, R5-MF | 5,000 | | 50 |
| R-20 Cluster (15,000 SF) | | | |
| R-15 Cluster (11,250 SF) | Provided in separate cluster provisions. | | |
| R-10 Cluster (7,500 SF) | | | |
| Office-1 | 5,000 | 5,000 if used for residential purposes | 50 |
| Office & Institutional-2 | 10,000 | | 75 |
| Business-1 | 6,000 | | 60 |
| Business-2 | 6,000 | | 60 |
| Business-3 | 220,000 | 10,000 if an outparcel or single store location | 400 |
| Business-4 | 10,000 | | 75 |
| Business-5 | No min. | | 60 |
| Central Business | No min. | 1,000 min. for residential | No min. |
| Central Business P | No min. | | No min. |
| Highway-115 | No min. | | No min. |
| Light Industrial | No min. | | No min. |
| Heavy Industrial I | No min. | | No min. |

## Shape

The shape of lots also may be prescribed. Side lot lines may be required to be near perpendicular to the adjacent street right-of-way, for example.

A commonly regulated lot shape is a flag lot. Usually not visible from the street, a flag lot is connected to the public right-of-way by a long, narrow strip of land. Flag lots allow a developer to meet frontage requirements without the cost of building streets to reach interior lots. The result can be an inefficient use of land with several duplicative private drives side-by-side.

An ordinance may prohibit or limit their use. Concord limits flag lots as follows: Subdivisions with up to twenty

**Table 6.2  Lot Dimensions under Chatham County's Subdivision Ordinance**

| Classification of Street Access | Frontage on Street of Access | Lot Width at Building Line | Usable Lot Area with Public Water and Sewer (sq. feet) | Usable Lot Area without Public Water or Sewer (sq. feet) | Usable Lot Area without Public Water and Sewer (sq. feet) |
|---|---|---|---|---|---|
| Major arterial | 300' | 75' | 40,000 | 40,000 | 65,340 |
| Minor arterial and major collector | 150' | 75' | 40,000 | 40,000 | 65,340 |
| Minor collector | 100' | 75' | 40,000 | 40,000 | 65,340 |
| Local road | 30' | 75' | 40,000 | 40,000 | 65,340 |

lots may include one flag lot; subdivisions with more than twenty lots may include one flag lot per every twenty lots. And, for those flag lots, the pole (or driveway portion of the lot) must be a minimum width of twenty-five feet for residential and thirty feet for non-residential subdivisions.[7]

## Future Division

When a division of land retains large lots, there is a good chance that those lots will be further subdivided as a result of future development. An ordinance may therefore require that the design of such large lots accommodate potential future subdivision and street right-of-way.[8]

Some ordinances call for a mid-block pedestrian way, or paseo, to break up longer blocks.

---

7. Concord Development Ordinance § 10.1.6 (also § 5.5.3).

8. Chatham County Subdivision Regulations § 7.4.B ("When land is subdivided into larger parcels than ordinary building lots, such parcels may be required to be arranged so as to allow for the opening of streets in the future and for logical further re-subdivision.")

## Block Size

Ordinances commonly set block length maximums and minimums.[9] For long blocks, the ordinance may require construction of a pedestrian way through the middle of the block and construction of street crosswalks mid-block. For residential development, ordinances often require two rows of lots within a block (lots abutting backyard to backyard), except for those blocks along the perimeter of the property.

## Non-residential Standards

Some jurisdictions have specific provisions for platting land for non-residential use, such as commercial, institutional, or industrial developments. Chatham County, for example, requires that such developments be designed for future expansion and arranged to prevent undue interference with through traffic; include an integrated parking area and buffers from present or future adjacent residences; and establish a stormwater plan pursuant to the stormwater ordinance.[10]

## Solar Design

Solar siting is a design concept that works through subdivision standards to regulate the layout and orientation of lots and buildings in order to maximize solar exposure for new and future development. Ordinances may address various related topics, including street design and layout, lot sizing and orientation, flexible setbacks to maximize solar access, and more. Some local governments have incorporated aspects of solar siting into approval processes. Fayetteville, for one, allows a density bonus of up to 20 percent if a project includes certain sustainable development practices. The menu of options includes solar access for 25 percent of the buildings in development and configuration on an east–west axis.[11] Chapel Hill's University-1 zoning district, a district correlated with development agreements

With solar siting requirements, lots and buildings are oriented to ensure optimal solar exposure.

---

9. Statesville Unified Development Code § 6.02.F (maximum block length of fifteen hundred feet, minimum of three hundred feet, "unless approved by the Planning Board to secure efficient use of land or to maintain desired features of street pattern").

10. Chatham County Subdivision Regulations § 7.4.C.3.

11. Code of Ordinances, City of Fayetteville, North Carolina, § 30-5-N (2014).

for university-related projects, includes provisions for such development to address the solar access and orientation of buildings within the district.[12]

## Transportation Network

### Dedication and Improvements

#### Subdivision Statutes

A local government may require both dedication of rights-of-way and construction of improvements in association with subdivision and development.[13] The state court of appeals has interpreted subdivision authority to be limited to requiring on-site improvements,[14] but fees may be used for off-site improvements and driveway permits may require off-site improvements. In addition, local authority other than subdivision regulation may provide for off-site improvements.

A city with a population of more than a quarter million may accept dedication of rights-of-way and maintain and improve streets within the city's extraterritorial planning jurisdiction, but the city must first enter into a memorandum of understanding with the NCDOT to provide for such maintenance.[15]

#### Future Corridors

In addition to the general authority for street alignment and dedication under the subdivision statutes, Article 3B of Chapter 136 of the General Statutes (hereinafter G.S.) authorizes a city or county to require, as part of the subdivision plat approval process, dedication of rights-of-way for future corridors and thoroughfares shown on an adopted comprehensive transportation plan adopted pursuant to G.S. 136-66.2 (described in the sidebar titled "Required Transportation and Land Use Planning"). As part of this process, the city or county may allow a developer to transfer density credits from the right-of-way area to contiguous land that the developer owns. The decision-making board must find that the dedication "does not result in the deprivation of a reasonable use of the original tract" and is either

1. reasonably related to the traffic generated by the proposed subdivision or

Street types

---

12. Chapel Hill, North Carolina, Code of Ordinances § 3.5.5(i) (2014).
13. G.S. 153A-331(a); G.S. 160A-372(a).
14. Buckland v. Town of Haw River, 141 N.C. App. 460 (2000).
15. G.S. 160A-296(a1).

2. use of the remaining land or the impact of the dedication is mitigated by measures provided in the local ordinance. (G.S. 136-66.10(a)(1)).

If the city or county does not require but the owner elects to dedicate the right-of-way, the local government may allow the density credit to be transferred to a non-contiguous property. G.S. 136-66.11 outlines procedures for establishing and transferring density credits.

Creating or expanding access to a public street typically requires a driveway permit and may require roadway improvements to accommodate the new traffic.

### Driveway Permits

A city may use a driveway permit to regulate the design and construction of connections to municipal streets and may require dedication of land for medians, turn lanes, or traffic lanes as well as construction of or reimbursement for those improvements. The improvements must be "reasonably attributable to the traffic using the driveway" and "serve the traffic of the driveway."[16]

For state roads (whether in a county or within a municipality), NCDOT is authorized to regulate driveway connections and to require the construction and dedication of medians, turn lanes, and traffic lanes on any federal, state, or secondary road routes with an average daily traffic volume of at least four thousand vehicles.[17]

Moreover, when a property abuts an NCDOT road, a municipality may require improvements by the developer to that state road.[18] First, through the development review process, such as subdivision plat review, the municipality must determine that improvements to the

---

**Required Transportation and Land Use Planning**

Article 3A of Chapter 136 concerns transportation systems in and around municipalities. Municipalities are required to develop and adopt comprehensive transportation plans; counties may develop comprehensive transportation plans. These plans are prepared in conjunction with a metropolitan planning organization (MPO) or with NCDOT (for municipalities and counties outside of an MPO area). Such plans must be based on growth projections, economic conditions, and patterns of land development, among other things. And, the plans must consider multiple modes of transportation, including streets, transit, bicycles, and pedestrian travel. Plans may include collector streets as part of the roadway element.

The transportation plan, once adopted by the applicable municipality or MPO and NCDOT, is the basis for future transportation improvements.

NCDOT participates in the creation and adoption of the transportation plan. Notably, though, the municipalities must have adopted a land development plan within the previous five years (or be in the process of developing a land development) before NCDOT can participate. NCDOT may not adopt or update a transportation plan until a local land development plan has been adopted.

---

16. G.S. 160A-307.
17. G.S. 136-18(29).
18. G.S. 136-66.3(d).

### Limits on Driveway Permits

The driveway permit authority is not unlimited. In *High Rock Lake Partners, L.L.C. v. N.C. Department of Transportation,*[†] the North Carolina Supreme Court found that N.C. DOT lacked statutory authority to condition approval of a driveway permit on offsite improvements and obtaining consent from a third party.

The developer had plans for a sixty-lot residential subdivision on 188 acres in Davidson County. The property is a peninsula jutting into High Rock Lake. It is accessed by State Road 1135, a 14-foot wide gravel road that crosses (at-grade) two sets of railroad tracks a quarter mile before it dead-ends into the property.

In 2005, after initial denial by the planning board, the developer obtained preliminary subdivision plat approval from the county board of commissioners. A representative from the railroad recommended denial, citing safety concerns relating to the railroad crossing. A DOT representative recommended that approval be conditioned on construction of a bridge at the railroad crossing.

The developer also sought a DOT driveway permit. The DOT district engineer denied the driveway permit, and the developer appealed to the DOT division engineer, who granted the permit with conditions to widen and pave the railroad crossing, widen and pave the road from the crossing to property (quarter mile), and negotiate with third parties (the N.C. Railroad Co. and Norfolk Southern) for consent for the crossing improvements. The third parties refused such approval, and the developer appealed to the Driveway Permit Appeals Committee, arguing that DOT lacked authority for the conditions. The committee upheld the permit, and the developer sought judicial review. After the trial court and court of appeals affirmed DOT's decisions, the N.C. Supreme Court ruled in favor of the developer.

Under the driveway permit statute (G.S 136-18(29)), DOT is authorized to establish policies and rules for driveway connections into any street or highway in the state highway system, including size, location, traffic flow, and construction standards. In addition, DOT may require improvements and dedication of turn lanes, additional lanes, and medians for roads used by at least four thousand cars per day. The court recognized this authority as balancing the public interest in safe highways and the private interest in access.

Under the plain language of the driveway permit statute, the court found no authority to require improvements away from the applicant's property, nor any authority to require an applicant seek consent from a third party.

[†]366 N.C. 315 (2012).

state highway system "are necessary to provide for the safe and orderly movement of traffic." The municipality may then itself build, or have built, those necessary improvements "in the vicinity of the development." Such improvements include, without limitation, "additional travel lanes, turn lanes, curb and gutter, drainage facilities, and other transportation system improvements." Any improvements must meet NCDOT construction standards.

## Fees

The subdivision ordinance may provide for fees in lieu of street construction. The formula to determine the fee must be based on trips generated from the subdivision or development. The ordinance can also require a combination—part dedication of constructed streets and part payment of fees in lieu of construction. In order to authorize such a combination, the governing board must determine that the combination is in the best interest of the citizens of the area to be served.[19]

Cities may use the fee in lieu of construction "for roads which serve more than one subdivision or development within the area." This language is interpreted by the courts to

---

19. G.S. 160A-372(c).

authorize expenditure of funds for off-site improvements.[20] The statute also provides that "funds received by the city pursuant to this paragraph shall be used only for development of roads, including design, land acquisition, and construction." But the city may undertake such activities in conjunction with and under agreement with NCDOT.[21]

The county authorization is slightly different from the city authorization: there is no specific mention of roads serving more than one subdivision. Funds received by a county for fees in lieu of construction must be transferred to a municipality for the development of roads pursuant to a mutual agreement between the county and municipality. Municipalities are authorized to receive such county funds and expend them outside of their corporate limits.[22]

In addition to these authorities for fees under the subdivision regulation authority, a municipality or NCDOT may also require a developer to reimburse the public for expenses for public improvements related to a driveway permit.[23] Improvements required in association with municipal driveway permits must be "reasonably attributable to the traffic using the driveway" and "serve the traffic of the driveway."[24] Also, certain local governments have been granted authority to charge additional fees for transportation improvements.[25]

## Transportation Design Standards

Subdivision ordinance requirements for transportation design include, among other things, standards for access, street alignment, street types, connectivity, and street names. Private streets may be held to the same standards as public streets, or an ordinance may establish separate standards for private streets.[26]

Transportation improvements must be built to specific technical standards, commonly municipal technical standards or NCDOT street standards that are merely referenced in the subdivision ordinance.[27] Such standards specify right-of-way width, travel lane dimensions, curb-and-gutter standards, grade and drainage minimums, paving requirements, and other minimum construction standards. The standards will vary based on context or street classification. In communities where private streets are permitted, specifications may be different for public streets and private streets. As examples, consider Statesville's dimensions for rights-of-way and pavement, as well as the city's pavement construction standards, presented in Table 6.3 and Table 6.4, respectively.[28]

Street signs and traffic signs, sidewalks, crosswalks, on-street parking standards, street trees, and other streetscape requirements also may be specified in a local ordinance.[29]

---

20. Buckland v. Town of Haw River, 141 N.C. App. 460, 463 (2000).

21. G.S. 160A-372(c).

22. G.S. 153A-331(c).

23. G.S. 160A-307; G.S. 136-18(29).

24. G.S. 160A-307.

25. S.L. 2006-103, for example, allows Chapel Hill to charge for transit as well as roads.

26. Statesville Unified Development Code § 8.06.B.1; Concord Development Ordinance § 10.2.5; Chatham County Subdivision Regulations § 7.2.D.3.

27. Wilson Unified Development Ordinance § 6.2.4.

28. Statesville Unified Development Code § 8.06, Table 8-1: Street Design Standards & Table 8-2: Street Composition.

29. Statesville Unified Development Code § 8.06.G; Wilson Unified Development Ordinance § 6.7.

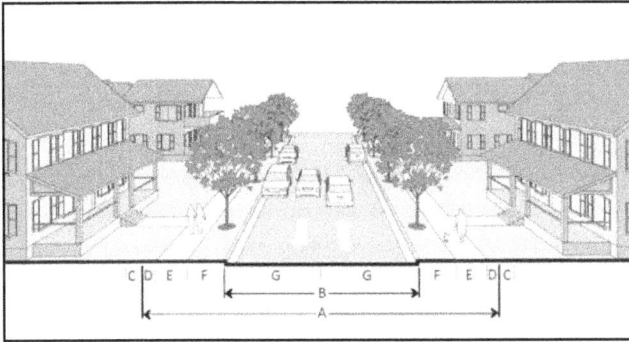

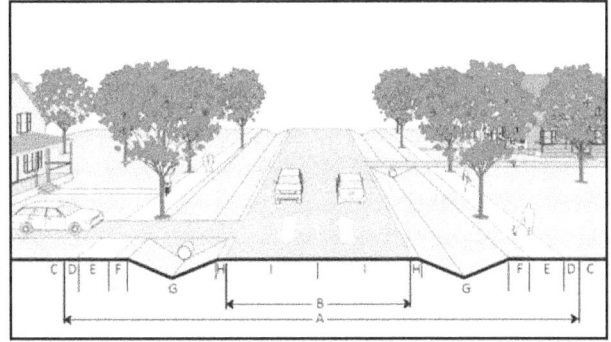

Street standards vary depending on the type of development, volume of traffic, and other context.
*Source*: City of Raleigh Unified Development Ordinance §§ 8.4.3, 8.4.4, 8.4.6. Reprinted with permission from the City of Raleigh, copyright 2013.

Guardhouses and neighborhood monument signs are handled differently by different communities, with some allowing and some prohibiting them.

Streets are the primary transportation element in most North Carolina subdivisions but certainly not the only element of a transportation network. Subdivision ordinances may include standards for greenways, transit shelters, bus turn-out lanes, future transit rights-of-way, or other aspects of the transportation network.[30] Greenway standards may include such amenities as waste and recycling baskets, water fountains, and bike racks.

In Wilson, residential projects comprising one hundred or more units, or one hundred thousand square feet of non-residential space are required to be reviewed by the city's transit manager for the inclusion of public space for a well-located transit shelter or bus stop.[31]

Sidewalks, greenways, transit shelters, and more are part of a subdivision's transportation network.

### Access

A subdivision ordinance typically includes minimum standards for access to developments. The most basic access concern is sufficient ingress and egress for emergency vehicles.

The level of access and street network improvements will depend on the size and nature of a project. In some cases, a traffic impact analysis is required. Under the Statesville ordinance, such an analysis is used to "(1) ensure that the transportation network has adequate capacity to handle projected transportation demand associated with the project, (2) identify problems with the transportation system, (3) delineate solutions to identified problems, and (4) identify improvements to be incorporated into the proposed development."[32] The standards for when a traffic impact analysis is required by the Wilson ordinance are presented in Table 6.5.[33]

Driveway permit standards (discussed above) also affect the type of access available to or required for a particular development.[34]

---

30. Wilson Unified Development Ordinance § 6.7.
31. Wilson Unified Development Ordinance § 6.4.5.
32. Statesville Unified Development Code § 8.06.H.
33. Wilson Unified Development Ordinance § 6.9 TIA.
34. Statesville Unified Development Code § 8.06.E.5.

**Table 6.3   Street Design Standards under Statesville's Unified Development Ordinance**

| Street Type | Minimum Right-of-Way Width | Minimum Pavement Width |
|---|---|---|
| Major thoroughfare/arterial street | As required by NCDOT | As required by NCDOT |
| Collector street (100+ dwellings) | 60 feet | 32 feet |
| Sub-collector (25–99 dwelling units) | 50 feet | 26 feet |
| Local street/dead-end street (10–24 dwelling units) | 50 feet | 22 feet |
| Minor (1–9 dwelling units) | 50 feet | 20 feet |
| Commercial/industrial street | Pavement and median width plus 24 feet | 12 feet per lane |
| Alley | 25 feet | 16 feet |
| Cul-de-sac | 90 feet in diameter | 70 feet in diameter |

**Table 6.4   Pavement Construction Standards under Statesville's Unified Development Ordinance**

| Options | Local Residential Streets Serving Fewer Than 100 Homes | Collector Streets Serving 100 or More Homes | Arterials and Other Streets Serving Office and Industrial Uses |
|---|---|---|---|
| 1 | • 1" Asphaltic concrete SF 9.5 A<br>• 1½" Asphaltic concrete S9.5 B<br>• 6" Crusher run or graded aggregate base for main line pavement.<br>• 24" curb and gutter<br>• Sidewalk on one side | • 1" Asphaltic concrete SF 9.5 A<br>• 1½" Asphaltic concrete S9.5 B<br>• 8" Graded aggregate or crusher run base course for main line pavement.<br>• 30" curb and gutter<br>• Base shall be compacted to 98% maximum dry density per standard proctor test ASTM D698.<br>• Sidewalk on both sides or per Sidewalk Masterplan | • 2" Asphaltic concrete S9.5 B<br>• 2" I19.0 B<br>• 5" B25.0 B or<br>• 10" Graded aggregate or crusher run base course compacted to 98% maximum dry density per standard proctor test ASTM D698.<br>• 30" curb and gutter<br>• Sidewalk on both sides<br>• Pavement design per minimum standards above or per NCDOT requirements |

Lot frontage is another basic and common requirement—each lot must abut a public right-of-way for a minimum number of linear feet.

Access to some lots may be limited. For example, lots along an existing or proposed major thoroughfare may be prohibited from accessing the thoroughfare; instead, the subdivision must be designed to provide those lots with access through a local street.[35] In some cases, the subdivider must establish a non-access easement restricting vehicle access from those lots to the thoroughfare.

---

35. Wilson Unified Development Ordinance § 6.4.1; Statesville Unified Development Code § 8.06.E.

**Table 6.5  Standards for When a Traffic Impact Analysis Is Required under the Wilson Unified Development Ordinance**

| Level of Study Required by Development Type | Residential | Office | Hotel | Industrial or Warehouse | Retail/ Shopping Center | Other |
|---|---|---|---|---|---|---|
| None (unless located in area of special concern) | < 200 units | < 50,000 sf. | < 100 rooms | < 150 employees | n/a | < 100 peak hour trips |
| Standard TIA | 200 to 500 units | 50,000 sf. to 350,000 sf. | 100 to 500 rooms | 150 to 1,000 employees | < 100,000 sf. | 100 to 500 peak hour trips |
| Enhanced TIA | > 500 units | > 350,000 sf. | > 500 rooms | > 1,000 employees | > 100,000 sf. | > 500 peak hour trips |

### Alignment

An ordinance may require that a subdivision be arranged to accommodate existing and planned streets and thoroughfares shown on adopted plans.

The subdivision ordinance may specify the design of intersections (for example, that the streets be laid out as near as possible to right angles and not less than 75 degrees). Spacing requirements may apply to intersections (minimum of one thousand feet between intersections with major thoroughfares, for example). Separate from the subdivision ordinance, municipal or NCDOT driveway permits may affect alignment and street layout.

### Special Street Types

Certain types of streets may have particular restrictions. Alleys are one such street type. Whereas some municipalities encourage or require alleys in residential subdivisions, others prohibit them in residential districts.[36] From a policy perspective, alleys may provide useful access for trash service, utilities, and garages in a relatively dense traditional neighborhood design. However, in large-lot residential subdivisions alleys may be unnecessary. Cul-de-sacs are another street type receiving particular attention. These dead-end streets with a turnaround are encouraged by some communities[37] and prohibited or discouraged by others.[38] Many municipalities limit the length of cul-de-sacs.[39] A vegetated island at the center of the cul-de-sac is sometimes required for the turnaround.[40]

Alleys can provide access for utilities, solid waste, garages, and emergency services, especially in small-lot neighborhoods.

---

36. Statesville Unified Development Code § 6.02.I.

37. Boone Unified Development Ordinance § 23.06.06 ("Cul-de-sacs and loop streets are encouraged so that through traffic on residential streets is minimized.").

38. Wilson Unified Development Ordinance § 6.4.1 ("In general, streets with one end permanently closed shall be avoided unless the design of the subdivision and the existing or proposed street system in the surrounding area clearly indicates that a through street is not essential at the location of the proposed cul-de-sac.").

39. Statesville Unified Development Code § 6.02.G.

40. Wilmington Land Development Code § 18-367.

**Designing for the Proposed Thoroughfare**

A landowner sought to develop eleven residential lots on twenty acres.[†] The town's thoroughfare plan, adopted as part of the comprehensive plan, included a future limited-access, two-lane parkway aligned through a portion of the property, but the landowner's proposed plat did not include the proposed parkway. The governing board denied the subdivision request for, among other reasons, failing to coordinate with existing and planned streets and highways. Lower courts found that the denial amounted to an unconstitutional taking, but the N.C. Supreme Court disagreed. It found that statutes clearly authorize local governments to require a developer to take present and future road development into account when designing subdivisions. Considering future road development in design, the court said, is not necessarily tantamount to a compulsory dedication. Having decided the case on state grounds, the court did not address the federal statutory and constitutional claims.

[†] Batch v. Town of Chapel Hill, 326 N.C. 1 (1989), *cert denied*, 496 U.S. 931 (1990).

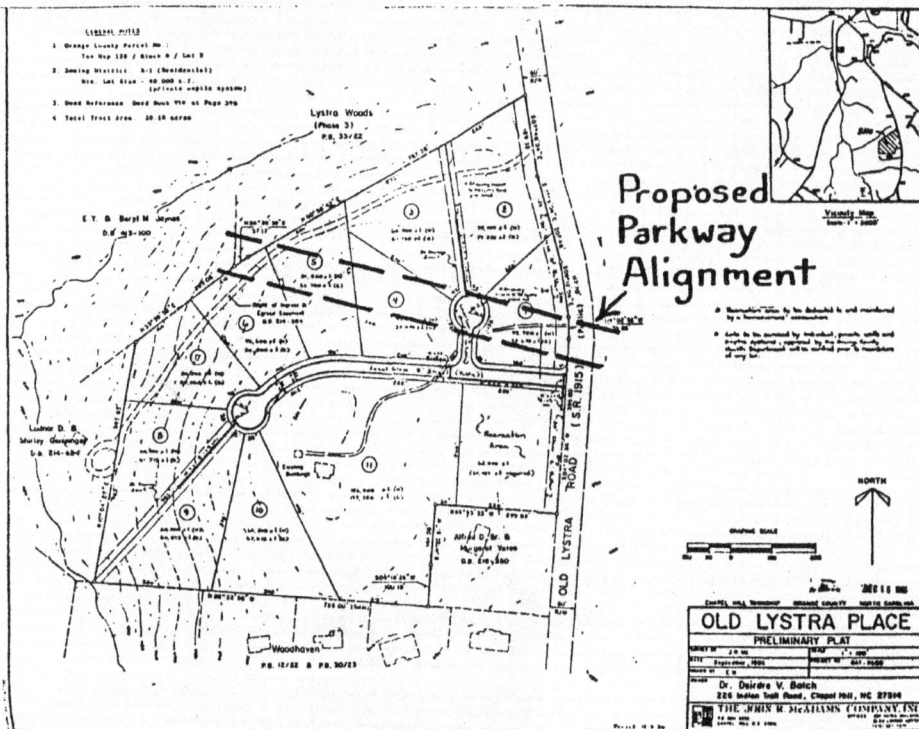

The proposed lot configuration for the Batch property and the (conflicting) proposed parkway alignment. The court found that designing a subdivision to accommodate proposed roadway alignment is not a taking but did not address whether compulsory dedication would amount to a taking.

### Connectivity

Greater connectivity serves two important public policy considerations: "improvement of traffic distribution to prevent unnecessary congestion and the improvement of public safety by providing increased access for law enforcement and emergency vehicles."[41] Some subdivision ordinances impose a general requirement for connectivity.[42] Others outline specific requirements for street connections and street stubs.[43]

---

41. Chatham County Subdivision Regulations § 7.2.B.

42. Pasquotank County Subdivision Ordinance § IV.1 ("All streets must provide for the continuation or appropriate projection or principal streets in the surrounding area and provide reasonable means of ingress and egress for surrounding acreage tracts.").

43. Wilson Unified Development Ordinance § 6.4.1; Statesville Unified Development Code § 8.06.B.5.

Stub roads are constructed to provide connectivity with future development on neighboring properties.

Stubs are created where a street extends to but terminates at the property line, thereby enabling future development on the neighboring property to connect into the street network. The ordinance may include prioritization for where stubs are to be located.

In addition, a subdivision ordinance may require a certain level of connectivity within a subdivision, the goal being to increase the network of well-connected streets within the development and to decrease the number of cul-de-sacs. As noted above, some communities prohibit cul-de-sacs unless necessitated by topography. Communities also apply a connectivity ratio (the ratio of streets to intersections) to set a minimum level of connectivity. (See "Connectivity Ratio" sidebar.) As an alternative to connectivity ratios, some ordinances increase connectivity by limiting block perimeter lengths. Raleigh, for example, sets limits on block perimeter, and those limits scale down for more dense developments.[44]

### Street Names

First responders need clear addresses in responding to emergency situations, so naming streets and establishing addresses are critical for public safety and important parts of the subdivision design review process. Subdivision names and street names need to be distinct from other names within the jurisdiction. When an existing street is extended into a subdivision, the developer may be required to maintain that name for the new portion.[45] Where the local ordinance calls for distinct subdivision names, the decision-making board has an obligation to observe that standard.[46]

### Private Streets

Subdivision street standards may apply to private streets as well as to streets that are intended to be dedicated to the public.[47] As has been noted, general authority for subdivision regulation states that, among other things, the ordinance may provide for orderly growth, coordination

44. www.raleighnc.gov/content/extra/Books/PlanDev/UnifiedDevelopmentOrdinance/#228.
45. Chatham County Subdivision Regulations § 7.4.C.
46. Springdale Estates Ass'n v. Wake Cnty., 47 N.C. App. 462 (1980).
47. Statesville Unified Development Code § 8.06.B.9.

## Connectivity Ratio

The goal of a connectivity ratio is to encourage a network of streets and intersections and to prevent a subdivision predominated by cul-de-sacs. The connectivity ratio is a calculation of the number of street links divided by number of nodes. A node is an intersection or cul-de-sac (a stub-out is not a node). A link is a section of street between nodes. A minimum ratio (1.4, for example) is required for a subdivision street layout. The specifics for calculation and the minimum ratios are refined by the various jurisdictions that use a connectivity ratio.

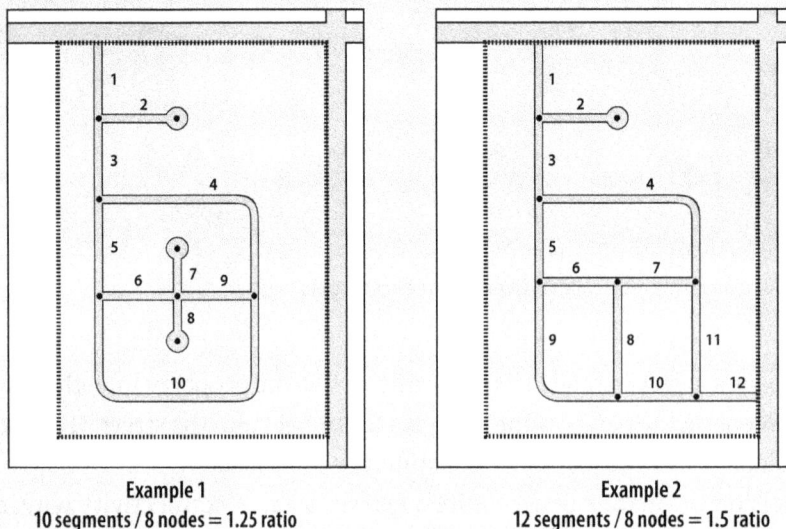

Example 1
10 segments / 8 nodes = 1.25 ratio

Example 2
12 segments / 8 nodes = 1.5 ratio

As shown in this example, from Section 6.4.3. of the Wilson Uniform Development Ordinance, the connectivity ratio increases with more intersections and fewer cul-de-sacs.

of transportation networks with other streets, and distribution of traffic to avoid congestion and to promote public health and safety.[48] These authorities are not limited to public streets; street design regulations may apply to private streets and parking lots as well.

Some ordinances allow access to be accomplished through private streets or easements. Private access could be used for a small subdivision or for other development types, such as a mobile home park, apartment complex, or commercial development. Concord, for example, requires every lot to "abut and have direct access to a publicly maintained street or other public right-of-way legally dedicated." Exceptions are permitted, however, for

1. parcels within nonresidential subdivisions, provided that adequate paved access is available for emergency and public safety vehicles and access;
2. town home lots where the individual lots are separated from a public right-of-way by a strip of land under common ownership by the owners of the town home lots; and
3. lots fronting on approved private streets.[49]

Chatham County allows private streets in conservation subdivisions, mobile home parks, apartment complexes, planned unit developments, and certain large-lot subdivisions.[50] Boone

---

48. G.S. 153A-331(a); G.S. 160A-372(a)
49. Concord Development Ordinance § 5.5.3.
50. Chatham County Subdivision Regulations § 7.2.D.

Some ordinances allow for private streets in order to provide necessary access. Private streets may be subject to the same standards as public streets.

allows private streets for access within residential developments, but the town may require dedication of streets shown on official town plans.[51]

When streets are maintained as private, the subdivision ordinance may require a legal entity (such as a homeowners association) to own and maintain them.[52]

For more on the control and maintenance of private streets, see the discussion in Chapter 9.

## Utilities

### Dedication and Improvements

Under the statutory authority to "substantially promote public health, safety, and the general welfare," to require dedication of easements for utilities, and for "construction of community service facilities," a subdivision ordinance may set minimum standards for the construction and dedication of water, sewerage, and other infrastructure.[53]

---

51. Boone Unified Development Ordinance § 23.01.03.

52. Concord Development Ordinance § 10.2.5 ("A legally responsible organization (i.e. homeowners association, other legally recognized association, etc.) as acceptable to the Administrator shall be established to maintain a private street(s). Documents to assure private responsibility of future maintenance and repair by a homeowners association or other legally recognized district shall be approved as to form by the City Attorney."); Chatham County Subdivision Regulations § 7.2.D.

53. G.S. 153A-331(a) & (c); G.S. 160A-372(a) & (c).

The General Statutes authorize cities and counties, through their public enterprise powers, to require property owners to connect to available water and sewer services and to pay a charge for the connection.[54] Alternatively, a city or county may require periodic payment of an availability charge instead of requiring connection to existing infrastructure. For counties, this authority is limited to properties that, as a result of their location, can be served by a county water or sewer line. For cities, this power is limited to properties within the corporate limits and within reasonable distance of a city water or sewer line.

Some communities—through the subdivision process—require a developer to connect to public water and/or sewer when available and to provide individual service connections to each lot. The connection requirement may be differentiated: all non-residential and major subdivisions must connect, for example.[55]

Similar to the approach for road standards, a subdivision ordinance commonly incorporates technical construction standards for water, sewer, and other utilities.[56]

Utility easement size and placement also may be specified by the subdivision ordinance—a five- or ten-foot easement, for example. Placement may be required or encouraged to follow street rights-of-way or property lines.[57] Some subdivision ordinances require utilities to be installed underground.[58]

In certain circumstances, North Carolina courts have interpreted "public easement" to permit multiple utility functions. In *Sampson v. City of Greensboro*,[59] a developer claimed a dedication was for a storm sewer, not a sanitary sewer as the city claimed. The court of appeals, though, found a dedicated easement and looked to the subdivision ordinance to determine that the necessary grants of easements were broad enough for a sanitary sewer. "In one breath, plaintiffs claim all the benefits that are afforded by the defendant's approval of their subdivision and, at the same time, seek to withdraw the burdens on the land that defendant required to be imposed thereon before it would approve the subdivision."[60] In *Beechridge Development Co., L.L.C. v. Dahners*,[61] a developer sought a declaratory judgment that a "public easement" noted on the plat of an existing adjacent subdivision could be used for a sanitary sewer line to serve the developer's new subdivision. The state supreme court stated that the term "public easement" "encompasses a wide variety of public uses, including a sanitary sewer line."[62]

For subdivisions outside of municipal boundaries (in either the county jurisdiction or the municipal extraterritorial jurisdiction), a subdivision ordinance may not require dedication of water systems or facilities as a condition of subdivision approval unless the municipality, county, or other public water system has agreed to begin operating and maintaining the water system within one year of the issuance of the first certificate of occupancy for a housing unit in the subdivision.[63]

---

54. G.S. 153A-284; G.S. 160A-317.
55. Statesville Unified Development Code §§ 8.01, 8.03.
56. Wilson Unified Development Ordinance § 6.2.4.
57. Statesville Unified Development Code § 6.02.K.
58. Statesville Unified Development Code § 8.01.G.
59. 35 N.C. App. 148 (1978).
60. *Id.* at 149.
61. 350 N.C. 583 (1999).
62. *Id.* at 584.
63. G.S. 160A-374.

The provision of adequate utilities is a fundamental element of subdivision control.

Private community water and wastewater systems raise particular issues, depending on the location of a project and the availability of public water and sewer. Private community systems may be a useful way to accommodate growth where no public system capacity is available, and some communities do rely on private systems for new growth. However, such an arrangement may raise concerns of oversight, maintenance, and long-term sustainability, which is one reason why some subdivision ordinances prohibit private community systems. Others require that they be designed for ultimate connection to the public system.[64]

Some subdivisions are designed for on-site wastewater treatment through septic systems. When on-site treatment is permitted, the subdivision ordinance may reference local or state environmental health standards for soils, and preliminary and final plat review may require confirmation that suitable soils are present for each proposed lot. Depending on the ordinance, confirmation could come from a North Carolina–licensed soil scientist hired by the developer, or certification could be evidenced by septic system permits from the local environmental health agency.

## Fees

In contrast to the transportation authority, the subdivision statutes do not specify the authority to charge fees in lieu of utility construction. Cities and counties, however, do have separate authority to charge fees related to the use of their public enterprise utilities, such as water, sewer, stormwater management, and even public transportation.[65] The full extent of that authority is not clear.

---

64. Statesville Unified Development Code § 8.03.A.
65. G.S. 153A-277; G.S. 160A-314.

Accommodating stormwater runoff is a major infrastructure and design consideration.

## Design Standards

Just as a subdivision ordinance may require a subdivision to coordinate subdivision streets with existing or planned roads, it also may require a subdivision to coordinate subdivision utilities with existing or planned public utilities.

Stormwater management also may drive design decisions for a subdivision. New development must address the increased stormwater runoff created by new roads, roofs, and other impervious surfaces. Federal and state regulations provide technical requirements for managing stormwater in a variety of ways: low-impact development to minimize the increased runoff, onsite collection and/or infiltration, neighborhood-scale stormwater pipes and ponds, and other individual and collective systems. Regardless of the approach, subdivision design is impacted by the need for space to accommodate such stormwater facilities.

## Recreation and Open Space

### Dedication and Improvements

The General Statutes authorize a subdivision ordinance to require dedication or reservation of recreation areas and to require the construction of community service facilities, such as playgrounds. The state supreme court has ruled that when a development creates a need for parks it is reasonable to require the developer to bear that cost.[66]

### Fees

As an alternative to dedication of recreation space, a subdivision ordinance may require the developer to contribute funds to be used by the local government to acquire recreational areas serving residents in the immediate area. The phrase "immediate area" is not defined,

---

66. River Birch Assocs. v. City of Raleigh, 326 N.C. 100 (1990).

but it is not necessarily limited to the particular subdivision. Some communities establish park service districts and apply the fees derived from that district to parks in that district.[67]

Notably, for counties, fees may be used only to *"acquire* recreational land or areas."[68] The city statute offers additional language. For cities, such funds "shall be used only for the acquisition *or development* of recreation, park, or open space sites."[69] In addition, the city statute specifies that any formula for determining funds is to be based on property tax values of the development or subdivision. Cities may require a mix of funds and land dedication from developers.

In *China Grove 152, L.L.C. v. Town of China Grove*, the court of appeals found that a local fee intended to cover the cost of increased needs for police, fire protection, and park space was not authorized by the subdivision statutes.[70] The court read G.S. 160A-372(c) to be permissive (the developer *may* pay) but not to authorize a local government to require park fees. The court, though, did not address the authority in G.S. 160A-372(a). Subsection (a), in contrast to subsection (c), states that "[a] subdivision control ordinance may provide . . . for the dedication or reservation of recreation areas serving residents of the immediate neighborhood within the subdivision or, alternatively, for provision of funds to be used to acquire recreation areas serving residents of the development or subdivision or more than one subdivision or development within the immediate area." Under the plain language of this authority in subsection (a), the local government can require dedication of recreation areas within the subdivision or, in lieu of such dedication, may require funds to acquire recreation areas.

Finally, note that certain counties have local legislation authorizing specific recreation fees.

## Design Standards

An ordinance may specify locations and characteristics for recreation space as well as open space. A preference may be given for smaller, dispersed playgrounds or, alternatively, for larger, consolidated parks. The ordinance may require that recreation space be located within a certain distance of every residence (a quarter mile, for example). Additional standards may address public or neighborhood access, acceptable facilities, and shape.[71] Ordinance requirements may call for open space to be designed to be contiguous with open space on neighboring properties.[72] In some cases, the open space requirement is really a buffering requirement.[73]

---

67. Chatham County Subdivision Regulations § 7.5.A ("In order to serve the public recreation needs of more than one development or subdivision, the County shall establish recreation service districts and fees paid in lieu of dedication hereunder shall be expended for acquisition or development of recreation or park facilities or areas.").

68. G.S. 153A-331(c).

69. G.S. 160A-372(c).

70. No. COA14-972, 2015 WL 4082073 (N.C. Ct. App. July 7, 2015).

71. Concord Development Ordinance § 10.5.7.

72. Statesville Unified Development Code § 6.06.G, H.

73. Pasquotank County Subdivision Ordinance § IV.18 ("Residential subdivisions are required to provide a 75' perpetually maintained vegetative buffer along all property lines that are located adjacent to existing agricultural uses. This buffer shall be permanently set aside as open space. Ownership and maintenance of the required open space shall be the responsibility of the developer and/or a Homeowner's Association.").

**Designing Recreation**

In *Messer v. Town of Chapel Hill*,[†] the town conditioned subdivision approval on relocating a neighborhood playground and dedicating it to the public. The developer challenged the condition as unauthorized and a taking of private property without just compensation. The N.C. Court of Appeals found sufficient statutory authority for the requirements to relocate the site and offer it for dedication.

[†]59 N.C. App. 692 (1982).

Open space may take many forms. It may be passive or natural, such as woodlands, wetlands, and stream buffers, or open space may be active recreation space, such as playgrounds, ball courts and fields, or pools. Moreover, open space may take many shapes: linear greenways or buffers, compact playgrounds or wooded areas, or large play fields or conservation area.

Recreation space requirements commonly are based on a calculation (0.03 acres of recreation space per dwelling unit, for example). Also, an ordinance may limit the percentage of passive recreation or the extent to which protected conservation areas (wetlands, marshes, etc.) count toward the recreation space standard. Stormwater ponds and required vegetative buffers may be excluded or limited from contributing toward recreation space area.[74] As an example, the open space requirements under Section 10.5.13 of the Concord Development Ordinance are presented in Table 6.6. Note, though, that required riparian buffers must be allowed toward applicable dimensional lot standards, such as open space and tree conservation areas.[75]

Ownership and maintenance of open space raises issues similar to those of streets. Some communities want to allow private ownership of open space but need to implement protections in order to assure proper maintenance. Concord's ordinance,[76] for example, allows one or a combination of the following:

1. Dedication to the City, an appropriate public agency, or a non-profit entity (such as a land conservancy) if such an agency or entity is willing to accept the dedication and is financially capable of maintaining such open space, or
2. Common ownership by a property owners' association, which assumes full responsibility for the maintenance of the open space. In the event the association fails to maintain the open space according to the standards of this Ordinance, the City may, following reasonable notice:
    a. Demand that the deficiency of maintenance be corrected; or
    b. Enter the open space to perform the needed maintenance. The cost of such maintenance shall be charged to the association.

---

74. See, for example, the Wilmington Land Development Code § 18-383 and the Concord Development Ordinance § 10.5.2.
75. G.S. 143-214.23A.
76. Concord Development Ordinance § 10.5.8.

**Table 6.6 Open Space Standards under the Concord Development Ordinance (§ 10.5.13)**

| Zoning District(s) | Total Percentage of Open Space |
|---|---|
| AG | N/A |
| RE, RL, RM-1, RM-2, RV, and RC | 8% (0–2 units per acre)<br>10% (2.1–4 units per acre)<br>12% (> 4 units per acre) |
| B-1, O-I, CC, C-1, C-2, I-1, and I-2 | N/A |
| PUD, PRD | 16% (0–2 units per acre)<br>20% (2.1–4 units per acre)<br>24% (> 4 units per acre) |
| TND | Specific provisions based on park type |

## Schools

### Reservation

The statutes specify procedures for required school reservation. As discussed in the Introduction, "reservation" is setting aside land for public purchase (in contrast to "dedication," when property is given to the public at no cost). For school site reservation, the governing board or planning board and the appropriate board of education "shall jointly determine the specific location and size of any school sites to be reserved."[77] Such sites will then appear in the approved comprehensive land use plan. If a subdivision plan includes all or part of an identified school site, the governing board or planning board must immediately notify the school board and the school board must promptly decide if it wants the site to be reserved. If the board of education wants the site, it will be reserved as such in the approved subdivision. The board of education has eighteen months from final approval of the subdivision to purchase the site or initiate condemnation proceedings. If no purchase takes place after eighteen months, the land is freed from the reservation.[78]

### Fees

As discussed in Chapter 8, school impact fees are not authorized under the General Statutes. Certain counties, though, have been authorized by local legislation to impose them.

## Additional Improvements Considerations

### Community Service Facilities

The General Statutes authorize local subdivision ordinances to require "the construction of community service facilities in accordance with municipal [or county] plans, policies, and standards."[79] This term, "community service facility," is not defined, nor has it been

---

77. G.S. 160A-372(c); *see also* G.S. 153A-331(c).
78. *Id.*
79. G.S. 160A-372(c); *see also* G.S. 153A-331.

interpreted by North Carolina courts. Nonetheless, in common practice such facilities include roads, sidewalks, and streetscaping, such as lights; infrastructure, such as water, sewer, and stormwater facilities; and recreation facilities, including playgrounds and greenways. In very large projects, community service facilities potentially could include community buildings, public safety stations, and other public improvements.

## Performance Guarantees

Policy and administrative issues related to performance guarantees are discussed in Chapter 9.

"To assure compliance with [community service facilities requirements] and other ordinance requirements, the ordinance may provide for performance guarantees to assure successful completion of required improvements."[80]

# Contracting for Improvements

Cities and counties may enter into agreements for certain improvements to be made by the developer. Statutory authority allows contracting for public enterprise improvements, roadway improvements (cities only), and general reimbursement agreements. These authorizations are distinct from the authority discussed in previous sections enabling a local government to require a property owner to construct and dedicate public improvements. These improvement agreements are described in Table 6.7.

## Public Enterprise Improvement Contracts

A city or county can contract with a developer or owner (or their contractor) for "public enterprise improvements that are adjacent or ancillary to a private land development project."[81] Public enterprises include water, wastewater, public transportation, parking, and stormwater management, among other things.[82] Under a public enterprise contract, the local government is to reimburse the private party for the cost of designing and constructing such improvements. This reimbursement, though, cannot pay the costs of improvements required by land development regulations.

A local government may adopt ordinances and policies to establish procedures, requirements, and terms for such agreements. If the public cost of a reimbursement contract does not exceed $250,000, the contract is not subject to the public bidding laws under Article 8 of Chapter 143, but the local government must find either that (1) the cost of the reimbursement contract will not exceed the estimated cost for such work through eligible force account qualified labor or through a bid contract; or (2) that coordination of separately constructed improvements would not be practical.

For public enterprise improvement contracts, the improvements may be on property owned by a private party or the local government. The private party can assist with obtaining easements across other private properties that will be necessary for or affected by the

---

80. *Id.*

81. G.S. 153A-280(a); G.S. 160A-320(a).

82. G.S. 160A-311; G.S. 153A-274.

### Table 6.7 Improvement Agreements Allowed for Cities and Counties

| | Public Enterprise Improvement Contract | Roadway and Intersection Improvement Contract | Reimbursement Agreement |
|---|---|---|---|
| **Statute** | 153A-280; 160A-320 | 160A-309 | 153A-451; 160A–499 |
| **Infrastructure** | Public enterprises including water, wastewater, public transportation, parking, and stormwater management, and others | Public intersection or roadway improvements | "Municipal infrastructure," including, among other things, water mains, sanitary sewer lines, lift stations, stormwater lines, streets, curb and gutter, sidewalks, traffic control devices |
| **Scope** | Cost of design and construction of the improvements; must be adjacent or ancillary to a private land development project; cannot pay for improvements required by development ordinances | Must be adjacent or ancillary to a private land development project | Improvement must be included in the local government's capital improvement plan and must serve the developer or property owner |
| **Authority** | City and county | City | City and county |
| **Private Party** | Developer, property owner, or private party under contract with developer or owner | Developer, property owner, or private party under contract with developer or owner | Developer or property owner |
| **Ordinance for Procedures and Terms** | May adopt | May adopt | Must adopt |
| **Bidding of Construction Work** | Contracts with public share less than $250,000 exempt, with proper findings | Contracts with public share less than $250,000 exempt, with proper findings | Agreement is exempt, but private party must solicit bids same as public body |
| **Property Acquisition** | Provisions for obtaining easements on third-party property | No specific authority | No specific authority |

improvements. The local government and private party may contract for reimbursement prior to acquisition of real property necessary for the project. That said, the authority is for "public enterprise improvements," so the improvements will need to be dedicated to the public.

## Roadway and Intersection Improvement Contracts

For roadway and intersection improvements, cities have contractual authority that is substantially similar to the authority to contract for public enterprise improvements.[83] There is no comparable authority for counties.

The roadway improvement contract may be with the developer, the property owner, or their contractor. The contract must be "for public intersection or roadway improvements that are adjacent or ancillary to a private land development project."[84] Contracts in which the public share is less than $250,000 are not subject to public bidding if the city makes the necessary determination that either (1) the cost of the reimbursement contract will not exceed the estimated cost for such work through eligible force account qualified labor or

---

83. G.S. 160A-309.
84. *Id.*

through a bid contract; or (2) that coordination of separately constructed improvements would not be practical.

The city may adopt ordinances or policies to set forth the details for such contracts.

In contrast to the public enterprise improvements authority, the roadway improvements authority does not have language specifically concerned with property acquisition.

## Reimbursement Agreements

In addition to the authority for contracting for public enterprise improvements and roadway improvements, cities and counties are authorized to enter reimbursement agreements for a developer or property owner to design and construct certain municipal infrastructure.[85] The reimbursement may be paid through any lawful source. The improvements may include, among other things, water mains, sanitary sewer lines, lift stations, stormwater lines, streets, curb and gutter, sidewalks, traffic control devices.

Statesville, as an example, provides that

> Streets, water lines, wastewater systems, drainage facilities, electric lines and telecommunications lines shall be constructed through new development to promote the logical extension of public infrastructure to serve future growth. The City may require the applicant for a subdivision to extend offsite improvements to reach the subdivision or to oversize required public facilities to serve anticipated future development as a condition of plat or plan approval. The City shall pay the cost of upsizing a utility line.[86]

Before entering into a reimbursement agreement, a city or county must adopt an ordinance "setting forth procedures and terms under which such agreements may be approved."[87] The specific improvement must be included in the local government's capital improvement plan (CIP) and must serve the developer or property owner.

A reimbursement agreement itself is not subject to public bidding laws, but the private party completing the work under the reimbursement agreement must "solicit bids in accordance with Article 8 of Chapter 143 of the General Statutes when awarding contracts for work that would have required competitive bidding if the contract had been awarded by the city [or county]."[88]

The county version of the statute, which perhaps was copied from the municipal version, refers to paying for "municipal infrastructure."[89] This terminology is confusing since the infrastructure is in the county, not a municipality, but two elements of the statute help clarify the meaning. First, the relevant infrastructure work must be included in the county's CIP, and a county's CIP will, by definition, be for county infrastructure, not the infrastructure of a nearby town. Second, the statute's definition of "municipal infrastructure" specifies particular facilities (water mains, sanitary sewer lines, streets, etc.), not that such facilities must be within a municipality. Thus, in this instance, the qualifier *municipal* in front of

---

85. G.S. 153A-451; G.S. 160A–499.
86. Statesville Unified Development Code § 8.01.H.
87. G.S. 160A-499(b).
88. G.S. 160A-499(d).
89. G.S. 153A-451(a).

*infrastructure* appears to describe a type of infrastructure and not the location of infrastructure. In other words, it is infrastructure traditionally considered to be an urban service.

County reimbursement authority is limited to infrastructure projects for which the county otherwise has statutory authority to undertake. This could raise concern about street construction, but the county reimbursement authority aligns with other county authority for funding road improvements constructed by other parties. Under G.S. 136-98, a "county is authorized to participate in the cost of rights-of-way, construction, reconstruction, improvement, or maintenance of a road on the State highway system under agreement with the Department of Transportation." And, under G.S. 153A-331, a county may use subdivision fees in lieu of construction to pay a municipality to perform street improvements.

Chapter 7

# Subdivision Design Concepts

Subdivision is a common and necessary tool for managing community growth, whether infill development in existing neighborhoods or new development in rural areas. Two broad design concepts warrant particular attention for how they manage growth and relate to subdivision ordinances: traditional neighborhood development and conservation subdivision.

## Traditional Neighborhood Development (TND)

The classic main streets and historic neighborhoods of North Carolina's cities and towns share common design elements, such as

- a mix of land uses, including commerce, residences, industry, and institutions;
- transportation options, including walking, biking, transit, and cars;
- interconnected streets within a grid network;
- a range of housing types, including mansions, cottages, townhomes, and apartments;
- access to public amenities, including parks and schools.

Contemporary city planning and development are returning to those elements of neighborhood design. Housing market preferences are increasingly shifting toward communities with mixed uses and walkable design, and developers are responding to those preferences. In addition, local governments are seeking to facilitate a growth model that takes many names, among them, *traditional neighborhood design, smart growth, new urbanism,* and *walkable urbanism.* While each term carries a slightly different connotation, the design elements underlying them are common. They are the design elements of North Carolina's historic main streets and neighborhoods (listed above). For simplicity of discussion, these design concepts will be referred to here as traditional neighborhood development or TND.

Conventional zoning and subdivision rules, unfortunately, can create barriers to such neighborhoods and communities. Common zoning strictly divides land uses, requires large setbacks, and demands a spread out, suburban style of development. Subdivision ordinances—working hand-in-hand with zoning—commonly require large lots, large blocks, over-sized streets, and auto-centric community design.

To accommodate TND design, communities may need to revise development ordinances—zoning, subdivision, and/or unified development ordinances.[1] In recent decades, developers

---

1. Statesville Unified Development Code Article 7 ("The provisions of this [TND] article describe a variety of desirable development patterns that generally are not facilitated by conventional zoning. These developments should be designed to enhance an improved living environment through open space/recreation, connectivity and architectural standards.")

Southern Village in Chapel Hill was designed with elements of traditional neighborhood development. Uses include a commercial village center, apartments, townhomes, and a mix of single-family homes, a school, and a church. The components of the neighborhood are integrated within a network of streets and trails. Substantial open space and recreation are provided throughout the development.

and local governments across the country have created exceptions to conventional zoning regulation through planned unit developments (PUDs) and conditional zoning. More recently, local governments have begun to adopt form-based codes to incorporate regulatory standards to allow or require mixed uses and traditional neighborhood development. Many of the necessary changes are zoning rules, but some are subdivision-specific or issues that impact zoning and subdivision.[2]

Thinking about subdivision specifically, TND design may require adjustments to lot and block size, street standards and connectivity, and the relation among lot types. An overarching theme of TND design is that it serves people, not just cars. So the design considers walking, biking, and transit as well as automobile transportation. Moreover, TND serves multiple needs of those people: commerce, recreation, and education as well as housing. This theme—serving people—plays out in the design.

## Lots and Blocks

TND design features a variety of lot types—large-lot residential, small-lot residential, townhomes, multifamily, commercial, office, and recreation. The subdivision ordinance must accommodate, even encourage, this mix of types. Some developments include very small lot single-family homes, perhaps built with zero lot line (no setback). The subdivision ordinance may need to make adjustments for this style of development (such as ensuring maintenance

---

2. For more on the elements of traditional neighborhood design and regulatory changes necessary to accommodate it, see DANIEL G. PAROLEK, KAREN PAROLEK, & PAUL C. CRAWFORD, FORM-BASED CODES: A GUIDE FOR PLANNERS, URBAN DESIGNERS, MUNICIPALITIES, AND DEVELOPERS (2008); DOUG FARR, SUSTAINABLE URBANISM: URBAN DESIGN WITH NATURE (2007); DANIEL K. SLONE & DORIS S. GOLDSTEIN, with W. ANDREW GOWDER, A LEGAL GUIDE TO URBAN AND SUSTAINABLE DEVELOPMENT FOR PLANNERS, DEVELOPERS AND ARCHITECTS (2008).

**Checklist of Elements Required by a Subdivision Ordinance**

In order to accommodate traditional neighborhood development, a subdivision ordinance needs to accommodate or require the following elements. Additional changes may be needed for zoning and other development regulations.

*Lots and blocks:*
- mix of lot types and sizes,
- zero lot line development,
- smaller blocks,
- flexible access standards (pedestrian-only front access possible),
- buildable area for building at or near the street (parking at rear).

*Street standards and connectivity:*
- narrower streets,
- on-street parking,
- alleys with garages,
- bike and pedestrian facilities,
- streetscaping (sidewalks and street trees),
- connectivity,
- streets in a grid,
- service alleys,
- reduced curb cuts.

*Relation among lot types:*
- variety of uses and lot types,
- reduced buffers and separation,
- neighborhood parks and common open space integrated into the neighborhood,
- shared parking,
- shared stormwater.

easements). Block size, too, is smaller in TND than in conventional suburban development. Minimum block size standards may need to be adjusted down.

## Street Standards and Connectivity

TND features narrower streets, on-street parking, alleys with garages, and an increase in pedestrian-related facilities, such as cross-walks, wider sidewalks, mid-block pedestrian ways, and signage and street furniture for pedestrians. Streetscaping with sidewalks and street trees is common. The subdivision ordinance must be adjusted to permit such development.

The traditional neighborhood features strong connectivity, with streets laid out in a grid, service alleys, and sidewalks and trails. The connectivity extends to neighboring developments—tying streets together and providing stub roads for future development. All of these features, of course, relate to standards set forth in the subdivision ordinance.

Lot access in a TND is more flexible than in conventional suburban development. In the latter, each lot has vehicular access through a driveway leading directly onto a neighborhood street. For the traditional neighborhood, each lot has street access but it may be in a variety of forms. A small-lot residential lot, for example, may have *pedestrian access* to the neighborhood street and sidewalk through the front yard but *vehicular access* via the alley at the rear yard. Similarly, a commercial lot may have pedestrian access at the front and

TND design commonly includes mixed-use buildings, minimal setbacks, pedestrian facilities, and on-street parking. Local subdivision and zoning ordinances may need to be revised in order to accommodate this style of development.

vehicular access through a shared parking lot at the rear. And, as a corollary, those lots do not require curb cuts and driveways at the front.

### Relation among Lot Types

A TND is intentionally diverse, featuring multiple housing types and land uses, and such diversity deserves thoughtful arrangement. A subdivision ordinance permitting or requiring TND needs to allow for a mix of lot types and sizes while also accommodating the infrastructure needs of more dense development. These may include shared parking (used for offices in the day and apartments at night) and shared stormwater maintenance (serving multiple property owners). Increased density, too, needs sufficient open space and recreational areas, both of which need to be requirements of the subdivision ordinance.

## Rural Development and Conservation Subdivision

In rural settings the subdivision ordinance is a useful tool in maintaining rural character even while allowing for modest levels of development. At the most basic level, limits on lot size and infrastructure will limit the density of development. But local policies for rural preservation can go much further, protecting natural resources, enabling cluster development, and encouraging continued agricultural production.

Balancing rural preservation and residential growth is a challenge for many North Carolina communities.

## Related Policies

Lot size is the primary restriction on density of development, but limiting water and sewer services to defined urban service areas also is an effective tool for guiding growth. These two tools—large lot size requirements and urban service boundaries—may be used together to protect rural landscapes and to focus development in more developed areas. In the 1980s, Orange County, Chapel Hill, and Carrboro entered into an inter-local agreement to establish a rural buffer with joint planning areas, lot minimums, and limited water or sewer service.[3]

A related but distinct tool is farmland preservation. The Agricultural Development and Farmland Preservation Enabling Act, outlined at Article 61 of Chapter 106 of the General Statutes, offers non-regulatory protection for agricultural land uses. Within voluntary agricultural districts water and sewer assessments may be limited, and a hearing is required before farmland can be condemned.

## Conservation Subdivision

Conservation subdivision is a broad term for a development model that emphasizes the preservation of open space and natural resources while still allowing for the subdivision and development of land. A conservation subdivision typically includes a substantial percentage of conserved open space (typically 30–50% of the development). While conservation development is commonly residential, it also may apply to mixed-use and TND.

---

3. *See* Richard D. Ducker, *The Orange County Joint Planning Agreement*, POPULAR GOV'T, Winter 1998, at 47.

Portions of the Johnston Mill Nature Preserve in Orange County were protected through conservation subdivision. As part of the county's flexible development regulation approval, the developer of the Creek Wood and North Field subdivisions granted a conservation easement to the Triangle Land Conservancy to protect portions of the property.

In order to maintain its development potential, a conservation development may have relaxed lot standards (allowing smaller lots) in exchange for open space conservation. So, for example, imagine a forty-acre tract of land. If the landowner subdivided under conventional rules, he or she might be required to divide the tract into twenty, two-acre parcels and provide extensive roads to serve those large, scattered lots. Fragmented ownership would, very likely, also fragment the tract's natural resources, whether natural woodlands or productive agricultural lands. A conservation subdivision, conversely, might allow for the same number of lots (twenty) but reduce lot size to one-half acre or one acre, thereby achieving the same density of development on a much smaller portion of the forty-acre tract. The remaining twenty to thirty acres of open space would be preserved for natural forestland or productive agriculture. Moreover, the conservation model would protect the rural character of the area and potentially reduce costs for the developer by requiring less infrastructure.

Many local ordinances prevent conservation development, just as they prevent TND. In order to allow—or require—conservation development, local governments must evaluate zoning and subdivision ordinances and make the necessary changes. Policy considerations include resource identification, design concepts, ownership alternatives, and ordinance administration.[4]

---

4. For more on conservation subdivisions, see, generally, RANDALL ARENDT, GROWING GREENER: PUTTING CONSERVATION INTO LOCAL PLANS AND ORDINANCES (1999); N.C. URBAN & CMTY. FORESTRY PROGRAM & NCSU FORESTRY & ENVTL. OUTREACH PROGRAM, CONSERVATION SUBDIVISION HANDBOOK: A GUIDE FOR NORTH CAROLINA COMMUNITIES IN THE USE OF

### Resource Identification

Policies to encourage conservation development must be grounded in the local ecology. A good policy begins with the identification and prioritization of natural resources in the area. Such resources include wetlands, floodplains and floodways, steep slopes, groundwater, woodlands, productive farmland, wildlife habitats, and cultural resources.[5]

Many of these resources have already been cataloged and are available from state and federal agencies. They also may be further highlighted and prioritized through local documents, such as the local comprehensive plan. Site-specific resource identification also can be accomplished through the preparation of an environmental impact statement.

For more on environmental impact statements, see the discussion in Chapter 5.

### Design Concepts

Several design concepts can facilitate conservation subdivision (see Table 7.1). The following discussion outlines some general design concepts, but the design of a particular site should emphasize conservation of critical resources and maintain cohesion of natural resources (for example, do not fragment a stream or wetland). The preferred concept depends on the site and the context.

Orange County, an early adopter of conservation subdivisions, has outlined several design options.[6] The first, estate design, is based on a typical large-lot subdivision in which a tract is divided into large lots that are sold and held by private owners. The difference for the conservation estate is that deed restrictions limit the buildable area of each lot in order to leave a smaller developmental footprint. In this way, private land agreements protect valuable natural resources.

Conservation design, like estate design, is based on a conventional large-lot subdivision but extends the protection and enforcement of estate design. Under this model, a third party holds a conservation easement applicable to the protected areas of the subdivision.

Cluster design shifts the placement of lots in the design model. Rather than spreading lots out evenly across the tract, a cluster design allows for smaller lot sizes, thereby enabling the same number of units to be developed on a smaller area of land. The open space may be held by a homeowners association or transferred to a third party by conservation easement or some other instrument.

The fourth design concept in conservation subdivision is the village design, which takes the cluster design and adds a mix of uses. Village design allows for even greater density (small-lots homes, townhomes, multi-family dwellings) as well as some commercial or institutional uses. Again, the protected open space may be held by the homeowners association or transferred to a third party by easement or other instrument.

---

CONSERVATION DESIGN FOR LAND USE PLANNING, http://content.ces.ncsu.edu/conservation-subdivision-handbook.pdf; N.C. WILDLIFE RES. COMM'N, GREEN GROWTH TOOLBOX: WILDLIFE AND NATURAL RESOURCE STEWARDSHIP IN PLANNING (2nd ed. 2013), www.ncwildlife.org/Conserving/Programs/GreenGrowthToolbox/DownloadHandbook.aspx).

    5. ARENDT, *supra* note 4, at 22–24.

    6. ORANGE CNTY., FLEXIBLE DEVELOPMENT STANDARDS FOR PRESERVING RURAL CHARACTER: A DESIGN MANUAL FOR CONSERVATION AND DEVELOPMENT IN ORANGE COUNTY, NORTH CAROLINA (1996).

**Table 7.1 Design Concepts That Facilitate Conservation Subdivision**

| | Estate Design | Conservation Design | Cluster Design | Village Design |
|---|---|---|---|---|
| Typical lot size | 5 acres | 3 acres | 1 acre | varied |
| Dwelling units per acre (based on tract) | 0.21 | 0.3 | 0.3 | 1.1 |
| Ownership of open space | Private lot owner | Private lot owner | Homeowners association | Homeowners association |
| Protection of open space | Deed restriction | Conservation easement held by third party | Conservation easement held by third party | Conservation easement held by third party |

In order to encourage open space conservation, an ordinance may provide incentives to the developer, including density bonuses, cluster development, and expedited permitting.[7] With a density bonus, the developer may add additional units to the development beyond what is permitted by right (i.e., 10–15% increase in density). Cluster development allows for reduced lot sizes so that the developer can achieve the same number of units as by right density but also set aside the open space. This flexibility preserves the developer's financial interests in the number of units but protects critical natural areas. Expedited permitting, reduced fees, and other procedural benefits also may serve as incentives.

### Ownership

As noted above, open space can be owned and maintained by private lot owners, owned and maintained by a homeowners association, or owned and maintained by a third party, such as a conservation trust or local government. Or, alternatively, open space can be handled through a combination of these. For example, conservation open space may be owned as a common area by a homeowners association but be maintained and secured by a conservation trust that holds a conservation easement.

### Administration

Like any new program, a conservation development ordinance requires some tailoring and education to be effective. Developers must be informed about the benefits of conservation development so that they will understand its purpose as well as its process. Some ordinances require an environmental inventory of the property as part of the development approval process. Standards and guidelines are needed to protect natural areas and preserve rural features.

For example, Chatham County's ordinance outlines provisions for conservation sub-divisions.[8] Forty percent of the project must be set aside as conservation, and of that conserved area, half of it must be contiguous. Riparian buffers and floodplain can count toward conservation. The conservation area must be protected by a legal Instrument for permanent protection: conservation easement, permanent restrictive covenant, or some comparable land use restriction. A conservation management plan is required. Motor vehicles, roads, parking, and impervious surfaces are prohibited in the conservation area. Permitted uses include conservation, agriculture, recreation, stormwater management, utility easements,

---

7. Chatham County Subdivision Regulations § 7.7.
8. Chatham County Subdivision Regulations § 7.7.

**Figure 7.1    Estate Option: Hall's Mill Inn**

### ESTATE OPTION
### Hall's Mill Inn

| Tract Size | 140.0 acres | Ownership of Open Space Private, individual ownership, subject to deed restrictions | |
|---|---|---|---|
| Number of Lots | 30 | **Residential Lots** Building Envelopes Restricted Area | **133.3 acres (95.2%)** 40.4 acres (29.9%) 92.9 acres (66.3%) |
| Average Lot Size | 4.7 acres | **Roads** | **6.7 acres (4.8%)** |

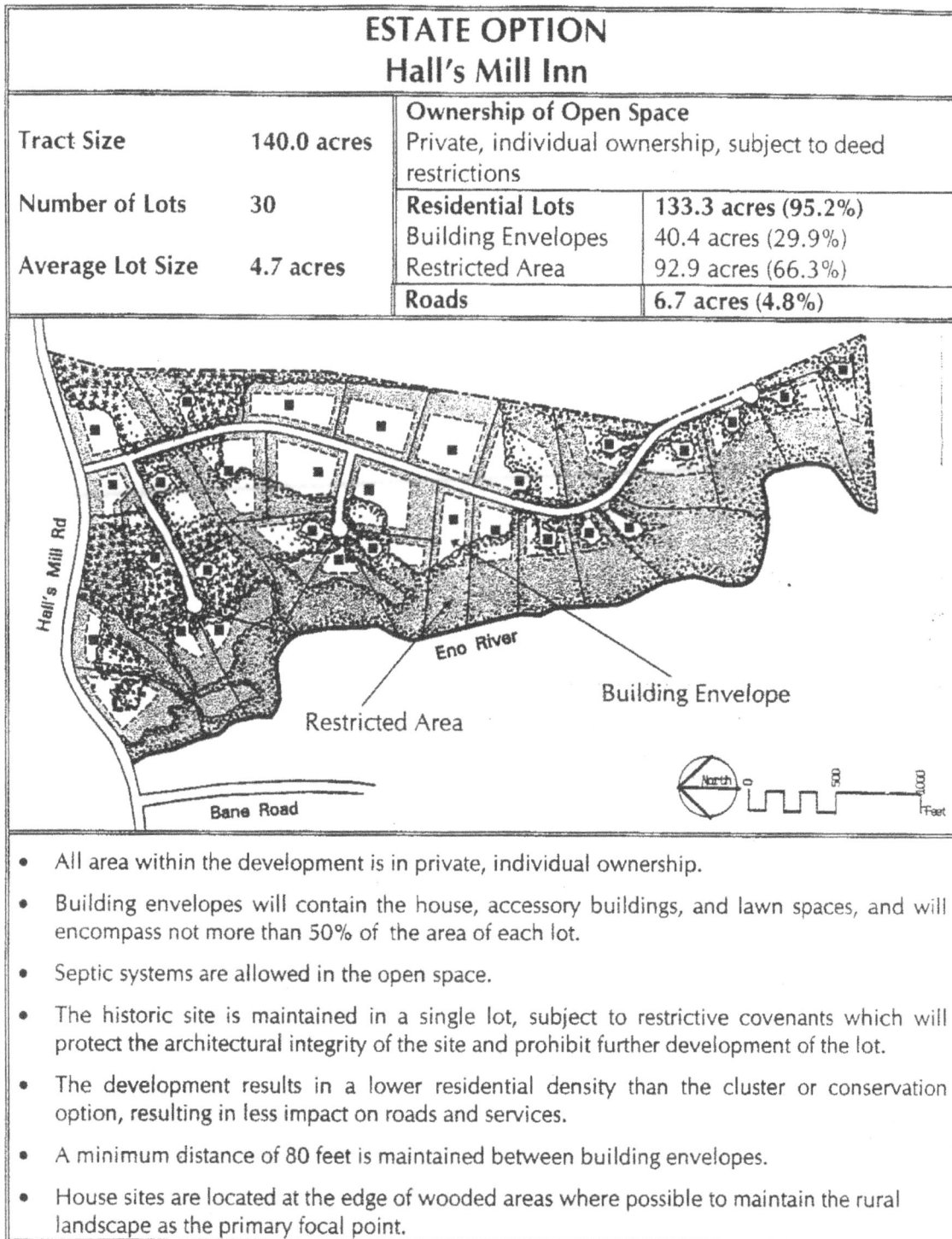

- All area within the development is in private, individual ownership.

- Building envelopes will contain the house, accessory buildings, and lawn spaces, and will encompass not more than 50% of the area of each lot.

- Septic systems are allowed in the open space.

- The historic site is maintained in a single lot, subject to restrictive covenants which will protect the architectural integrity of the site and prohibit further development of the lot.

- The development results in a lower residential density than the cluster or conservation option, resulting in less impact on roads and services.

- A minimum distance of 80 feet is maintained between building envelopes.

- House sites are located at the edge of wooded areas where possible to maintain the rural landscape as the primary focal point.

water, septic and sewer systems, and trails. There is no minimum lot size, and setbacks may be reduced to as little as five feet, but "the majority of lots should abut open space to provide residents with direct views and access."[9] Conservation subdivisions with fifteen lots or fewer may be approved administratively.

---

9. *Id.*

**Figure 7.2    Conservation Option: Hall's Mill Inn**

# CONSERVATION OPTION
## Hall's Mill Inn

| Tract Size | 140.0 acres | Ownership of Open Space |  |
|---|---|---|---|
| | | Private, individual ownership, subject to conservation easement held by Orange County or other entity. | |
| Number of Lots | 42 | | |
| | | **Residential Lots** | **133.3 acres (95.2%)** |
| Average Lot Size | 3.2 acres | Buildable Area | 75.4 acres (53.9%) |
| | | Conservation Easement | 57.9 acres (41.3%) |
| Conservation Easement | 57.9 acres | **Roads** | **7.3 acres (4.8%)** |

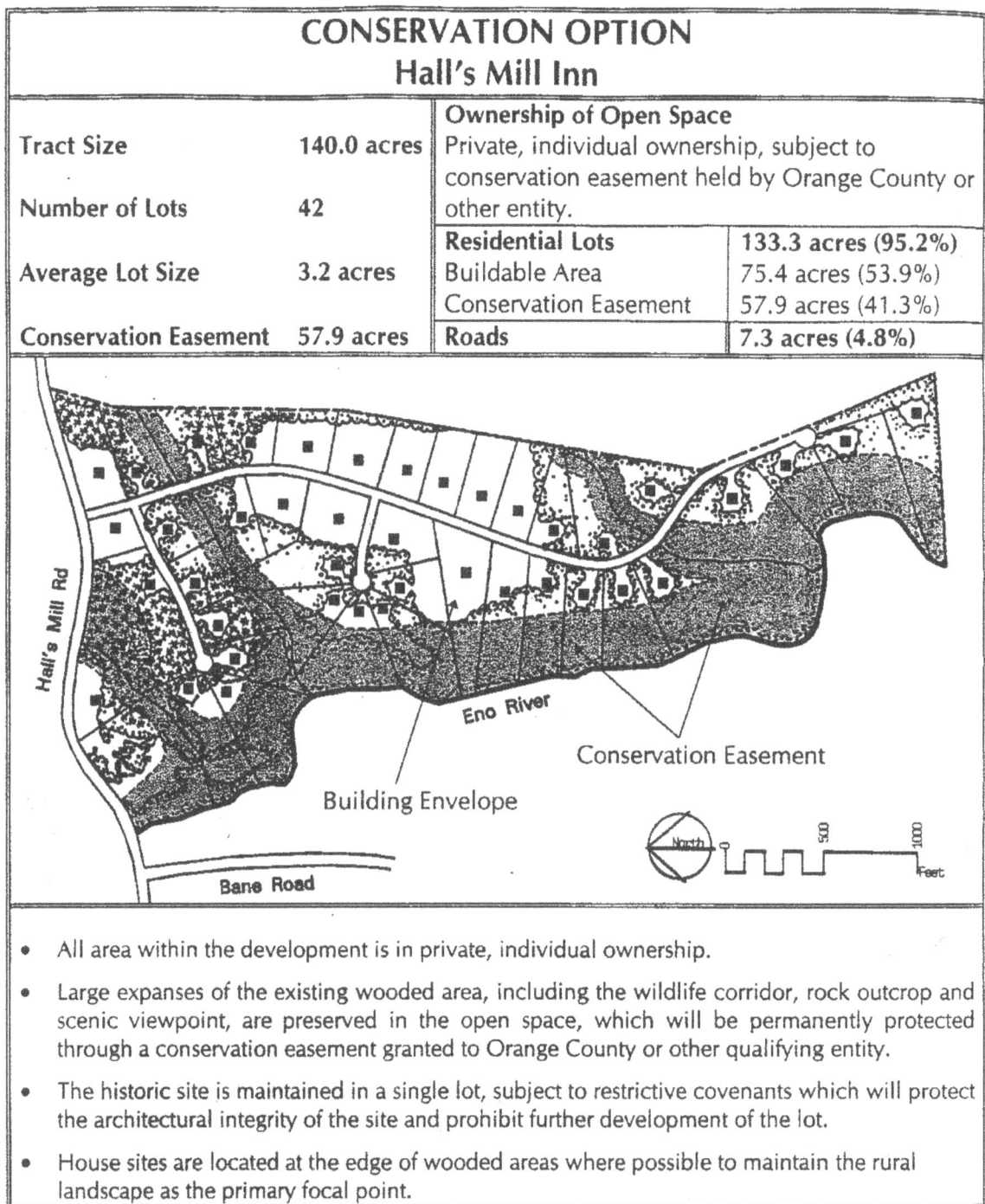

- All area within the development is in private, individual ownership.

- Large expanses of the existing wooded area, including the wildlife corridor, rock outcrop and scenic viewpoint, are preserved in the open space, which will be permanently protected through a conservation easement granted to Orange County or other qualifying entity.

- The historic site is maintained in a single lot, subject to restrictive covenants which will protect the architectural integrity of the site and prohibit further development of the lot.

- House sites are located at the edge of wooded areas where possible to maintain the rural landscape as the primary focal point.

**Figure 7.3 Cluster Option: Hall's Mill Inn**

## CLUSTER OPTION
### Hall's Mill Inn

| | | | |
|---|---|---|---|
| Tract Size | 140.0 acres | **Conservation Area** | **97.5 acres (70%)** |
| | | Primary | 27.1 acres (20%) |
| Number of Lots | 42 | Secondary | 70.4 acres (50%) |
| | | **Ownership of Conservation Area** | |
| Average Lot Size | .84 acres | Owned by homeowners association, with conservation easement held by Orange County or other entity | |
| Open Space | 97.5 acres | | |
| | | **Developed Area** | **42.5 acres (30%)** |
| | | Residential Lots | 35.2 acres (25%) |
| | | Roads | 7.3 acres (5%) |

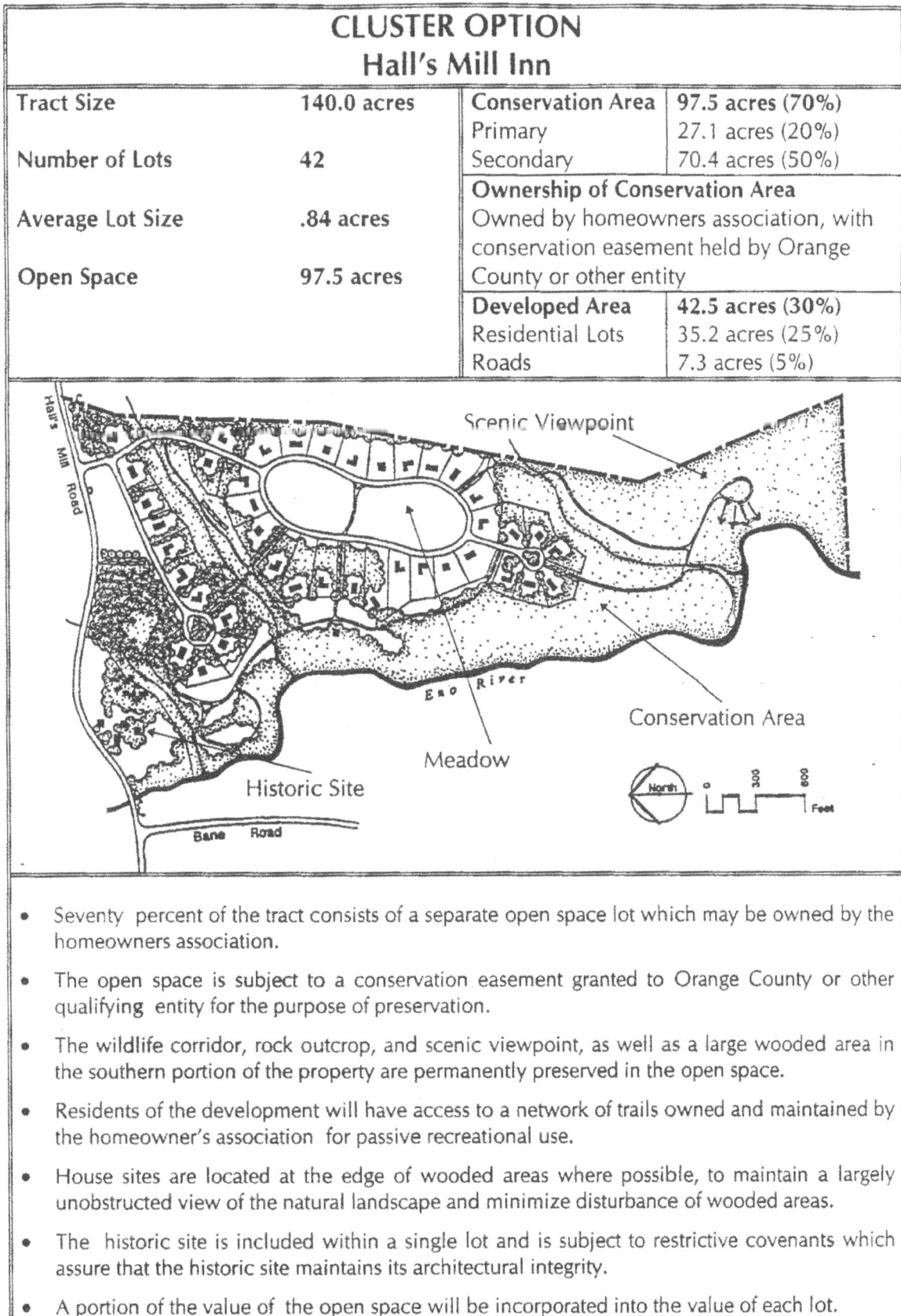

- Seventy percent of the tract consists of a separate open space lot which may be owned by the homeowners association.

- The open space is subject to a conservation easement granted to Orange County or other qualifying entity for the purpose of preservation.

- The wildlife corridor, rock outcrop, and scenic viewpoint, as well as a large wooded area in the southern portion of the property are permanently preserved in the open space.

- Residents of the development will have access to a network of trails owned and maintained by the homeowner's association for passive recreational use.

- House sites are located at the edge of wooded areas where possible, to maintain a largely unobstructed view of the natural landscape and minimize disturbance of wooded areas.

- The historic site is included within a single lot and is subject to restrictive covenants which assure that the historic site maintains its architectural integrity.

- A portion of the value of the open space will be incorporated into the value of each lot.

**Figure 7.4    Village Option (without density bonus): McGowan Creek Village**

## VILLAGE OPTION (without density bonus)
## McGowan Creek Village

| | | | |
|---|---|---|---|
| Total Acreage | 257.0 | Village Conservancy | 214.0 acres (83.3%) |
| Right-of-way Acreage | 15.2 | Primary | 40.6 acres (15.8%) |
| Net Acreage | 241.8 | Secondary | 170.3 acres (66.3%) |
| | | Other | 3.1 acres (1.2%) |
| | | Village Proper | 43 acres (16.7%) |
| Total Units | 262 | Civic | 7.8 acres (3.0%) |
| | | Storefront | 1.3 acres (.5%) |
| | | Commercial | 55,724 sf |
| Density | 1du/.92 acres | Residential | 61 units (900 sf) |
| | | Residential | 20.5 acres (8.0%) |
| | | Townhouse | 2.1 acres (.8%) |
| | | Single-Family | 18.4 acres (7.2%) |

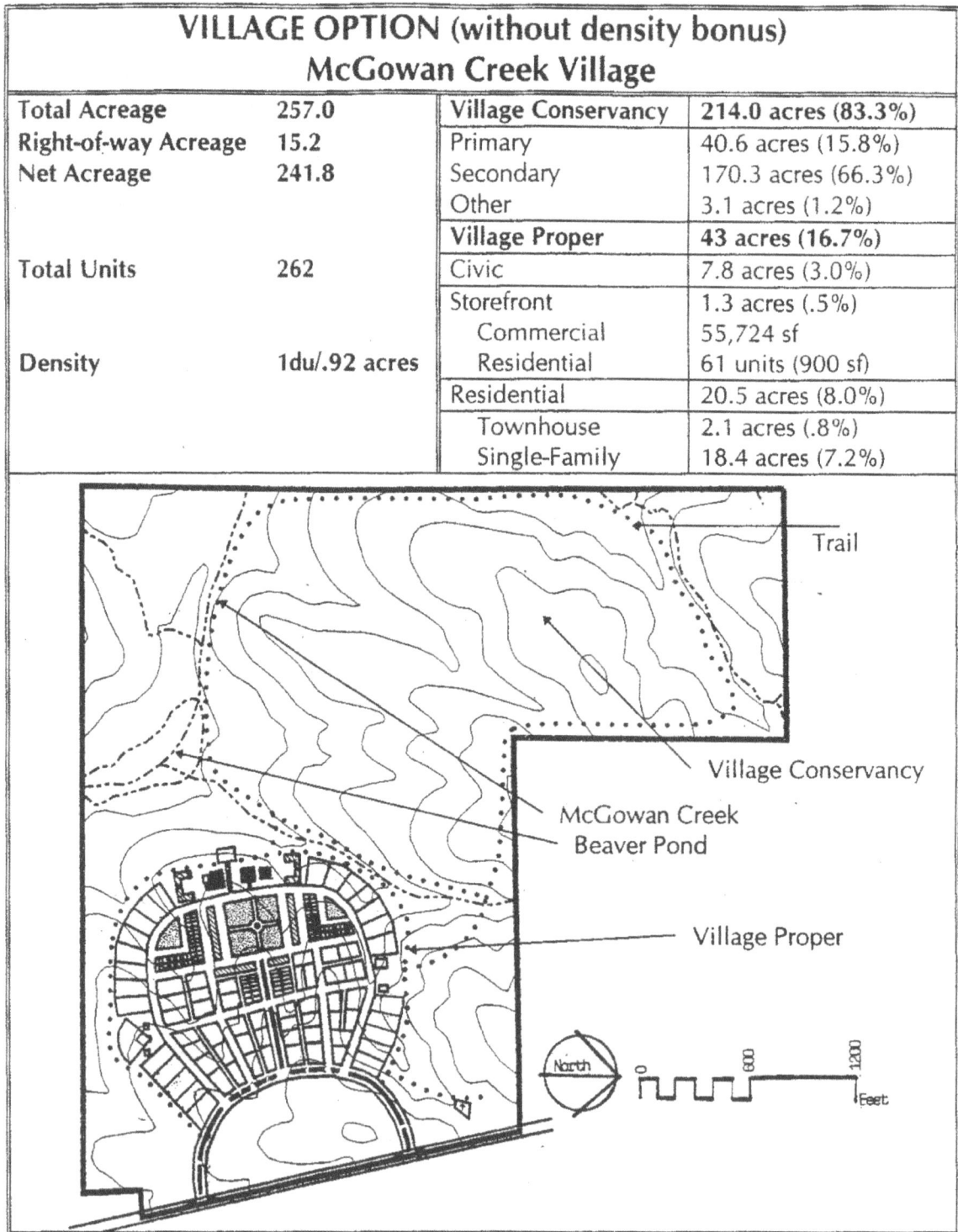

Trail

Village Conservancy

McGowan Creek
Beaver Pond

Village Proper

North

0      600      1200
Feet

**Figure 7.4    Village Option (without density bonus): McGowan Creek Village** (*continued*)

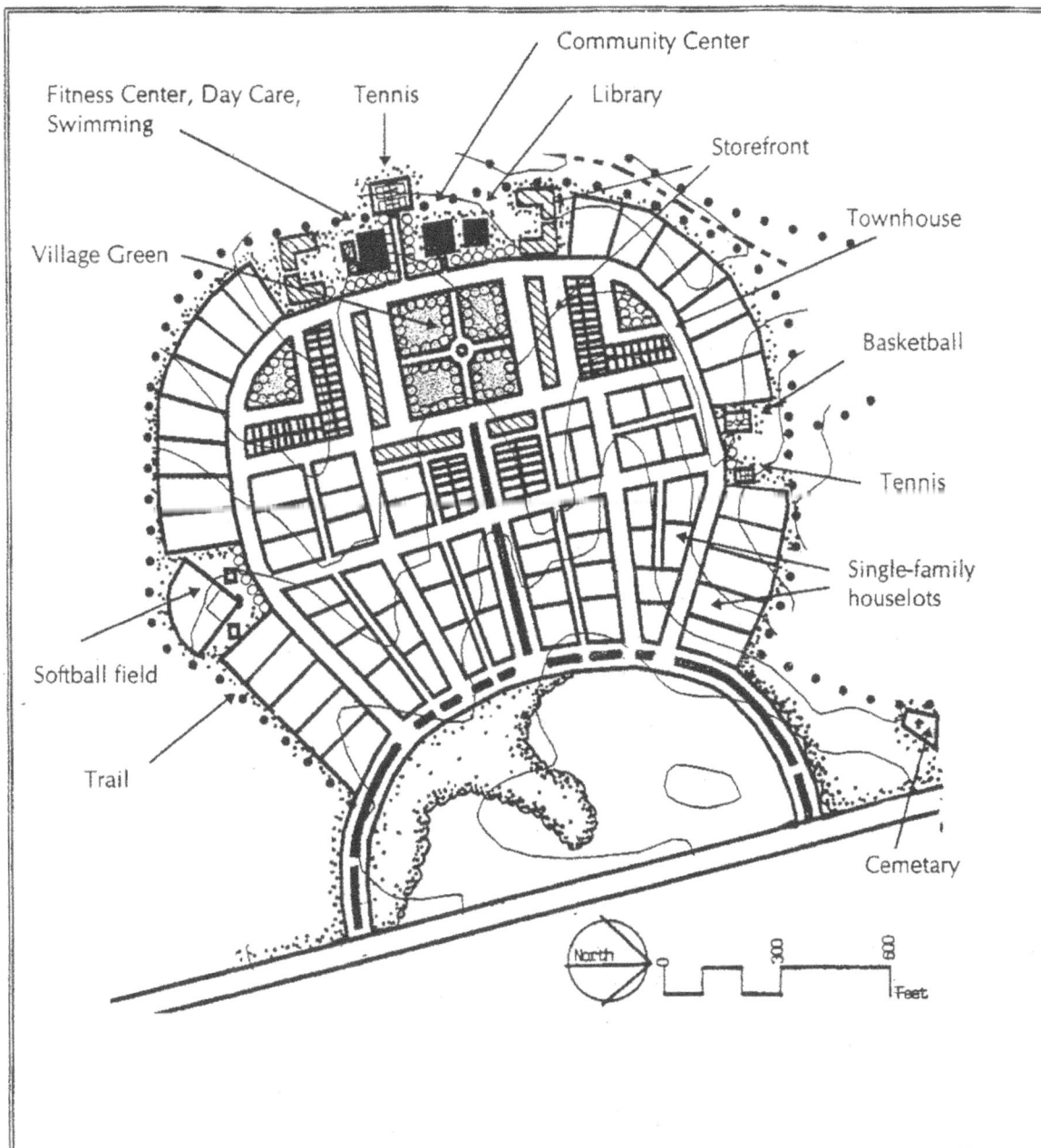

- Development is concentrated to preserve a large area of contiguous open space.
- Construction of infrastructure such as roads and utilities is minimized through efficient land use design.
- .The amount of area preserved as open space is maximized.
- Active and passive recreational opportunities are provided.
- Residents can walk to recreational, civic and commercial areas, reducing reliance on the automobile.
- Businesses within the village center may provide job opportunities for village residents

**Figure 7.5    Village Option (with density bonus): McGowan Creek Village**

## VILLAGE OPTION with Density Bonus
## McGowan Creek Village

| | | | |
|---|---|---|---|
| Total Acreage | 257.0 | **Village Conservancy** | **189.4 acres (73.7%)** |
| Right-of-way acreage | 20.0 | Primary | 40.6 acres (15.8%) |
| Net Acreage | 237.0 | Secondary | 145.7 acres (56.7%) |
| | | Other | 3.1 acres (1.2%) |
| | | **Village Proper** | **67.6 acres (26.3%)** |
| Total Units | 308 | Civic | 7.8 acres (3.0%) |
| | | Storefront | 1.3 acres (.4%) |
| | | Commercial | 55,724 sf |
| Density | 1.3du/.acre | Residential | 61 units (900 sf) |
| | | Residential | 63.7. acres (24.8%) |
| | | Townhouse | 2.1 acres (.8%) |
| | | Single-Family | 61.6 acres (24.0%) |

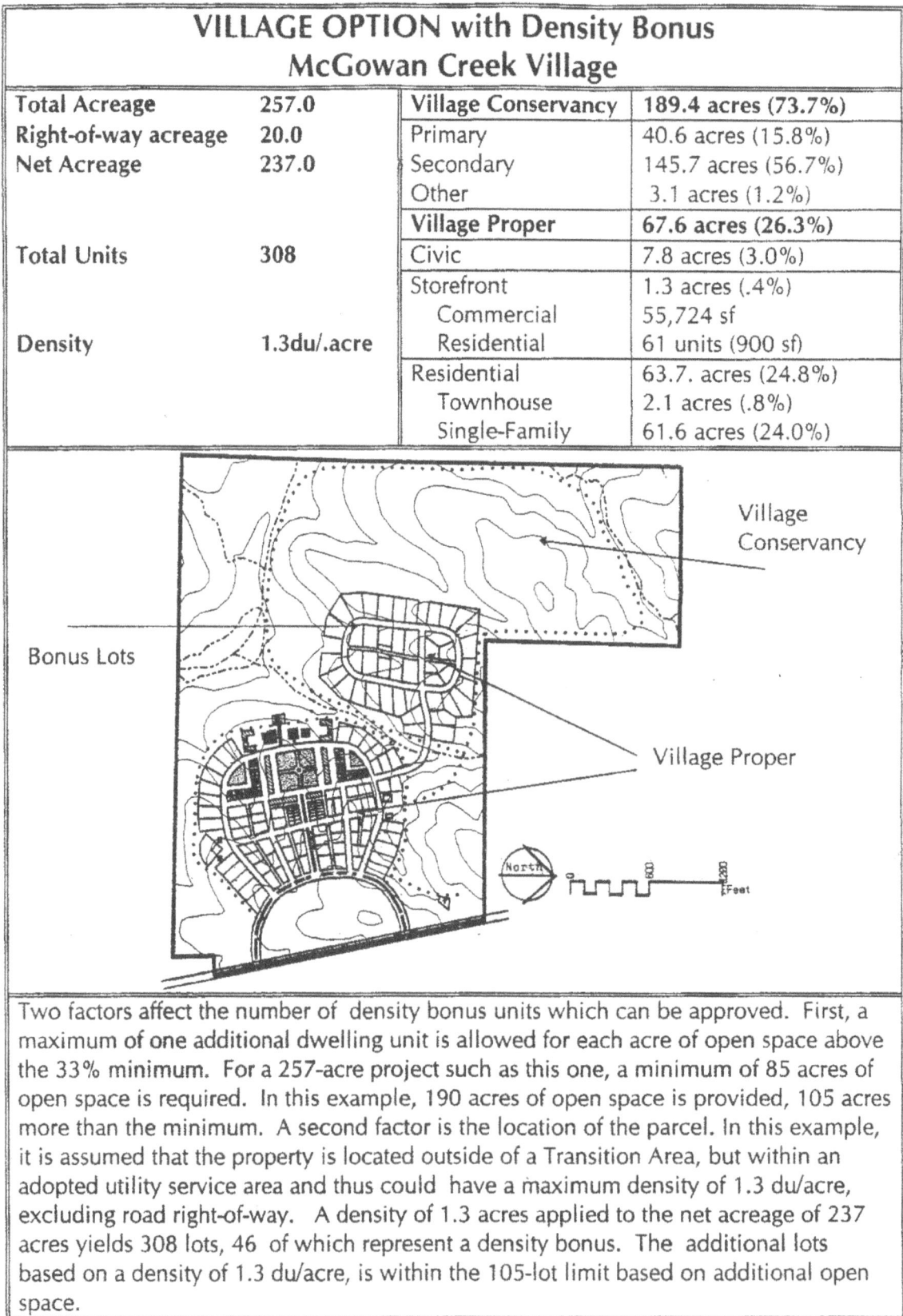

Village Conservancy

Bonus Lots

Village Proper

North    Feet

Two factors affect the number of  density bonus units which can be approved.  First, a maximum of one additional dwelling unit is allowed for each acre of open space above the 33% minimum.  For a 257-acre project such as this one, a minimum of 85 acres of open space is required.  In this example, 190 acres of open space is provided, 105 acres more than the minimum.  A second factor is the location of the parcel.  In this example, it is assumed that the property is located outside of a Transition Area, but within an adopted utility service area and thus could  have a maximum density of 1.3 du/acre, excluding road right-of-way.   A density of 1.3 acres applied to the net acreage of 237 acres yields 308 lots, 46  of which represent a density bonus.  The  additional lots based on a density of 1.3 du/acre, is within the 105-lot limit based on additional open space.

*Source for figures 7.1–7.5*: Orange County, *Flexible Development Standards for Preserving Rural Character: A Design Manual for Conservation and Development in Orange County, North Carolina* (1996).

# Chapter 8

# Exaction Authority and Limits

When a developer must fund, construct, or dedicate improvements for the public as a condition of a development approval, that condition is an exaction. Authorized by statute and recognized by the U.S. Supreme Court as a fundamental element of local land development regulation, exactions are legal but not without limits. An exaction must be authorized by statute, rationally related to the impacts of the development, and roughly proportional to the impacts of the development.

This section explores several important elements: What are exactions? What are not exactions (e.g., regulatory authority)? What is authorized by statute? And what are the constitutional limits?

Exactions—such as dedication of infrastructure to the public as a condition of permit approval—are legal but subject to specific statutory and constitutional limits.

## In General

By way of definition, the N.C. Court of Appeals adopted the following explanation from the UNC School of Government's Richard Ducker:

> [A]n exaction is a condition of development permission that requires a public facility or improvement to be provided at the developer's expense. Most exactions fall into one of four categories: (1) requirements that land be dedicated

for street rights-of-way, parks, or utility easements and the like; (2) requirements that improvements be constructed or installed on land so dedicated; (3) requirements that fees be paid in lieu of compliance with dedication or improvement provisions; and (4) requirements that developers pay "impact" or "facility" fees reflecting their respective prorated shares of the cost of providing new roads, utility systems, parks, and similar facilities serving the entire area.[1]

A land *reservation* is the setting aside of land for a public entity to purchase. Reservation is qualitatively different from formal exaction because the public must pay for the land. Still, reservation is commonly discussed alongside pure exactions.

## Distinguishing Regulatory Authority and Exaction Authority

When is a condition an exaction? Here is the test question: If the local government demands the certain condition separate from development approval, would that demand qualify as a taking of property and require just compensation under the Fifth Amendment of the U.S. Constitution? For example, if a city simply required a property owner to dedicate land for a park, would the city have to pay just compensation? Yes, of course. So, if a property owner is required to dedicate land for a park as a condition of getting a permit from the city, then that dedication is an exaction.

Alternatively, suppose that a city required a property owner to *provide* private parking sufficient for the development on the property. Is that a taking requiring just compensation? No. It is a regulation on land use.[2] The owner is required to meet a certain condition related to use of the property, but no property right is granted to the public. Therefore, if a property owner seeks a development approval and the city requires as a condition of that approval that the property owner provide sufficient parking, such a condition is not an exaction.

It is critical to distinguish the authority to *regulate* land development from the authority to *require exactions*. While in practice they may be linked, these are two distinct authorities for local governments in North Carolina. Provisions of G.S. 143-214.23A emphasize this distinction with regard to the regulation of riparian buffers. "Cities and counties shall not treat the land within a riparian buffer area as if the land is the property of the State or any of its subdivisions unless the land or an interest therein has been acquired by the State or its subdivisions by a conveyance or by eminent domain."

This distinction is especially important in discussions of adequate public facilities ordinances (APFOs). In plain terms, an APFO requires that essential public services must be available for a particular development approval. Requiring that infrastructure be sufficient to support development is a fundamental element of land development regulation. Adequacy

---

1. Franklin Rd. Props. v. City of Raleigh, 94 N.C. App. 731, 736 (1989) (quoting Richard D. Ducker, *"Taking" Found for Beach Access Dedication Requirement:* Nollan v. California Coastal Commission, 30 Local Gov't Law Bull. 2 (Aug. 1987)).

2. It is worth noting that regulation can go too far. If regulation is so burdensome that a property owner is left with no beneficial use, it amounts to a taking and requires just compensation.

reviews may be incorporated as part of subdivision or zoning approvals, and some local governments formalize the adequacy review into a related APFO.

The enabling legislation for subdivision and zoning ordinances each authorize regulating development to ensure adequate infrastructure and to avoid overcrowding. Ordinances established through subdivision authority may provide for the orderly growth and development; coordination of infrastructure within the subdivision with existing and planned public infrastructure; and distribution of population and traffic in a manner to avoid congestion and overcrowding and to substantially promote the public health and welfare.[3] Under their zoning authority, cities and counties are authorized to adopt ordinances for the following public purposes, among others: "to prevent the overcrowding of land; . . . to lessen congestion in the streets; to secure safety from fire, panic, and dangers; and to facilitate the efficient and adequate provision of transportation, water, sewerage, schools, parks, and other public requirements."[4] In other words, these enabling statutes for subdivision and zoning clearly authorize regulation of land division and use based on adequacy of infrastructure.

In *Tonter Investments, Inc. v. Pasquotank County*,[5] the N.C. Court of Appeals upheld a zoning requirement for residential structures to be within a thousand feet of a public water supply and on a lot with public frontage. The court found that the "goal of ensuring that all new structures in Pasquotank County will have adequate access to drinking water, as well as roads that can handle traffic and emergency vehicles" clearly fit within the permissible goals of zoning.[6]

To be sure, adequacy standards must be based on clear metrics, and adequacy decisions must be based on sufficient evidence. In *Blue Ridge Co., L.L.C. v. Town of Pineville*,[7] the town denied a subdivision request based on general conformity standards as well as inadequacy of roads and school capacity. The N.C. Court of Appeals found the conformity standard requiring the "most advantageous development" to be vague. As for schools, although the standard called for consistency with adopted plans and policies, the court did not find a clearly adopted school-crowding policy, nor did the ordinance require a school-impact study. The court ruled that denial based on school impact was not supported by the evidence. Moreover, for roads the court found insufficient evidence to deny the subdivision. The applicant's engineer provided expert testimony concerning the modesty of traffic impacts, and the opponents rebutted with general perceptions that were not enough to overcome the expert testimony.

The regulatory authority for a local government to ensure adequate infrastructure does not imply authority to charge fees to resolve any inadequacy. In North Carolina, a local government must have express authority to charge a fee for infrastructure capacity. North Carolina courts have struck down APFOs that the courts viewed as de facto fee schemes. In

---

3. Sections 153A-331(a) and 160A-372(a) of the North Carolina General Statutes (hereinafter G.S.).

4. G.S. 153A-341; G.S. 160A-383.

5. 199 N.C. App. 579 (2009).

6. *Tonter*, 199 N.C. App. at 584. Subsequent adoption of G.S. 153A-340(j) limits the ability of a county to regulate residential structures on lots greater than ten acres. While this changes the statutory authority, it does not alter the underlying legal principle that ensuring an adequate water supply and service roads is within the permissible goals of land use regulation.

7. 188 N.C. App. 466, 473 (2008).

2009, the N.C. Court of Appeals rejected the voluntary mitigation payment included in Union County's APFO.[8] In that case, the court reviewed the zoning and subdivision authority and noted that limited regulatory tools were available to achieve the stated purposes of zoning and subdivision. As the court stated, a county "may not use the APFO to obtain indirectly the payment of what amounts to an impact fee given that defendant lacks the authority to impose school impact fees directly."[9] And in 2012, the N.C. Supreme Court addressed the question. Reviewing an APFO that included a mitigation payment for school capacity, the court stated clearly, "APFOs that effectively require developers to pay an adequate public facilities fee to obtain development approval are invalid as a matter of law."[10]

These decisions reflect a clear view of the courts: A local government may not impose an impact fee unless it is clearly authorized, and in cases where an APFO is effectively a fee requirement, the court will strike it down. These decisions, however, do not alter the clear statutory authority for regulating land use and land division based on the adequacy of public facilities. If there is insufficient public facility capacity, the local government may not have the authority to charge a fee, but it does have the authority to say no to the development.

## Statutory Authority for Exactions

More details about each of these authorities—and the procedures that accompany them—are outlined in Chapter 5.

Under the statutes authorizing subdivision regulation, North Carolina cities and counties can require dedication of certain property rights to the public in connection with land subdivision. These include

- dedication or reservation of recreation areas within the subdivision;
- funds to be used to acquire recreation areas within the immediate area;
- dedication or reservation of rights-of-way or easements for streets and utility purposes;
- funds for the acquisition, design, and construction of roads to serve the development;
- construction of community service facilities in accordance with local plans, policies and standards;
- reservation of school sites in accordance with local plans.

In addition to subdivision regulation, development projects commonly trigger other related regulations—such as driveway permits, zoning, and utility approvals—that have independent exaction authority. For example, development, whether or not it is a subdivision, commonly requires a driveway permit from the municipality or NCDOT. Statutory authority for driveway permits includes additional authority for dedication and construction or reimbursement for medians, turn lanes, and traffic lanes.[11]

---

8. Union Land Owners Ass'n v. Cnty. of Union, 201 N.C. App. 374 (2009); *see also* Durham Land Owners Ass'n v. Cnty. of Durham, 177 N.C. App. 629, *writ denied, review denied*, 360 N.C. 532 (2006).

9. *Union Land Owners Ass'n*, 201 N.C. App. at 381.

10. Lanvale Props., L.L.C. v. Cnty. of Cabarrus, 366 N.C. 142, 163 (2012).

11. G.S. 160A-307; G.S. 136-18(29).

Zoning authority also allows for certain exactions. Conditional use permits and special use permits may include reasonable and appropriate conditions, including conditions for dedication of street and utility rights-of-way and provision of recreational space and facilities.[12] Special or conditional use districts and conditional zoning districts also may include conditions "that address the conformance of the development and use of the site to county ordinances and an officially adopted comprehensive or other plan and those that address the impacts reasonably expected to be generated by the development or use of the site."[13]

In addition, cities and counties have authority to charge fees related to their public enterprise utilities, such as water, sewer, stormwater management, and even public transportation.[14] Sections 160A-314 and 153A-277 of the North Carolina General Statutes (hereinafter G.S.) authorize cities and counties to establish and revise "schedules of rents, rates, fees, charges, and penalties for the use of or the services furnished by any public enterprise." The N.C. Court of Appeals has found that "a municipal body may include not only operating expenses and depreciation, but also capital cost associated with actual or anticipated growth or improvement of the facilities required for the furnishing of such services."[15] Thus, in addition to basic usage charges, this statutory language gives fairly broad authority to charge fees related to the capital costs of infrastructure, sometimes termed connections fees, tap fees, capacity fees, or cost-recovery fees. Notably, though, this case was limited to charges to current customers, not new connections. The full breadth of this fee authority is not clear.

A series of North Carolina court cases have emphasized that school impact fees must be clearly authorized by statute in order for a local government to be allowed to impose them. Through this line of litigation, courts have ruled that school impact fees are not authorized under either the general authority for administrative fees or the broad construction of G.S. 153A-4 and G.S. 160A-4;[16] that school impact fees may not be imposed indirectly through adequate public facilities ordinances;[17] that school impact fees may not be required by local custom;[18] and that school impact fees may not be framed as "voluntary mitigation payments."[19]

Local legislation provides additional authority for certain local governments to exact specific dedications, improvements, and fees. These include impact fees for streets, parks, open spaces, recreational facilities, and stormwater facilities as well as emergency medical facilities, fire stations, schools, libraries, water, sewer, and solid waste facilities.[20]

---

12. G.S. 153A-340(c1); G.S. 160A-381(c).

13. G.S. 153A-342(b); G.S. 160A-382(b).

14. G.S. 153A-277; G.S. 160A-314.

15. Town of Spring Hope v. Bissette, 53 N.C. App. 210, 213 (1981), *aff'd*, 305 N.C. 248 (1982).

16. Durham Land Owners Ass'n v. Cnty. of Durham, 177 N.C. App. 629, *writ denied, review denied*, 360 N.C. 532 (2006).

17. Union Land Owners Ass'n v. Cnty. of Union, 201 N.C. App. 374 (2009).

18. Amward Homes, Inc. v. Town of Cary, 206 N.C. App. 38 (2010).

19. Lanvale Props., L.L.C. v. Cnty. of Cabarrus, 366 N.C. 142, 163 (2012).

20. *See, for example*, S.L. 1985-498 (for Raleigh: roads, drainage, and open space); S.L. 1985-536 (for Dare County municipalities: streets, open space, water access, fire department, emergency refuge shelters); S.L. 1986-936 (for Chapel Hill and Hillsborough: streets, bridges, sidewalks, bikeways, drainage, and recreation); S.L. 1987-705 (for Hickory: streets, sidewalks, water and sewer, drainage, parks, open space, and recreation); S.L. 1987-801 (for Cary: roads); S.L. 1987-802 (for Durham: streets, sidewalks, parks, recreation, drainage, and open space). *See also*, S.L. 1987-460

## Constitutional Limits

Even if authorized by statute, exactions must still adhere to constitutional limits. When a government agency requires an exaction there must be an "essential nexus" and "rough proportionality" between the condition of dedication and the impact of the development necessitating the dedication. Moreover, the requirement to pay cash exactions must meet the test for nexus and proportionality.

### *Nollan* and Essential Nexus

The essential nexus test arose from the case of *Nollan v. California Coastal Commission.*[21] The Nollans proposed to tear down their small bungalow and build a larger home on beachfront property in California. Such construction required a coastal development permit. As a condition of approval, the coastal commission required a public easement across the Nollans' property along the beachfront, between the mean high tide line and the seawall. To support the need for the easement, the commission cited the cumulative effect of the wall of residential development. The commission found that it created a visual and psychological barrier between the ocean and individuals on the street side of the property and burdened the public's ability to traverse and access the beach.

The U.S. Supreme Court rejected the exaction because the easement was insufficiently related to the impact of the development. The Court has "long recognized that land-use regulation does not effect a taking if it substantially advance[s] legitimate state interests and does not den[y] an owner economically viable use of his land. . . . [And] a broad range of governmental purposes and regulations satisfies these requirements."[22] Thus, in order to preserve the view of the ocean from the street, the Court stated that the commission likely could have placed height and width restrictions, a ban on fences, or refused to issue the permit for construction.

Once a condition requires the dedication of property, however, additional analysis is needed. In such cases, an essential nexus or link must be found between the development regulation and the exaction condition. The coastal commission may have been justified, the Court stated, to require a viewing deck on the street side for the public to see the ocean. "Although such a requirement, constituting a permanent grant of continuous access to the property, would have to be considered a taking if it were not attached to a development permit, the Commission's assumed power to forbid construction of the house in order to protect the public's view of the beach must surely include the power to condition construction upon some concession by the owner, even a concession of property rights, that serves the same end."[23]

Without an essential nexus, however, the requirement for an easement is merely a taking without compensation. For the Nollans' property, the Court found no essential nexus

---

(for Chatham and Orange counties: school impact fees). For more on local authority, see David W. Owens, Land Use Law in North Carolina 65 n.49 (2d ed. 2011).

21. 483 U.S. 825 (1987).

22. *Id.* at 834–35 (quotations and citations omitted).

23. *Id.* at 836.

between the valid governmental purpose of reducing obstacles for viewing the beach from the street and the requirement that people already on the beach be allowed to walk across the Nollans' beachside property.

## *Dolan* and Rough Proportionality

The decision of *Dolan v. City of Tigard*[24] further refined the constitutional limits of exactions and extended the essential nexus test to include proportionality.

The property owner, Dolan, proposed to expand her plumbing and electric supply store that sat on a 1.67-acre parcel along a creek in downtown Tigard, Oregon. The redevelopment would double the size of the store and pave a 39-space parking lot.

The city had previously adopted a pedestrian/bicycle pathway plan, and the development code required new development to dedicate land for pathways as shown on that plan, which was based on a transportation study. The city also adopted a drainage plan that noted flooding along the adjacent creek and that an increase in impervious surfaces would exacerbate flooding problems. The plan called for stream improvements and assurances that the floodplain would remain free of structures.

As a condition of permit approval, the planning commission required Dolan to dedicate the portion of her property within the 100-year floodplain for use as a public greenway with storm drainage improvements and to dedicate an additional fifteen-foot strip of land adjacent to the floodplain for a pedestrian/bicycle pathway.

The U.S. Supreme Court first considered "whether the 'essential nexus' exists between the 'legitimate state interest' and the permit condition exacted by the city."[25] The Court easily affirmed the legitimate public interest and its nexus with the permit conditions.

> Undoubtedly, the prevention of flooding along Fanno Creek and the reduction of traffic congestion in the Central Business District qualify as the type of legitimate public purposes we have upheld. It seems equally obvious that a nexus exists between preventing flooding along Fanno Creek and limiting development within the creek's 100-year floodplain. . . . The same may be said for the city's attempt to reduce traffic congestion by providing for alternative means of transportation.[26]

The Court then turned to "determine whether the degree of the exactions demanded by the city's permit conditions bears the required relationship to the projected impact of petitioner's proposed development." In other words, whether there was rough proportionality. In determining rough proportionality, the city must have more than "very generalized statements as to the necessary connection between the required dedication and the proposed development" but need not "demonstrate that its exaction is directly proportional to the specifically created need."[27]

---

24. 512 U.S. 374 (1994).
25. *Id.* at 386.
26. *Id.* at 387 (citation omitted).
27. *Id.* at 390–91.

The Court looked to the city's justification for the exactions. In terms of the public greenway, the Court affirmed that prohibiting construction in the floodplain is acceptable regulation, but the city cited no justification for requiring that the area be dedicated as a public greenway (open to the "recreational visitors trampling along the petitioner's floodplain easement"[28]).

As for the justification for the pedestrian/bicycle pathway, the Court found that "on the record before us, the city has not met its burden of demonstrating that the additional number of vehicle and bicycle trips generated by petitioner's development reasonably relate to the city's requirement for a dedication of the pedestrian/bicycle pathway easement. The city simply found that the creation of the pathway 'could offset some of the traffic demand . . . and lessen the increase in traffic congestion.'"[29] The Court reiterated that "No precise mathematical calculation is required, but the city must make some effort to quantify its findings in support of the dedication for the pedestrian/bicycle pathway beyond the conclusory statement that it could offset some of the traffic demand generated."[30]

### *Koontz* and Cash Exactions

In *Koontz v. St. Johns River Water Management District*,[31] the U.S. Supreme Court extended the *Nollan* and *Dolan* test to demands for property prior to permit approval (not just exactions that attach to approved permits) and to conditions for cash payment (rather than just interests in real property).

For a bit of background, in the 1990s Koontz sought to develop about four acres of his nearly fifteen-acre tract of land in Florida. State regulation required him to obtain certain wetlands permits from the water management district. In seeking the permit to develop, Koontz proposed to grant a conservation easement on eleven acres of his property to prevent any future development. The district found the conservation easement to be inadequate to offset the impacts of the proposed development; it suggested other mitigation conditions that would be acceptable. Koontz felt that the requests for additional mitigation were excessive, accepted his permit rejection, and commenced litigation.

The Supreme Court affirmed the role of exactions in local land use regulation: Government agencies may still apply conditions to prevent a development from imposing costs on the public as long as the conditions meet the test of "nexus" and "rough proportionality." As Justice Alito noted in the majority opinion, "[i]nsisting that landowners internalize the negative externalities of their conduct is a hallmark of responsible land-use policy, and we have long sustained such regulations against constitutional attack." But, while a government may require a developer to mitigate impacts, the conditions may not amount to "'out-and-out . . . extortion' that would thwart the Fifth Amendment right to just compensation."[32]

While an agency may say no or apply conditions to a development approval, such conditions may not force an individual to waive a constitutional right. The *Nollan/Dolan* test applies to demands for property attached to approved permits *and* to demands an applicant

---

28. *Id.* at 393.
29. *Id.* at 395.
30. *Id.* at 395–96.
31. 133 S. Ct. 2586, 2591 (2013).
32. *Id.* at 2595.

refuses to accept. Thus, an applicant may challenge the denial of a permit on the ground that the government agency's demand for property does not have a "nexus" and "rough proportionality" with the impacts of the development. But, as long as a government agency provides at least one option that would satisfy *Nollan/Dolan*, an applicant does not have a claim of unconstitutional conditions.[33]

Notably, when challenging a denied permit, the claim is not for an uncompensated taking, but for damages caused by an unconstitutional condition. The remedy may be money damages but will not be "just compensation" for a taking.[34]

Cash exactions are subject to the *Nollan/Dolan* test. While prior Supreme Court decisions found that a financial obligation for money is not a taking of an identified property interest under the Fifth Amendment, in *Koontz* the Court viewed "in lieu of" fees as a commonplace land use exaction that burdens the applicant's real property (the Court related the burden to a lien on the property). Thus, conditions for cash imposed as a condition on a permit are subject to the test for "nexus" and "rough proportionality."[35]

In North Carolina, the statutory enabling authority may clarify this issue.

## Constitutional Exactions in North Carolina

N.C. courts have, on occasion, taken up questions of constitutional authority for exactions in addition to questions of statutory limits for exactions (see the section titled "Statutory Authority for Exactions," above).

In *River Birch Associates v. City of Raleigh*,[36] the N.C. Supreme court echoed the federal ruling from *Nollan*. In *River Birch*, the developer sought to develop an area previously set aside for open space. The court found the existing requirement—and the denial of the new request—to be reasonable and not a taking.

> A requirement of dedication of park space for subdivision approval does not necessarily constitute a taking. Where the subdivider creates the specific need for the parks, it is not unreasonable to charge the subdivider with the burden of providing them. Here, the increased density of development renders necessary the setting aside of open space.[37]

In *Franklin Road Properties v. City of Raleigh*,[38] a developer challenged the city's authority to condition approval of a development permit on dedicating and widening an adjacent public road. The court of appeals found that the developer, having accepted the benefits of the variance, was precluded from attacking the validity of the ordinance. But the court

---

33. *Id.* at 2598 ("We agree with respondent that, so long as a permitting authority offers the landowner at least one alternative that would satisfy *Nollan* and *Dolan,* the landowner has not been subjected to an unconstitutional condition.").

34. Because *Koontz* arose from a state cause of action, the Supreme Court remanded the case back to the Florida courts to determine, among other things, the appropriate remedy for the injury. In future cases, as with Koontz's claim, the remedy will depend on the specific cause of action, state or federal.

35. *Koontz*, 133 S. Ct. at 2599.

36. 326 N.C. 100 (1990).

37. *Id.* at 122 (citations omitted).

38. 94 N.C. App. 731 (1989).

remanded the case, instructing the trial court to apply a rational nexus test to a road-widening requirement. "To aid a trial court in determining whether an exaction is an unconstitutional taking, [the court of appeals] adopted the following rational nexus test:

> To determine whether an exaction amounts to an unconstitutional taking, the court shall: (1) identify the condition imposed; (2) identify the regulation which caused the condition to be imposed; (3) determine whether the regulation substantially advances a legitimate state interest. If the regulation substantially advances a legitimate state interest, the court shall then determine (4) whether the condition imposed advances that interest; *and* (5) whether the condition imposed is proportionally related to the impact of the development."[39]

In *Batch v. Town of Chapel Hill*,[40] a landowner challenged the town's authority to require that subdivision be designed to accommodate a future thoroughfare across the property. The governing board denied the subdivision request because, among other reasons, the development did not have streets that coordinated with existing and planned streets and highways. The N.C. Supreme Court found that statutes clearly authorize local governments to require a developer to take present and future road development into account when designing subdivisions. Considering future road development in design is not necessarily tantamount to a compulsory dedication. While the landowner argued (and the court of appeals agreed) that the conditions amounted to an unconstitutional taking under *Nollan*, the N.C. Supreme Court found that there was no taking.

In *Batch*, the subdivision request was denied, so no exaction ever applied. The subsequent *Koontz* decision from the U.S. Supreme Court may require additional analysis in such a case.

Certain statutes concerning exactions address a calculation for exactions. For municipalities, fees in lieu of recreation facilities must be based on "the value of the development or subdivision for property tax purposes."[41] Also, for municipalities and counties, the "formula adopted to determine the amount of funds the developer is to pay in lieu of required street construction shall be based on the trips generated from the subdivision or development."[42] Improvements required in association with municipal driveway permits must be "reasonably attributable to the traffic using the driveway" and "serve the traffic of the driveway."[43] These likely meet the *Nollan/Dolan* test for essential nexus and rough proportionality.

---

39. *Id.* at 736 (citation omitted).
40. 326 N.C. 1 (1990).
41. G.S. 160A-372(c).
42. *Id.*
43. G.S. 160A-307.

Chapter 9

# Enforcement

## Ordinance Enforcement

A municipality or county may take several actions to ensure compliance with the subdivision ordinance. Under its subdivision regulation authority, a local government may seek court orders, withhold building permits, or seek criminal prosecution.[1] Moreover, the general authority for land development regulations allows subdivision ordinances to be enforced as any other local ordinance. This includes some overlapping and additional authority, such as fines, civil penalties, and court orders of injunction or abatement.[2] A local government, through its ordinance, may use any of these actions or a combination to enforce the subdivision ordinance.

## Withhold Permits

A local government may refuse to issue building permits for lots that have been illegally subdivided.[3] Although prior versions of the statute did not include this authority,[4] amendments clearly authorize a local government to withhold building permits for subdivision enforcement. Some ordinances call for withholding other permits, including permits for installation or connection to water and sewer facilities (public or private).[5]

The certificate of compliance or occupancy offers an additional layer of subdivision enforcement. Under the applicable statutes, the inspector, at the conclusion of permitted building work, must make final inspection and confirm that the completed work complies with all applicable state and local laws as well as with the terms of the permit.[6] In *First American Federal Savings & Loan Association v. Royall*,[7] a subdivision approval included the requirement that the developer install, in conformance with city standards, a water line that would serve the overall office park. After conveyance, the purchaser could not obtain a certificate of occupancy because the required water infrastructure was not complete (withholding the certificate of occupancy was authorized under Section 160A-423 of the North Carolina General Statutes (hereinafter G.S.)).

---

1. Sections 153A-334(a) and 160A-375(a) of the North Carolina General Statutes (hereinafter G.S.).
2. G.S. 153A-324 & -123; G.S. 160A-365 & -175.
3. G.S. 153A-334(a); G.S. 160A-375(a).
4. Town of Nags Head v. Tillett, 314 N.C. 627 (1985).
5. Wilson Unified Development Ordinance § 6.2.2.B; Chatham County Subdivision Regulations § 1.14.C.
6. G.S. 153A-363; G.S. 160A-423.
7. 77 N.C. App. 131 (1985).

Recent statutory amendments state that unless otherwise authorized by law, a local government may not withhold a building permit or certificate of occupancy in order to compel compliance with a permit or ordinance on another property.[8] The precise application in the case of building permits on subdivision lots is not clear. To be legally subdivided, a lot must have been created as part of a lawful subdivision—one that complies with the procedural and substantive standards of the local ordinance and state regulations.

## Civil Penalty

A local government may impose civil penalties for violation of the ordinance. If the offender does not pay the penalty within a prescribed time, the local government may bring a civil action to recover the fee as a debt.[9]

Pasquotank County imposes $100 per offense, and each day's continuing violation is a separate and distinct offense.[10] Chatham County imposes civil penalties that increase with subsequent violations, as follows:

- first violation, $50 per day;
- same violation (within six years of remedy of first occurrence), $100 per day;
- same violation (within six years of remedy of second occurrence), $200 per day;
- same violation (within six years of remedy of third occurrence), $500 per day.

Violation of a stop work order in Chatham County is $500 per day.[11]

## Court Order

In addition, a local government may seek a court order to prevent illegal subdivision or to correct a violation. Under the subdivision enabling statutes, a local government "may bring an action for injunction of any illegal subdivision, transfer, conveyance, or sale of land, and the court shall, upon appropriate findings, issue an injunction and order requiring the offending party to comply with the subdivision ordinance."[12] Notably, the statute creates the obligation that the court *shall* issue an injunction requiring compliance upon appropriate findings.

Under the general ordinance enforcement statutes, a local government "may secure injunctions and abatement orders to further insure compliance with its ordinance."[13] Also, an "ordinance may provide that it may be enforced by an appropriate equitable remedy issuing from a court of competent jurisdiction. In such case, the General Court of Justice shall have jurisdiction to issue such orders as may be appropriate, and it shall not be a defense to the application of the city for equitable relief that there is an adequate remedy at law."[14]

For ordinances that regulate "a condition existing upon or use made of real property,"[15] the ordinance may be enforced by injunction and order of abatement. When an unlawful

---

8. G.S. 153A-357; G.S. 160A-417.

9. G.S. 153A-324 & -123(c); G.S. 160A-365 & -175(c).

10. Pasquotank County Subdivision Ordinance § 204.

11. Chatham County Subdivision Regulations § 1.14.F.

12. G.S. 153A-334(a); G.S. 160A-375(a).

13. G.S. 153A-324 & -123(a); G.S. 160A-365 & -175(a).

14. G.S. 153A-324 & -123(d); G.S. 160A-365 & -175(d).

15. G.S. 153A-324 & -123(e); G.S. 160A-365 & -175(e).

condition or use occurs, the local government may seek a court order "for a mandatory or prohibitory injunction and order of abatement commanding the defendant to correct the unlawful condition upon or cease the unlawful use of the property."[16] The statute dictates that such actions are governed by the Rules of Civil Procedure (Chapter 1A of the General Statutes), in particular Rule 65 on injunctions.

The order of abatement may require, among other things, that buildings be closed, removed, or demolished; that improvements or repairs be made; "or that any other action be taken that is necessary to bring the property into compliance with the ordinance."[17] If the owner fails to comply with the injunction or order of abatement, the owner may be cited for contempt of court, and the local government may execute the order of abatement. The local government will then have a lien on the property comparable to that of a mechanic's or materialman's lien for the cost of abatement. The owner can cancel the order of abatement by paying all costs of the proceedings and posting a bond for compliance. If the order of abatement is canceled, though, that action neither suspends nor cancels the injunction.[18]

Can the court consider the cost and burden placed on the landowner by complying with the applicable subdivision ordinance requirements? It is not clear. "The North Carolina courts have not addressed . . . whether a trial court entering an injunction pursuant to these statutes must still balance the equities of the parties."[19] Courts in other states are split on this issue. In the zoning context, the N.C. Supreme Court rejected an argument that the court must consider economic waste in considering abatement orders for zoning violations. In *Town of Pine Knoll Shores v. Evans*,[20] the court upheld an injunction and order of abatement requiring a property owner to remove a deck that was illegally constructed within the zoning setback. "To apply that theory [of economic waste] in the context presented here would be novel and far-reaching and would substantially erode powers the General Assembly has granted to municipalities."[21]

## Criminal Prosecution

A local government may impose criminal fines or prosecution for failure to comply. If a landowner (or owner's agent) subdivides land or transfers land without proper approval under the subdivision ordinance, the owner or agent is guilty of a Class 1 misdemeanor.[22] A transfer may be unlawful if it references an unapproved plat or if the transferred property is described by metes and bounds.

The ordinance may provide that each day's continuing violation is a separate and distinct offense.[23] The ordinance may set maximum fines and imprisonments that are less than the maximums set by statute under G.S. 14-4.[24]

---

16. *Id.*
17. *Id.*
18. *Id.*
19. Town of Pinebluff v. Marts, 195 N.C. App. 659, 665 (2009).
20. Town of Pine Knoll Shores v. Evans, 331 N.C. 361 (1992).
21. *Id.* at 366–67.
22. G.S. 153A-334(a); G.S. 160A-375(a).
23. G.S. 153A-324 & -123(g); G.S. 160A-365 & -175(g).
24. G.S. 153A-324 & -123(b); G.S. 160A-365 & -175(b).

Criminal arrest for subdivision violations is rare. If a local government pursues such action, it should make sure to follow the proper procedures, including the proper allegations for the warrant.[25]

## Alternative Enforcement

"In addition to other remedies, a city may institute any appropriate action or proceedings to prevent the unlawful subdivision of land, to restrain, correct, or abate the violation, or to prevent any illegal act or conduct."[26] If enforcement is not available under the subdivision ordinance, other development regulations may apply.

In *Town of Nags Head v. Tillett*,[27] enforcement was not authorized under the subdivision ordinance, but the court upheld enforcement under the zoning ordinance. Similarly, in *Tonter Investments, Inc. v. Pasquotank County*,[28] the subdivision was exempt, but the local government could still enforce the zoning ordinance.

In addition to these public enforcement options, property purchasers may have claims against the developer that will enforce the subdivision requirements. Private claims are discussed more in the section below titled "Property Owner Obligations."

## Performance Guarantees

### Authority

City and county subdivision regulations may require specific infrastructure improvements in conjunction with subdivision approval. Such improvements commonly include installation of adequate water and sewer, construction and dedication of subdivision streets that meet town or NCDOT standards, and provision of parks and recreation space. Moreover, as previously discussed, the statutes authorize subdivision ordinances to require the construction of "community service facilities," a broad category encompassing stormwater facilities, sedimentation and erosion controls, sidewalks and trails, and more. Depending on the jurisdiction and the type of development, such improvements may be dedicated to the public or maintained as private.

Several enforcement tools are available to ensure compliance with improvement requirements. One option is to refuse final plat approval until all infrastructure is complete. That gives certainty of completion but may hinder development. Another option is to issue approvals for phases such that all improvements for one phase must be complete before final plat approval for that particular phase. In addition, cities and counties may withhold building permits, seek injunctive relief, or bring other actions to ensure compliance with the sub-

25. State v. McBane, 276 N.C. 60 (1969).
26. G.S. 153A-334(a); G.S. 160A-375(a).
27. 314 N.C. 627 (1985).
28. 199 N.C. App. 579 (2009).

A performance guarantee is financial security to finish subdivision improvements if the developer fails to do so.

division ordinance.[29] Even if a local government allowed a performance guarantee to lapse, the other remedies may still be available.[30]

Beyond these enforcement options, cities and counties are authorized to require performance guarantees for required improvements: "To assure compliance with these and other ordinance requirements, the ordinance may provide for performance guarantees to assure successful completion of required improvements."[31] Under the statutes, if such a guarantee is required, the developer must be allowed to choose from a range of assurance types, including

a. a surety bond issued by any company authorized to do business in the state,
b. a letter of credit issued by any financial institution licensed to do business in the state, or
c. any other form of guarantee that provides security equivalent to a surety bond or letter of credit.

The statutes authorizing performance guarantees explicitly prohibit maintenance bonds. "[T]he performance guarantee shall only be used for completion of the required improvements *and not for repairs or maintenance after completion.*"[32] Separately, local governments have explicit authority to enter into financial arrangements to ensure adequate maintenance and replacement of stormwater management facilities.[33] There is no such explicit authority for maintenance bonds for private streets or recreation facilities.

---

29. G.S. 160A-375 & G.S. 153A-334.
30. Town of Pinebluff v. Marts, 195 N.C. App. 659 (2009).
31. G.S. 160A-372; G.S. 153A-331.
32. G.S. 160A-372; G.S. 153A-331 (emphasis added).
33. G.S. 153A-454; G.S. 160A-459.

## Terms

Courts enforce the authorized and agreed upon terms of the performance guarantee, so getting the terms right in the ordinance and any contract is critical. "Under North Carolina law . . . 'a public performance bond is a contract, governed by the law of contracts. Parties entering into public performance bond are free to contract for any terms they so desire.' Therefore, the contractual terms of the Bonds are controlling. . . . "[34]

Following is a discussion of some of the topics and terms to consider.

### When Does It Become Available?

The local government may set minimum criteria that must be met before a performance guarantee is an option. Chatham County, for example, requires that before a developer may use a performance guarantee, the developer must have

1. completed 75 percent of the required improvements,
2. provided all weather vehicle access for emergency vehicles, and
3. completed all waterlines.[35]

### How Much May It Require?

Subdivision ordinances commonly require that the applicant provide a work plan and cost estimate signed and sealed by a licensed engineer, land surveyor, or landscape architect. The ordinance, then, may require a stated percentage of that estimate. Jurisdictions may require some amount above the estimate up to 125 percent to address the risk of increased costs over time.

### What Is Its Term and Extension?

If improvements are not complete as the expiration of a guarantee is approaching, "the performance guarantee shall be extended, or a new performance guarantee issued, for an additional period until such required improvements are complete."[36] Given the statutory context and the practical mechanics of performance guarantees, this section appears to create an obligation for the developer to obtain an extension or newly issued financial instrument if the current instrument is set to expire. But that language—"the performance guarantee shall be extended"—could be read to require the local government to allow extensions so long as the developer shows reasonable good faith progress toward completing the improvements.

In the event that a developer fails to meet milestones set through the performance guarantee agreement, and the developer is not making good faith efforts, a local government can call the guarantee and use the funds to complete the unfinished improvements.

If an extension is allowed, the amount of the renewed performance guarantee is capped at 125 percent of the improvements yet to be completed. In other words, the amount must be reduced for improvements that have been completed.

---

34. Cnty. of Brunswick v. Lexon Ins. Co., 425 F. App'x 190, 192 (4th Cir. 2011) (unpublished) (quoting Town of Pineville v. Atkinson/Dyer/Watson, Architects P.A., 114 N.C. App. 497 (1994)).
35. Chatham County Subdivision Regulations § 3.1.B.
36. G.S. 160A-372; G.S. 153A-331.

**The Terms Matter**

Two recent cases emphasize that courts will enforce the terms of the guarantee and financial instrument, regardless of which party that benefits.

In *Synovus Bank v. County of Henderson*,[†] the contractual terms of the bond stated that the sum was a penal sum (a penalty amount). Thus, upon nonperformance the county was owed the full amount of the bond. As the court stated, "The plain meaning of 'penal sum' is an amount awarded to a beneficiary as a penalty if some obligation is not performed. The term 'penal sum' suggests the entire $6,000,000.00 was due once [the developer] failed in the performance of the duties enumerated in the performance bond."

By contrast, in *Developers Surety & Indemnity Co. v. City of Durham*,[‡] the city argued that the bonds must pay for all necessary construction for facilities to meet city standards to be accepted by the city. The surety companies argued that the bonds only cover minimal completion of facilities already constructed. For Street and Sidewalk Bonds, the court found the plain reading of the bond language to cover only the completion of unfinished sidewalks and the final inch of asphalt for roads (not full construction of un-improved roads). The court rejected the city's argument that the surety had the same obligations as the developer. The court found that the surety had the obligations specified in the bond language.

[†]729 S.E.2d 731 (N.C. Ct. App. 2012), *review withdrawn*, 366 N.C. 411 (2012).
[‡]No. 1:11CV515, 2014 WL 4677181 (M.D.N.C. Sept. 18, 2014).

Note that both federal and North Carolina courts have found that the Permit Extension Act of 2009 did not modify a bond company's obligations to pay subdivision performance bonds upon default by the developer.[37]

### What Triggers Default?

It is plain that a local government should have the right to call in the financial assurance if a developer fails to complete the agreed upon improvements by the deadline. But at what point is the developer in default, and what is the procedure for calling in the financial assurance? Does the local government have an obligation to notify the developer or the financial institution? The performance guarantee and financial instrument should have clearly defined criteria for default and a process for calling in the funds. If the terms of a performance bond grant the surety an opportunity to complete the improvements, the local government will need to provide appropriate notice of default as well as give the surety an opportunity to satisfy the obligation.[38]

Local governments may be wise to include additional triggers leading them to call in the assurance, such as failure of the developer to renew an expiring financial instrument, developer insolvency or bankruptcy, or foreclosure on the property. Additional terms might smooth out the enforcement process. For example, the agreement may grant appropriate public bodies (the municipality, the county, NCDOT, or their contractors) the right to enter the property and complete construction of the improvements. Some local governments

---

37. *See Brunswick*, 425 F. App'x at 192; Synovus Bank v. Cnty. of Henderson, 222 N.C. App. 319 (2012) (unpublished), *review withdrawn*, 366 N.C. 411 (2012).

38. Cnty. of Brunswick v. Lexon Ins. Co., 710 F. Supp. 2d 520 (E.D.N.C. 2010), *aff'd*, 425 F. App'x 190 (4th Cir. 2011).

even include terms that authorize the release of funds to an applicable property owners association to oversee the remaining construction. Practically speaking this may be a useful tool, but the rights and obligations of the association would need to be clearly contracted. Moreover, there is an underlying question of authority to assign financial assurances to a third party, as discussed below.

Under Statesville's ordinance, if a developer fails to complete improvements, the city may

1. declare the development in default and require all public improvements be installed regardless of the extent of completion of the development;
2. collect funds pursuant to the guaranty and complete the public improvements;
3. assign its rights in the guarantee in whole or in part to any third party, including a subsequent owner of the subdivision, in exchange for that party's agreement to complete the improvements; and/or
4. exercise any other rights available under state law.[39]

### Obligations upon Default

What obligation does the surety have after a developer defaults? Courts will impose those obligations that are spelled out in the terms, but no more. In *Developers Surety & Indemnity Co. v. City of Durham*,[40] for example, the city argued that the surety companies had the same obligations as the developer and must pay for all necessary construction to bring facilities up to city standards in order to be accepted. The court, however, ruled in favor of the sureties, enforcing the limited obligations of the clear bond language (complete unfinished sidewalks, apply the final inch of asphalt to constructed streets, and maintain already constructed stormwater ponds).

### Criteria to Release

After acknowledgment by the local government that the improvement is complete, the local government must return or release the performance guarantee in a timely manner. Prior to the release of any performance guarantee, the local government needs confirmation that the improvements have been completed and built to the required standards. Jurisdictions may require a letter from a licensed professional (engineer, surveyor, landscape architect) certifying completion. Following the certification, local government staff will inspect the improvements for confirmation.

Some jurisdictions have drafted form performance guarantees to make sure appropriate terms are specified. The model language for public construction performance bonds, provided at G.S. 44A-33, may be instructive but will not cover the distinct issues of subdivision performance guarantees.

## Administration and Enforcement

Even if the terms of a performance guarantee are clear and comprehensive, practical administration and enforcement deserve some extra consideration.

---

39. Statesville Unified Development Code § 2.03.E.8.i.
40. No. 1:11CV515, 2014 WL 4677181 (M.D.N.C. Sept. 18, 2014).

***Who is administering?*** Performance agreements require careful administration. Development milestones will come and go, guarantees will approach expiration, and a local government official will occasionally need to call in a financial assurance. Who is responsible for taking this action? The attorney who approved the agreement, the finance department, inspections, public works, or planning? Clear roles and responsibility could save a local government millions of dollars.

***What if the financial assurance is more than the cost of improvements?*** It depends on the terms of the contract. Some ordinances specify that excess funds must be returned to the developer. A general performance bond (or indemnity bond) will cover the cost of completing the improvements. A penal bond, in contrast, will pay the full stated amount, regardless of the actual cost of improvements. The N.C. Court of Appeals considered this terminology. Although the surety argued that the actual cost of improvements would be less than the bond amount, the contractual terms of the bond stated that the sum included a penal sum. Thus, upon nonperformance, the county was owed the full amount of the bond. As the court stated, "The plain meaning of 'penal sum' is an amount awarded to a beneficiary as a penalty if some obligation is not performed. The term 'penal sum' suggests the entire $6,000,000.00 was due once Seven Falls failed in the performance of the duties enumerated in the performance bond."[41] If, however, the developer never commenced development, the local government may not have a claim to the financial assurance.[42]

***What if the financial assurance is less than the cost of improvements?*** Would the local government have to complete the infrastructure? The statutory purpose and authority of a performance guarantee is for the developer to insure the completion of required improvements related to a subdivision approval. A performance guarantee does not create an obligation on the local government to expend funds beyond the guarantee. That said, local governments should have standards in place from the start to ensure that available funds are adequate if needed.

***What are the rights of third parties?*** That depends on the facts of the case and the terms of the guarantee, but third parties will need clear authority and distinct interests in order to have a proper claim. Funds from a subdivision financial assurance cannot be used to pay contractors for work already completed—the statutory authorization for performance guarantees does not include payment bonds.[43] A property owners association may have a recognizable interest, but it will depend on the facts. Consider the federal district court's ruling in a recent North Carolina case. The court initially allowed an association to intervene as having interests adverse to the county based on the association's intent to assert a claim of declaratory relief to ensure that any funds secured from the bonds would be used for infrastructure in the subdivision. However, when the association failed to make that claim, the court granted the defendant's motion to dismiss the association. The court looked at the terms of the ordinance and contract to find, among other things, that the association's

---

41. *Synovus Bank*, 729 S.E.2d at 731.

42. Westchester Fire Ins. Co. v. City of Brooksville, 731 F. Supp. 2d 1298 (M.D. Fla. 2010) *aff'd*, 465 F. App'x 851 (11th Cir. 2012).

43. *In re* Versant Props., L.L.C., 1:10CV98, 2011 WL 1131057 (W.D.N.C. Mar. 25, 2011) (not reported).

interest was not adverse to that of the county as well as a claim of breach of contract as a third-party beneficiary.[44]

***Does a local government have authority to assign rights from a performance guarantee?*** There is no express statutory authority to assign the rights to third parties, but it may be reasonably necessary and within the contracting rights of a local government to do so. Consider a county that has called in a subdivision performance bond for incomplete subdivision streets. If that money had been obtained as a fee-in-lieu of construction, the county would be required to transfer the funds to a municipality to develop the roads. G.S. 153A-331(c). A similar transfer may be reasonably necessary and appropriate for funds called in from a performance guarantee. And, as noted above, "[p]arties entering into public performance bond are free to contract for any terms they so desire."[45]

***If the financial assurance is called in and used for construction, is that work subject to public bidding requirements?*** The answer depends on how the financial assurance is called in and the construction contract is structured. Generally it is the expenditure of public funds on a contract for construction that triggers bidding. If the public entity calls in the financial assurance and contracts for the construction, then it is subject to typical bidding requirements. If the public entity calls in the financial assurance and then contracts with a private entity (such as a subsequent developer) to complete the improvements, that too is subject to bidding—it is a contract for construction using public funds. If the financial assurance was structured to go directly to the homeowners association, the association's contract for construction may not be subject to bidding requirements. If costs are less than $250,000, the local government may be able to avoid bidding requirements by structuring the transfer of funds as a reimbursement agreement under G.S. 160A-499 & -320 or G.S. 153A-451 & -280.

## Property Owner Obligations

This book is focused on the public role in land subdivision regulation, but that discussion necessarily includes a discussion of private actors, private rights, and private responsibilities, especially when it comes to enforcement. This section considers three topics of private rights and responsibilities: (1) lot purchaser rights against a developer, (2) obligations of property owners and owner associations to comply with regulations, and (3) enforcement tools for when private parties fail to comply.

### Private Rights

When a developer plats a subdivision and then sells lots in reference to that plat, the lot purchasers have rights in development depicted on the plat. Such rights cannot be altered except by agreement of the owners or estoppel.

> The right of the lot owners to the use of the streets, parks and playgrounds
> may not be exitinguished [*sic*], altered or diminished except by agreement or

---

44. Rutherford Cnty. v. Bond Safeguard Ins. Co., 1:09CV292, 2011 WL 809821 (W.D.N.C. Mar. 2, 2011).

45. Cnty. of Brunswick v. Lexon Ins. Co., 425 F. App'x 190, 192 (4th Cir. 2011)(unpublished).

estoppel. This is true because the existence of the right was an inducement to and a part of the consideration for the purchase of the lots. Thus, a street, park or playground may not be reduced in size or put to any use which conflicts with the purpose for which it was dedicated.[46]

The rights of purchasers are greater than the rights of the general public. Lot owners may maintain an easement even when an offer of dedication to the public has been withdrawn.[47] These rights in the plat are enjoyed by all of the owners, including the developer who retains some ownership.[48]

Purchasers have rights to use the streets depicted on the plat. Those rights may remain even if the developer changes the plat.[49] Purchasers also have rights in open space depicted on the plat. Where property was platted for use as a golf course, a country club cannot permit a road across the golf course property with approval from those with rights under the plat.[50]

In contrast, in *Harry v. Crescent Resources, Inc.*,[51] a developer subdivided a tract into five residential building lots and four remnant lots. (The remnant lots were small, oddly shaped parcels that may have seemed undevelopable individually.) Several purchasers bought the residential lots. One purchaser bought the remnant lots and sought to develop them. The residential lot purchasers claimed a negative easement to require the remnants to remain as open space because they appear as open space on the plat (which was referenced in deeds), but the court found that the plat did not designate the remnant parcels for any specific purpose (such as street, park, beach, or playground).

The clarity of elements on a plat can affect the rights of parties. Consider *Stines v. Willyng*[52] in contrast to *Shear v. Stevens Building Co.*[53] (discussed in the accompanying text box titled "Implied Open Space Easement"). If an area identified for dedication lacks clear boundaries on the plat, for example, it may be impossible to define the area, making the dedication impossible to enforce. In *Stines*, the plat clearly designated two areas for "Park Property." But, while the boundary of one area was clear, the boundary of the second area was vague (there was no boundary along the edge of the plat). The court enforced the clearly defined area but found the unbounded area to be "patently ambiguous" and the plat designation unenforceable.

A developer's failure to meet subdivision standards may amount to an encumbrance on the property. If so, the purchaser may have a contract claim. In *First American Federal Savings & Loan Association v. Royall*,[54] a developer agreed to sell a lot in an office park. The conveyance was to be a general warranty deed providing that "title is marketable and free and clear of all encumbrances." Subdivision approval included the requirement that the developer install a water line, in conformity with city standards, that would serve the

---

46. Cleveland Realty Co. v. Hobbs, 261 N.C. 414, 421 (1964) (citations omitted).
47. Stephens v. Dortch, 148 N.C. App. 509, 510 (2002).
48. *Cleveland Realty*, 261 N.C. at 414.
49. Home Real Estate Loan & Ins. Co. v. Town of Carolina Beach, 216 N.C. 778 (1940).
50. *Cleveland Realty*, 261 N.C. at 414 (1964).
51. 136 N.C. App. 71 (1999).
52. 81 N.C. App. 98, 99 (1986).
53. 107 N.C. App. 154 (1992).
54. 77 N.C. App. 131, 132 (1985).

### Implied Open Space Easement

In 1957, a developer recorded a plat for a new development that was to include three hundred lots, streets, a lake, and undeveloped area around the lake.† The deeds for the lots referenced the plat but made no reference to an easement for homeowner access to the lake nor a restriction on use of the lake. Homeowners, claiming there were verbal representations by the developer that the lake was for the use of the residents, used the lake until no trespassing signs were erected in the 1980s. After notice that the dam was in disrepair, the developer lowered the water level of the lake and submitted a plat to subdivide and develop an additional twenty-four lots on the undeveloped land. The court of appeals found, in this particular case, that an easement implied by dedication enabled the homeowners to access the lake and surrounding undeveloped property. "[A]n easement may be created by dedication. This dedication may be either a formal or informal transfer and may be either implied or express." The court required the developer to return the lake to the prior level and required the homeowners to maintain the lake and surrounding undeveloped land.

†Shear v. Stevens Bldg. Co., 107 N.C. App. 154 (1992).

overall office park. After conveyance, however, the purchaser was unable to obtain a certificate of occupancy because the required water infrastructure had not been completed. The developer's failure to provide the required water infrastructure was an encumbrance on the property and amounted to a violation of the covenant against encumbrances on the contract and warranty deed.

Moreover, purchasers may seek specific performance for the developer to complete the promised improvements. In *Lyerly v. Malpass*,[55] the developer indicated by contracts, plat, restrictive covenants, and oral representations that the subdivision would include a boat basin and channel at least six feet deep and a private road built to NCDOT standards. As it turned out, the developer provided a channel that was impassable at low tide and the road was substandard. The developer claimed that these were merely maintenance issues and the responsibility of the homeowners association. The court stated, however, that a "developer may not by the use of recorded plats and restrictive covenants create the illusion of a high quality subdivision and then shield itself from responsibility by claiming that it did not promise to construct the amenities implied by the restrictive covenants and that these covenants do not give rise to an affirmative obligation."[56] The court allowed the remedy of specific performance requiring the developer to perform the necessary improvements.

When a property owner is seeking to clarify rights among private parties, such as rights in an easement, all necessary parties (including all affected owners) must be party to the action.[57]

Homeowners associations may seek enforcement, but questions of standing may arise. An association may seek judicial relief to enforce the rights of the association as an entity. An association also may seek declaratory or injunctive relief for its members if the remedy will benefit those association members who were actually injured. But, if an association seeks damages, standing is an issue. In *River Birch Associates v. City of Raleigh*, the court determined that the homeowners association did not have standing for claims of fraud or unfair

55. 82 N.C. App. 224 (1986).
56. *Lyerly*, 82 N.C. App. at 229.
57. Rice v. Randolph, 96 N.C. App. 112 (1989).

trade practices because the claimed damages were not common to the entire membership and were not shared to the same degree among the membership.[58]

## Deed Restrictions and Property Owners Associations

The ownership and maintenance of many improvements and common areas required by the subdivision ordinance are governed by private governance, such as deed restrictions and property owners associations.

### Planned Community Act

The North Carolina Planned Community Act (Chapter 47F of the General Statutes) applies to residential subdivisions with more than twenty lots. A planned community is defined as real estate (except cooperatives and condominiums) where deed restrictions require an owner to contribute toward the maintenance of common areas, such as roads, parks, and stormwater facilities. The act outlines, among other things, organization of the association and obligations for upkeep of common areas.

The Planned Community Act does not modify local subdivision rules, but the statute does state that a zoning or subdivision ordinance may not prohibit or impose "any requirement upon a planned community which it would not impose upon a substantially similar development under a different form of ownership or administration."[59] Generally applicable subdivision standards—for roads, parks, stormwater facilities, recreation facilities, or other improvements—may impact the fees and maintenance obligations of the planned community, if those improvements will be private and held as common area.

### Subdivision Standards and Private Agreement

For certain improvements, there is specific statutory authority for imposing requirements through deed restrictions. Local governments are authorized, for example, to require deed restrictions and protective covenants for stormwater management and financial arrangements for adequate maintenance and replacement.[60] Some subdivision ordinances require homeowners association ownership and governance for those community facilities not dedicated to the public.

> Property owners' association covenants shall be established and recorded that guarantee the association's responsibility for the ongoing liability, taxes, and maintenance of recreational and other common facilities, including private streets, which are not dedicated to the city. Prior to approval of any final plat, the Administrator shall review the covenants of any property owners' association to ensure compliance with city requirements.[61]

---

58. 326 N.C. 100, 130 (1990).

59. G.S. 47F-1-106.

60. G.S. 153A-454; G.S. 160A-459; Statesville Unified Development Code § 8.05.E ("The owner of a non-residential facility and the owner, homeowners association or similar entity of a facility serving a residential development shall be responsible for the maintenance and repair of the stormwater detention facility." Also, "The owner of a private facility serving multiple lots shall provide and maintain sufficient financial guarantees in an amount approved by the City Engineer to ensure that maintenance and repair will be provided for the facility." *Id.* at § 8.05.E.b).

61. Wilson UDO § 6.2.2.B

Even without explicit authority, the N.C. Supreme Court has found the requirement for a developer to convey property to a homeowners association to be reasonably necessary and expedient in order to carry out the general subdivision authority. In *River Birch*, subdivision approval required the developer to convey recreation areas to the homeowners association. The developer challenged the required conveyance, but the court found "that the requirement of a conveyance of the common recreation areas to the home owners' association of a subdivision is an 'additional and supplementary' power 'reasonably necessary or expedient' to carry into effect the legislative intent to secure to the residents of the subdivision the benefits of the recreation areas."[62]

## Public Remedies

Consider a scenario. Twenty years ago a county approved a residential subdivision. Its fifty lots are served by private roads, one of which connects to the adjacent state road controlled by NCDOT. As is typical, a homeowners association was formed, the developer completed the roads and sold all of the lots, and the roads were turned over to the association. In the early years everything was fine; the homeowners association collected dues and contracted for minor maintenance needs. As the years passed by, though, some homeowners fell behind on their dues and the association was lax about enforcing dues payment. At the same time, the roads began to crumble from normal wear and tear. Now, the association cannot afford the major paving maintenance that is needed. What to do?

This scenario—a common one across the state and the country—raises two interrelated issues of governance and public policy. First, in the balance of community interest and private rights, what infrastructure should be considered as public and what should be viewed as private? And second, once the policy decision is made to allow private infrastructure, who is ultimately responsible for its maintenance? When should the public step in to assist a private concern? There is, of course, no single answer for these questions. Different communities approach these issues differently. But it is critical for good and fair governance that decision-makers consider the implications up front.

With that in mind, consider some of the statutory tools for acquiring public assistance from cities and counties. Note that these tools, generally, are limited to use for public improvements. Thus, in the case of a crumbling private street, the street would have to be made public before some of these tools could be used. G.S. 136-96.1 authorizes a special court proceeding for a group of landowners to petition for a private right-of-way on an unrecorded plat to be dedicated to the public.

### Maintenance Bonds

Local governments have explicit authority to enter into financial arrangements to ensure the availability of adequate funds for maintenance and replacement of stormwater management facilities.[63] The general authority for performance guarantees expressly prohibits the provision of maintenance bonds.[64]

---

62. *River Birch*, 326 N.C. at 109.
63. G.S. 153A-454; G.S. 160A-459.
64. G.S. 160A-372; G.S. 153A-331.

### Special Assessment

Local governments have limited authority to provide improvements and then charge the benefitting property owners for those improvements.

Article 10 of Chapter 160A authorizes cities to impose special assessments for certain improvements within the municipal corporate limits. Improvements may include streets, curbs and gutters, sidewalks, water systems, sewer systems, and stormwater facilities. This power, though, is limited to public improvements.

The article outlines detailed procedural requirements for exercising this authority, including notice, hearings, resolutions, assessment calculations, and more. Assessments for street and sidewalk improvements must be requested by petition of the property owners.

Counties, too, can use special assessments for certain improvements.[65] For counties, the authority allows assessments to fund water systems, sewage systems, beach erosion control, flood and hurricane protection, watershed and drainage improvements, streets, and street lights. Several of these categories have specific requirements in addition to the general procedures. Notably, G.S. 153A-205 authorizes counties to pay for the local share of the cost of improvements to private roads to bring them up to NCDOT standards, after which the county can levy a special assessment on the property owners for the cost of the local share.

### Service Districts

Cities and counties may create special taxing districts called service districts to finance, provide, and maintain certain facilities within that district. Under Article 16 of Chapter 153A, counties may establish service districts to finance, provide, and maintain a variety of public improvements and services, including

*In all counties*:
- water and sewer,
- recreation,
- beach erosion control,
- fire, ambulance, rescue (and law enforcement in certain counties),
- solid waste.

*In addition, in coastal counties*:
- removal of junk automobiles and
- street maintenance.

*And, in mountain counties*:
- street maintenance.

City authority for service districts is more limited. The General Statutes grant the authority for specified areas, such as historic districts and urban revitalization areas, as well as for beach erosion, sewer, and drainage improvements. There also is authority for converting private residential streets to public streets, but that authority is available only to a certain set of cities.[66]

---

65. G.S. 153A-185–206.

66. G.S. 160A-536(e). This authority is limited to cities that straddle the county line between two counties, one county with population of a quarter million and the other with a population of three quarters of a million. This perhaps applies only to Morrisville.

### Eminent Domain

Finally, in the case of community improvements that homeowners have failed to maintain, a city or county may use its authority under eminent domain to take the property and improvements to be used for a public purpose.[67]

---

67. See, generally, Charles Szypszak, Eminent Domain for North Carolina Local Governments, Law and Practice (2008).

Chapter 10

# Appeals and Judicial Review

Appeals of subdivision decisions may arise in several different ways. From the outset, a party could challenge the adoption or amendment of the subdivision ordinance for unconstitutionality, lack of statutory authority, or failure to adhere to procedural requirements. Alternatively, a party could challenge the decision of a particular subdivision plat review. The appeal process, then, will depend on the type of decision—quasi-judicial or administrative. And, finally, a party could challenge an enforcement action under the subdivision ordinance. Each of these avenues of appeal is discussed below, as are their respective statutes of limitations.

It is worth noting that certain challenges may be barred after a developer has obtained approval and enjoyed the benefits of that approval. "It is well established that the acceptance of benefits under a statute or ordinance precludes an attack upon it. . . . A party may, by his or her conduct, be estopped to assert both statutory and constitutional rights."[1]

Pursuant to Section 6-21.7 of the North Carolina General Statutes (hereinafter G.S.), if a court finds that a local government acted outside the scope of its legal authority, the court *may* award reasonable attorneys' fees to the party challenging the local government. If the court finds further that the local government action was "an abuse of its discretion" the court *shall* award attorneys' fees. This authority for awarding attorneys' fees may apply to challenges of ordinance validity as well as to plat decisions.

## Appeals of Legislative Decisions

Legislative decisions—adopting or amending the subdivision ordinance—may be challenged as either (1) failing to meet statutory procedural challenges or (2) beyond the scope of local government authority.

A challenge to a subdivision ordinance based on a defect in the adoption process must be brought within three years.

A challenge to a subdivision ordinance as being beyond the scope of authority may be framed a few ways: The ordinance runs afoul of the U.S. Constitution or the N.C. Constitution or is beyond the authority granted to the local government by the applicable statutes. A challenge to the validity of a stand-alone subdivision ordinance must be brought within the general three-year period established at G.S. 1-52(5). This stands in contrast to the shorter statutes of limitation for challenges to the zoning ordinance. But, as noted by the court of appeals, "the limitations period relating to challenges to 'zoning ordinances' set out in N.C.

---

1. Franklin Rd. Props. v. City of Raleigh, 94 N.C. App. 731, 735 (1989) (citations and quotations omitted).

Gen.Stat. § 1–54.1 and N.C. Gen.Stat. § 160A–364.1 simply does not apply to challenges to the constitutionality of subdivision ordinance provisions."[2]

Notably, however, subdivision provisions built into a unified development ordinance may be subject to the zoning statutes of limitations. Challenges to the validity of a subdivision provision in a unified development ordinance must be brought within one year of the party having standing to appeal.

A court may strike down an ordinance that it determines to be invalid. Separation of powers, however, prevents courts from requiring a local government to adopt particular ordinances or provisions unless such provisions are required by statute.[3]

## Appeals of Quasi-Judicial Plat Decisions

Similar to other quasi-judicial decisions, quasi-judicial plat decisions made by the governing board or planning board are appealed to superior court. The rules outlined at G.S. 160A-388 and -393 apply. The statute excludes from this provision appointed boards made up solely of planning staff members. The inference and implication are that decisions by staff-only subdivision review boards must be based on administrative standards, not quasi-judicial discretion.[4]

Appeals of quasi-judicial decisions may be filed with the clerk of the superior court within thirty days of notice or the effective date of the decision. The appeal is called a petition for writ of certiorari, and it sets forth the petitioner's claims for standing, the grounds upon which the petitioner claims error or conflicts of interest by the board, and the relief sought.

G.S. 160A-393 also sets forth requirements for standing, responding parties, intervening parties, and answers to the petition for writ as well as for sufficiency of evidence, scope of review, and standard of review. The court reviews the decisions to ensure that a quasi-judicial decision was not

a. in violation of constitutional provisions, including those protecting procedural due process rights;
b. in excess of the statutory authority conferred upon the city or the authority conferred upon the decision-making board by ordinance;
c. inconsistent with applicable procedures specified by statute or ordinance;
d. affected by other error of law;
e. unsupported by substantial competent evidence in view of the entire record; or
f. arbitrary or capricious.[5]

Appeals of quasi-judicial decisions are heard on the record. The record for appeal consists of all documents and exhibits submitted to the decision-making board for the decision that is being appealed as well as the minutes of the meeting at which the decision was made. The record may include an audio or videotape of the meeting and/or a transcript of the proceeding.

---

2. Coventry Woods Neighborhood Ass'n, Inc. v. City of Charlotte, 202 N.C. App. 247, 254 (2010).
3. Marriott v. Chatham Cnty., 187 N.C. App. 491 (2007).
4. Sections 153A-336(a) and 160A-377(a) of the North Carolina General Statutes (hereinafter G.S.).
5. G.S. 160A-393(k)(1).

The court may allow supplemental evidence on matters of standing, conflicts of interest, or questions of constitutional protections or exceeding statutory authority.[6]

## Appeals of Administrative Decisions

Appeals of administrative decisions, arguably, may follow a couple of routes. First, the subdivision statutes specifically authorize appeal to superior court. Applicants have a right to approval if they meet the applicable standards, and any party aggrieved by such administrative decisions may appeal the decision to superior court seeking appropriate declaratory or equitable relief. Such appeal must be filed within the time frame set forth for appeals of quasi-judicial decisions (thirty days from the effective date of the decision or receipt of notice of the decision).[7]

Alternatively, an administrative subdivision decision made by a staff person could be appealed to the board of adjustment under G.S. 160A-388(b1), which states that the board of adjustment shall hear appeals related to enforcement of the zoning ordinance or the unified development ordinance and "may hear appeals *arising out of any other ordinance that regulates land use or development.*" That would include the subdivision ordinance. Indeed, the provision for appealing administrative decisions specifically references notice of a "Subdivision Decision." Appeals to the board of adjustment must be filed within thirty days of notice of the decision. And, parties may appeal the board of adjustment's decision to the superior court.

It is not clear from the General Statutes which of these administrative appeal options applies or who gets to choose. Arguably the local ordinance could choose which appeal process applies. Practically speaking, it makes sense to have staff decisions appealed to the board of adjustment (as with other staff decisions related to land use issues) and board decisions (such as a planning board decision on a preliminary plat) appealed straight to superior court.

## Statutes of Limitations

The statute of limitation to challenge the adoption of a subdivision ordinance depends on the type of challenge and format of the ordinance (either as a stand-alone subdivision ordinance or as part of a unified development ordinance) (see Table 10.1).

---

6. G.S. 160A-393(i) & (j).
7. G.S. 153A-336(b); G.S. 160A-377(b).

**Table 10.1   Statutes of Limitation for Challenges**

| Challenge | Time Period | Statute |
| --- | --- | --- |
| Defect in the adoption process | 3 years | G.S. 153A-348(b); G.S. 160A-364.1(b) |
| Validity of stand-alone subdivision ordinance provision | 3 years | G.S. 1-52(5) |
| Validity of subdivision ordinance provision in unified development ordinance | 1 year | G.S. 153A-348(b); G.S. 160A-364.1(b) |
| Quasi-Judicial plat decision | 30 days | G.S. 153A-336(a); G.S. 160A-377(a) |
| Administrative plat decision | 30 days | To board of adjustment: G.S. 160A-388(b1) To superior court: G.S. 153A-336(b); G.S. 160-377(b) |

# Appendix A: City and County Statutes Authorizing Land Subdivision Regulation

| Municipalities | Counties |
|---|---|
| § 160A-371. Subdivision regulation. | § 153A-330. Subdivision regulation. |

A city may by ordinance regulate the subdivision of land within its territorial jurisdiction.

A county may by ordinance regulate the subdivision of land within its territorial jurisdiction.

If a county, pursuant to G.S. 153A-342, has adopted a zoning ordinance that applies only to one or more designated portions of its territorial jurisdiction, it may adopt subdivision regulations that apply only within the areas so zoned and need not regulate the subdivision of land in the rest of its jurisdiction.

In addition to final plat approval, the ordinance may include provisions for review and approval of sketch plans and preliminary plats. The ordinance may provide for different review procedures for differing classes of subdivisions. The ordinance may be adopted as part of a unified development ordinance or as a separate subdivision ordinance. Decisions on approval or denial of preliminary or final plats may be made only on the basis of standards explicitly set forth in the subdivision or unified development ordinance. Whenever the ordinance includes criteria for decision that require application of judgment, those criteria must provide adequate guiding standards for the entity charged with plat approval.

In addition to final plat approval, the ordinance may include provisions for review and approval of sketch plans and preliminary plats. The ordinance may provide for different review procedures for differing classes of subdivisions. The ordinance may be adopted as part of a unified development ordinance or as a separate subdivision ordinance. Decisions on approval or denial of preliminary or final plats may be made only on the basis of standards explicitly set forth in the subdivision or unified development ordinance. Whenever the ordinance includes criteria for decision that require application of judgment, those criteria must provide adequate guiding standards for the entity charged with plat approval.

| Municipalities | Counties |
|---|---|
| § 160A-372 | § 153A-331 |

(a) A subdivision control ordinance may provide for the orderly growth and development of the city;

for the coordination of transportation networks and utilities within proposed subdivisions with existing or planned streets and highways and with other public facilities;

for the dedication or reservation of recreation areas serving residents of the immediate neighborhood within the subdivision or,

alternatively, for provision of funds to be used to acquire recreation areas serving residents of the development or subdivision or more than one subdivision or development within the immediate area,

and rights-of-way or easements for street and utility purposes including the dedication of rights-of-way pursuant to G.S. 136-66.10 or G.S. 136-66.11;

and for the distribution of population and traffic in a manner that will avoid congestion and overcrowding and will create conditions that substantially promote public health, safety, and the general welfare.

(b) The ordinance may require a plat be prepared, approved, and recorded pursuant to the provisions of the ordinance whenever any subdivision of land takes place.

The ordinance may include requirements that plats show sufficient data to determine readily and reproduce accurately on the ground the location, bearing, and length of every street and alley line, lot line, easement boundary line, and other property boundaries, including the radius and other data for curved property lines, to an appropriate accuracy and in conformance with good surveying practice.

---

(a) A subdivision control ordinance may provide for the orderly growth and development of the county;

for the coordination of transportation networks and utilities within proposed subdivisions with existing or planned streets and highways and with other public facilities;

for the dedication or reservation of recreation areas serving residents of the immediate neighborhood within the subdivision

[*See (c) below.*]

and of rights-of-way or easements for street and utility purposes including the dedication of rights-of-way pursuant to G.S. 136-66.10 or G.S. 136-66.11;

and for the distribution of population and traffic in a manner that will avoid congestion and overcrowding and will create conditions that substantially promote public health, safety, and the general welfare.

(b) The ordinance may require that a plat be prepared, approved, and recorded pursuant to the provisions of the ordinance whenever any subdivision of land takes place.

The ordinance may include requirements that the final plat show sufficient data to determine readily and reproduce accurately on the ground the location, bearing, and length of every street and alley line, lot line, easement boundary line, and other property boundaries, including the radius and other data for curved property lines, to an appropriate accuracy and in conformity with good surveying practice.

| Municipalities | Counties |
|---|---|
| | (c) A subdivision control ordinance may provide that a developer may provide funds to the county whereby the county may acquire recreational land or areas to serve the development or subdivision, including the purchase of land that may be used to serve more than one subdivision or development within the immediate area. [*Comparable municipal authority above at (a) and below in (c).*] |
| (c) The ordinance may provide for the more orderly development of subdivisions by requiring the construction of community service facilities in accordance with municipal plans, policies, and standards. | (e) The ordinance may provide for the more orderly development of subdivisions by requiring the construction of community service facilities in accordance with county plans, policies, and standards. |
| To assure compliance with these and other ordinance requirements, the ordinance may provide for performance guarantees to assure successful completion of required improvements at the time the plat is recorded as provided in subsection (b) of this section. | To assure compliance with these and other ordinance requirements, the ordinance may provide for performance guarantees to assure successful completion of required improvements at the time the plat is recorded as provided in subsection (b) of this section. |
| For any specific development, the type of performance guarantee shall be at the election of the developer.<br>[*See definition of "performance guarantee" in Section (g) below.*] | For any specific development, the type of performance guarantee from the range specified by the county shall be at the election of the developer.<br>[*See definition of "performance guarantee" in Section (g) below.*] |
| (d) The ordinance may provide for the reservation of school sites in accordance with comprehensive land use plans approved by the council or the planning board. In order for this authorization to become effective, before approving such plans the council or planning board and the board of education with jurisdiction over the area shall jointly determine the specific location and size of any school sites to be reserved, which information shall appear in the comprehensive land use plan. | (f) The ordinance may provide for the reservation of school sites in accordance with comprehensive land use plans approved by the board of commissioners or the planning board. For the authorization to reserve school sites to be effective, the board of commissioners or planning board, before approving a comprehensive land use plan, shall determine jointly with the board of education with jurisdiction over the area the specific location and size of each school site to be reserved, and this information shall appear in the plan. |
| Whenever a subdivision is submitted for approval which includes part or all of a school site to be reserved under the plan, the council or planning board shall | Whenever a subdivision that includes part or all of a school site to be reserved under the plan is submitted for approval, the board of commissioners or the |

## Municipalities

immediately notify the board of education and the board of education shall promptly decide whether it still wishes the site to be reserved.

If the board of education does not wish to reserve the site, it shall so notify the council or planning board and no site shall be reserved. If the board of education does wish to reserve the site, the subdivision shall not be approved without such reservation.

The board of education shall then have 18 months beginning on the date of final approval of the subdivision within which to acquire the site by purchase or by initiating condemnation proceedings. If the board of education has not purchased or begun proceedings to condemn the site within 18 months, the subdivider may treat the land as freed of the reservation.

(e) The ordinance may provide that a developer may provide funds to the city whereby the city may acquire recreational land or areas to serve the development or subdivision, including the purchase of land that may be used to serve more than one subdivision or development within the immediate area.

All funds received by the city pursuant to this paragraph shall be used only for the acquisition or development of recreation, park, or open space sites. Any formula enacted to determine the amount of funds that are to be provided under this paragraph shall be based on the value of the development or subdivision for property tax purposes. The ordinance may allow a combination or partial payment of funds and partial dedication of land when the governing body of the city determines that this combination is in the best interests of the citizens of the area to be served.

## Counties

planning board shall immediately notify the board of education. The board of education shall promptly decide whether it still wishes the site to be reserved and shall notify the board of commissioners or planning board of its decision.

If the board of education does not wish the site to be reserved, no site may be reserved. If the board of education does wish the site to be reserved, the subdivision may not be approved without the reservation.

The board of education must acquire the site within 18 months after the date the site is reserved, either by purchase or by exercise of the power of eminent domain. If the board of education has not purchased the site or begun proceedings to condemn the site within the 18 months, the subdivider may treat the land as freed of the reservation.

*[repeated from above]*
*(c) A subdivision control ordinance may provide that a developer may provide funds to the county whereby the county may acquire recreational land or areas to serve the development or subdivision, including the purchase of land that may be used to serve more than one subdivision or development within the immediate area.*

## Municipalities

(f) The ordinance may provide that in lieu of required street construction, a developer may be required to provide funds that the city may use for the construction of roads to serve the occupants, residents, or invitees of the subdivision or development and these funds may be used for roads which serve more than one subdivision or development within the area.

All funds received by the city pursuant to this paragraph shall be used only for development of roads, including design, land acquisition, and construction. However, a city may undertake these activities in conjunction with the Department of Transportation under an agreement between the city and the Department of Transportation.

Any formula adopted to determine the amount of funds the developer is to pay in lieu of required street construction shall be based on the trips generated from the subdivision or development. The ordinance may require a combination of partial payment of funds and partial dedication of constructed streets when the governing body of the city determines that a combination is in the best interests of the citizens of the area to be served.

(g) For purposes of this section, all of the following shall apply with respect to performance guarantees:
  (1)  The term "performance guarantee" shall mean any of the following forms of guarantee:
    a.  Surety bond issued by any company authorized to do business in this State.
    b.  Letter of credit issued by any financial institution licensed to do business in this State.
    c.  Other form of guarantee that provides equivalent security to a surety bond or letter of credit.

## Counties

*(d) The ordinance may provide that in lieu of required street construction, a developer may provide funds to be used for the development of roads to serve the occupants, residents, or invitees of the subdivision or development.*

*All funds received by the county under this section shall be transferred to the municipality to be used solely for the development of roads, including design, land acquisition, and construction. Any municipality receiving funds from a county under this section is authorized to expend such funds outside its corporate limits for the purposes specified in the agreement between the municipality and the county.*

*Any formula adopted to determine the amount of funds the developer is to pay in lieu of required street construction shall be based on the trips generated from the subdivision or development. The ordinance may require a combination of partial payment of funds and partial dedication of constructed streets when the governing body of the county determines that a combination is in the best interest of the citizens of the area to be served.*

(g) Any performance guarantee shall comply with G.S. 160A-372(g).

## Municipalities

## Counties

(2) The performance guarantee shall be returned or released, as appropriate, in a timely manner upon the acknowledgement by the city or county that the improvements for which the performance guarantee is being required are complete. If the improvements are not complete and the current performance guarantee is expiring, the performance guarantee shall be extended, or a new performance guarantee issued, for an additional period until such required improvements are complete. A developer shall demonstrate reasonable, good faith progress toward completion of the required improvements that are the subject of the performance guarantee or any extension. The form of any extension shall remain at the election of the developer.

(3) The amount of the performance guarantee shall not exceed one hundred twenty-five percent (125%) of the reasonably estimated cost of completion at the time the performance guarantee is issued. Any extension of the performance guarantee necessary to complete required improvements shall not exceed one hundred twenty-five percent (125%) of the reasonably estimated cost of completion of the remaining incomplete improvements still outstanding at the time the extension is obtained.

(4) The performance guarantee shall only be used for completion of the required improvements and not for repairs or maintenance after completion.

## Municipalities

**§ 160A-373. Ordinance to contain procedure for plat approval; approval prerequisite to plat recordation; statement by owner.**

Any subdivision ordinance adopted pursuant to this Part shall contain provisions setting forth the procedures to be followed in granting or denying approval of a subdivision plat prior to its registration.

The ordinance may provide that final decisions on preliminary plats and final plats are to be made by:
 (1) The city council,
 (2) The city council on recommendation of a designated body, or
 (3) A designated planning board, technical review committee, or other designated body or staff person.

From and after the effective date of a subdivision ordinance that is adopted by the city, no subdivision plat of land within the city's jurisdiction shall be filed or recorded until it shall have been submitted to and approved by the council or appropriate agency, as specified in the subdivision ordinance, and until this approval shall have been entered on the face of the plat in writing by an authorized representative of the city.

## Counties

**§ 153A-332. Ordinance to contain procedure for plat approval; approval prerequisite to plat recordation; statement by owner.**

A subdivision ordinance adopted pursuant to this Part shall contain provisions setting forth the procedures to be followed in granting or denying approval of a subdivision plat before its registration.

The ordinance shall provide that the following agencies be given an opportunity to make recommendations concerning an individual subdivision plat before the plat is approved:
 (1) The district highway engineer as to proposed State streets, State highways, and related drainage systems;
 (2) The county health director or local public utility, as appropriate, as to proposed water or sewerage systems;
 (3) Any other agency or official designated by the board of commissioners.

The ordinance may provide that final decisions on preliminary plats and final plats are to be made by:
 (1) The board of commissioners,
 (2) The board of commissioners on recommendation of a designated body, or
 (3) A designated planning board, technical review committee, or other designated body or staff person.

From the effective date of a subdivision ordinance that is adopted by the county, no subdivision plat of land within the county's jurisdiction may be filed or recorded until it has been submitted to and approved by the appropriate board or agency, as specified in the subdivision ordinance, and until this approval is entered in writing on the face of the plat by an authorized representative of the county.

## Municipalities

The Review Officer, pursuant to G.S. 47-30.2, shall not certify a plat of a subdivision of land located within the territorial jurisdiction of a city that has not been approved in accordance with these provisions, nor shall the clerk of superior court order or direct the recording of a plat if the recording would be in conflict with this section.

## Counties

The Review Officer, pursuant to G.S. 47-30.2, shall not certify a plat of a subdivision of land located within the territorial jurisdiction of the county that has not been approved in accordance with these provisions, and the clerk of superior court may not order or direct the recording of a plat if the recording would be in conflict with this section.

| Municipalities | Counties |
|---|---|
| **§ 160A-374. Effect of plat approval on dedications.** | **§ 153A-333. Effect of plat approval on dedications.** |

**Municipalities**

**§ 160A-374. Effect of plat approval on dedications.**

The approval of a plat shall not be deemed to constitute or effect the acceptance by the city or public of the dedication of any street or other ground, public utility line, or other public facility shown on the plat.

However, any city council may by resolution accept any dedication made to the public of lands or facilities for streets, parks, public utility lines, or other public purposes, when the lands or facilities are located within its subdivision-regulation jurisdiction. Acceptance of dedication of lands or facilities located within the subdivision-regulation jurisdiction but outside the corporate limits of a city shall not place on the city any duty to open, operate, repair, or maintain any street, utility line, or other land or facility, and a city shall in no event be held to answer in any civil action or proceeding for failure to open, repair, or maintain any street located outside its corporate limits. Unless a city, county or other public entity operating a water system shall have agreed to begin operation and maintenance of the water system or water system facilities within one year of the time of issuance of a certificate of occupancy for the first unit of housing in the subdivision, a city or county shall not, as part of its subdivision regulation applied to facilities or land outside the corporate limits of a city, require dedication of water systems or facilities as a condition for subdivision approval.

**Counties**

**§ 153A-333. Effect of plat approval on dedications.**

The approval of a plat does not constitute or effect the acceptance by the county or the public of the dedication of any street or other ground, public utility line, or other public facility shown on the plat and shall not be construed to do so.

## Municipalities

### § 160A-375. Penalties for transferring lots in unapproved subdivisions.

(a) If a city adopts an ordinance regulating the subdivision of land as authorized herein, any person who, being the owner or agent of the owner of any land located within the jurisdiction of that city, thereafter subdivides his land in violation of the ordinance or transfers or sells land by reference to, exhibition of, or any other use of a plat showing a subdivision of the land before the plat has been properly approved under such ordinance and recorded in the office of the appropriate register of deeds, shall be guilty of a Class 1 misdemeanor.

The description by metes and bounds in the instrument of transfer or other document used in the process of selling or transferring land shall not exempt the transaction from this penalty.

The city may bring an action for injunction of any illegal subdivision, transfer, conveyance, or sale of land, and the court shall, upon appropriate findings, issue an injunction and order requiring the offending party to comply with the subdivision ordinance.

Building permits required pursuant to G.S. 160A-417 may be denied for lots that have been illegally subdivided.

In addition to other remedies, a city may institute any appropriate action or proceedings to prevent the unlawful subdivision of land, to restrain, correct, or abate the violation, or to prevent any illegal act or conduct.

(b) The provisions of this section shall not prohibit any owner or its agent from entering into contracts to sell or lease by reference to an approved preliminary plat for which a final plat has not yet been properly approved under the subdivision ordinance or recorded with the register of deeds, provided the contract does all of the following:

## Counties

### § 153A-334. Penalties for transferring lots in unapproved subdivisions.

(a) If a person who is the owner or the agent of the owner of any land located within the territorial jurisdiction of a county that has adopted a subdivision regulation ordinance subdivides his land in violation of the ordinance or transfers or sells land by reference to, exhibition of, or any other use of a plat showing a subdivision of the land before the plat has been properly approved under the ordinance and recorded in the office of the appropriate register of deeds, he is guilty of a Class 1 misdemeanor.

The description by metes and bounds in the instrument of transfer or other document used in the process of selling or transferring land does not exempt the transaction from this penalty.

The county may bring an action for injunction of any illegal subdivision, transfer, conveyance, or sale of land, and the court shall, upon appropriate findings, issue an injunction and order requiring the offending party to comply with the subdivision ordinance.

Building permits required pursuant to G.S. 153A-357 may be denied for lots that have been illegally subdivided.

In addition to other remedies, a county may institute any appropriate action or proceedings to prevent the unlawful subdivision of land, to restrain, correct, or abate the violation, or to prevent any illegal act or conduct.

(b) The provisions of this section shall not prohibit any owner or its agent from entering into contracts to sell or lease by reference to an approved preliminary plat for which a final plat has not yet been properly approved under the subdivision ordinance or recorded with the register of deeds, provided the contract does all of the following:

## Municipalities

(1)  Incorporates as an attachment a copy of the preliminary plat referenced in the contract and obligates the owner to deliver to the buyer a copy of the recorded plat prior to closing and conveyance.

(2)  Plainly and conspicuously notifies the prospective buyer or lessee that a final subdivision plat has not been approved or recorded at the time of the contract, that no governmental body will incur any obligation to the prospective buyer or lessee with respect to the approval of the final subdivision plat, that changes between the preliminary and final plats are possible, and that the contract or lease may be terminated without breach by the buyer or lessee if the final recorded plat differs in any material respect from the preliminary plat.

(3)  Provides that if the approved and recorded final plat does not differ in any material respect from the plat referred to in the contract, the buyer or lessee may not be required by the seller or lessor to close any earlier than five days after the delivery of a copy of the final recorded plat.

(4)  Provides that if the approved and recorded final plat differs in any material respect from the preliminary plat referred to in the contract, the buyer or lessee may not be required by the seller or lessor to close any earlier than 15 days after the delivery of the final recorded plat, during which 15-day period the buyer or lessee may terminate the contract without breach or any further obligation and may receive a refund of all earnest money or prepaid purchase price.

(c)  The provisions of this section shall not prohibit any owner or its agent from entering into contracts to sell or lease land by reference to an approved

## Counties

(1)  Incorporates as an attachment a copy of the preliminary plat referenced in the contract and obligates the owner to deliver to the buyer a copy of the recorded plat prior to closing and conveyance.

(2)  Plainly and conspicuously notifies the prospective buyer or lessee that a final subdivision plat has not been approved or recorded at the time of the contract, that no governmental body will incur any obligation to the prospective buyer or lessee with respect to the approval of the final subdivision plat, that changes between the preliminary and final plats are possible, and that the contract or lease may be terminated without breach by the buyer or lessee if the final recorded plat differs in any material respect from the preliminary plat.

(3)  Provides that if the approved and recorded final plat does not differ in any material respect from the plat referred to in the contract, the buyer or lessee may not be required by the seller or lessor to close any earlier than five days after the delivery of a copy of the final recorded plat.

(4)  Provides that if the approved and recorded final plat differs in any material respect from the preliminary plat referred to in the contract, the buyer or lessee may not be required by the seller or lessor to close any earlier than 15 days after the delivery of the final recorded plat, during which 15-day period the buyer or lessee may terminate the contract without breach or any further obligation and may receive a refund of all earnest money or prepaid purchase price.

(c)  The provisions of this section shall not prohibit any owner or its agent from entering into contracts to sell or lease land by reference to an approved

## Municipalities

preliminary plat for which a final plat has not been properly approved under the subdivision ordinance or recorded with the register of deeds where the buyer or lessee is any person who has contracted to acquire or lease the land for the purpose of engaging in the business of construction of residential, commercial, or industrial buildings on the land, or for the purpose of resale or lease of the land to persons engaged in that kind of business, provided that no conveyance of that land may occur and no contract to lease it may become effective until after the final plat has been properly approved under the subdivision ordinance and recorded with the register of deeds.

## Counties

preliminary plat for which a final plat has not been properly approved under the subdivision ordinance or recorded with the register of deeds where the buyer or lessee is any person who has contracted to acquire or lease the land for the purpose of engaging in the business of construction of residential, commercial, or industrial buildings on the land, or for the purpose of resale or lease of the land to persons engaged in that kind of business, provided that no conveyance of that land may occur and no contract to lease it may become effective until after the final plat has been properly approved under the subdivision ordinance and recorded with the register of deeds.

## Municipalities

### § 160A-376. Definition.

(a) For the purpose of this Part, "subdivision" means all divisions of a tract or parcel of land into two or more lots, building sites, or other divisions when any one or more of those divisions is created for the purpose of sale or building development (whether immediate or future) and shall include all divisions of land involving the dedication of a new street or a change in existing streets;

but the following shall not be included within this definition nor be subject to the regulations authorized by this Part:

(1) The combination or recombination of portions of previously subdivided and recorded lots where the total number of lots is not increased and the resultant lots are equal to or exceed the standards of the municipality as shown in its subdivision regulations.

(2) The division of land into parcels greater than 10 acres where no street right-of-way dedication is involved.

(3) The public acquisition by purchase of strips of land for the widening or opening of streets or for public transportation system corridors.

(4) The division of a tract in single ownership whose entire area is no greater than two acres into not more than three lots, where no street right-of-way dedication is involved and where the resultant lots are equal to or exceed the standards of the municipality, as shown in its subdivision regulations.

(b) A city may provide for expedited review of specified classes of subdivisions.

## Counties

### § 153A-335. "Subdivision" defined.

(a) or purposes of this Part, "subdivision" means all divisions of a tract or parcel of land into two or more lots, building sites, or other divisions when any one or more of those divisions are created for the purpose of sale or building development (whether immediate or future) and includes all division of land involving the dedication of a new street or a change in existing streets;

however, the following is not included within this definition and is not subject to any regulations enacted pursuant to this Part:

(1) The combination or recombination of portions of previously subdivided and recorded lots if the total number of lots is not increased and the resultant lots are equal to or exceed the standards of the county as shown in its subdivision regulations.

(2) The division of land into parcels greater than 10 acres if no street right-of-way dedication is involved.

(3) The public acquisition by purchase of strips of land for widening or opening streets or for public transportation system corridors.

(4) The division of a tract in single ownership the entire area of which is no greater than two acres into not more than three lots, if no street right-of-way dedication is involved and if the resultant lots are equal to or exceed the standards of the county as shown by its subdivision regulations.

(b) A county may provide for expedited review of specified classes of subdivisions.

## Municipalities

### § 160A-377. Appeals of decisions on subdivision plats.

(a) When a subdivision ordinance adopted under this Part provides that the decision whether to approve or deny a preliminary or final subdivision plat is to be made by a city council or a planning board, other than a planning board comprised solely of members of a city planning staff, and the ordinance authorizes the council or planning board to make a quasi-judicial decision in deciding whether to approve the subdivision plat, then that quasi-judicial decision of the council or planning board shall be subject to review by the superior court by proceedings in the nature of certiorari.

The provisions of G.S. 160A-381(c), 160A-388(e2), and 160A-393 shall apply to those appeals.

(b) When a subdivision ordinance adopted under this Part provides that a city council, planning board, or staff member is authorized to make only an administrative or ministerial decision in deciding whether to approve a preliminary or final subdivision plat, then any party aggrieved by that administrative or ministerial decision may seek to have the decision reviewed by filing an action in superior court seeking appropriate declaratory or equitable relief.

Such an action must be filed within the time frame specified in G.S. 160A-381(c) for petitions in the nature of certiorari.

(c) For purposes of this section, an ordinance shall be deemed to authorize a quasi-judicial decision if the city council or planning board is authorized to decide whether to approve or deny the plat based not only upon whether the application complies with the specific requirements set forth in the ordinance, but also on whether the application complies with one or more generally stated standards requiring a discretionary decision to be made by the city council or planning board.

## Counties

### § 153A-336. Appeals of decisions on subdivision plats.

(a) When a subdivision ordinance adopted under this Part provides that the decision whether to approve or deny a preliminary or final subdivision plat is to be made by a board of commissioners or a planning board, other than a planning board comprised solely of members of a county planning staff, and the ordinance authorizes the board of commissioners or planning board to make a quasi-judicial decision in deciding whether to approve the subdivision plat, then that quasi-judicial decision of the board of commissioners or planning board shall be subject to review by the superior court by proceedings in the nature of certiorari.

The provisions of G.S. 153A-340(f), 153A-345(e2), and 153A-349 shall apply to those appeals.

(b) When a subdivision ordinance adopted under this Part provides that a board of commissioners, planning board, or staff member is authorized to make only an administrative or ministerial decision in deciding whether to approve a preliminary or final subdivision plat, then any party aggrieved by that administrative or ministerial decision may seek to have the decision reviewed by filing an action in superior court seeking appropriate declaratory or equitable relief.

Such an action must be filed within the time frame specified in G.S. 153A-340(f) for petitions in the nature of certiorari.

(c) For purposes of this section, an ordinance shall be deemed to authorize a quasi-judicial decision if the board of commissioners or planning board is authorized to decide whether to approve or deny the plat based not only upon whether the application complies with the specific requirements set forth in the ordinance, but also on whether the application complies with one or more generally stated standards requiring a discretionary decision to be made by the board of commissioners or planning board.

# Appendix B:    North Carolina Case Summaries

## N.C. Supreme Court

### Stephens Co. v. Myers Park Homes Co., 181 N.C. 335 (1921)
*Review; phasing; improvements; private claims*

The developer sought to subdivide and sell lots from an eleven-hundred-acre tract of land. The developer used a key map for the overall concept plan, but lots were sold with reference to detailed subdivision plats of smaller areas. For the lot in question, the first recorded plat showed a 110-foot-wide, curved right-of-way over and adjacent to the lot. Thereafter, a revised plat was recorded showing a straight eighty-foot-wide right-of-way. A lot purchaser argued that the developer was obligated to complete the road as shown on the original plat because lots had been sold from the overall development (even though none were sold from the original plat). The court found that the development should not be treated as one unit merely because there was a key map. The key map was a general depiction of the various tracts, not sufficiently detailed to correctly describe lots and blocks.

### Irwin v. City of Charlotte, 193 N.C. 109 (1927)
*Dedication*

This case concerned a dispute as to whether or not property was dedicated as a city park. Among other things the court emphasized that a dedication is not complete until it is formally accepted by the public body, that the public bears no burden or benefit of dedication until formal acceptance and that an offer to dedicate is revocable until accepted.

### Home Real Estate Loan and Insurance Co. v. Town of Carolina Beach, 216 N.C. 778 (1940)
*Streets; dedication*

The developer platted lots and streets and sold lots in reference to that map. As such, the developer dedicated the streets to the use of the lot purchasers and the public. The purchasers maintain their rights, even if the developer subsequently changes the plat.

### Sheets v. Walsh, 217 N.C. 32 (1940)
*Dedication; private easements*

Within a subdivision certain property was dedicated to the public but never formally accepted or improved. The owner entered into a contract to sell the dedicated property, took action to declare withdrawal of the dedication, and tendered a deed to the purchaser. The purchaser refused to pay the purchase price, citing a lack of good title. Other lot owners, the purchaser argued, bought lots by reference to the maps showing the streets and were vested with easements over those streets. The court found that under the former statute other lot purchasers previously had easements but that the statute of limitations to assert those rights had run out. Having had a reasonable time to assert rights, the other lot owners were not deprived of their due process.

### Russell v. Coggin, 232 N.C. 674, 675 (1950)
*Dedication; withdrawal of*
A developer platted lots and streets and then sold lots in reference to the recorded plat. Later, the developer declared withdrawal of the dedication of the streets and conveyed that property to a purchaser. A prior lot purchaser challenged the withdrawal and purchase, arguing that the lot purchasers owned the street to the centerline, subject to the easement to the public and other lot owners. The court found that lots were conveyed by block and lot number (no rights in the streets) and that the dedicators were individuals (not a corporation that has become nonexistent). The provisions of G.S. 136-96 authorize the developer (the original dedicator), under the specified circumstances, to withdraw the offer of dedication to public use.

### Wilson Realty Co. v. City and County Planning Board for City of Winston-Salem and Forsyth County, 243 N.C. 648 (1956)
*Exactions; roads*
In its review of a subdivision plat application, the planning board insisted that the developer reserve right-of-way through the property for a four-lane divided highway that would serve as a beltline thoroughfare on the western outskirts of the city. The right-of-way ranged from 110 to 240 feet wide and consumed a six-acre strip through the seventy-acre property. The property owner refused to designate such a reservation, arguing that the submitted plat proposal (without the highway reservation) met the standards for a subdivision and that denial is beyond the board's authority. The court remanded the case on procedural grounds (distinguishing the standards of review for writ of certiorari and writ of mandamus). Nevertheless, the court expressed that the facts and legal authority favored the landowner. G.S. 136-44.50–54 authorizes cities, counties, and other transportation authorities to reserve roadways by official map.

### Roberts v. Town of Cameron, 245 N.C. 373, 375 (1957)
*Dedication*
Lots and streets were plotted on a map, and lots were sold, but particular streets were not accepted or improved by the town. A lot owner placed a fence across a portion of property dedicated for a street and used the area as a pasture. After decades without accepting or improving the dedicated street property, the town adopted a resolution to open the unopened streets, set stakes and markers, and began grading. The court found that a mere delay in accepting an offer of dedication does not constitute a bar of acceptance unless: (1) the property is claimed by adverse possession for purposes inconsistent with the street use or (2) the dedication is withdrawn. In this case, the lot owner could not claim adverse possession because the pasture use was permissive (not adverse).

## Steadman v. Town of Pinetops, 251 N.C. 509 (1960)

*Dedication*

The town was platted with streets and lots in the 1910s. Decades later the property owner sought to enforce a declaration of withdrawal of dedication for certain streets adjoining the owner's property, but the parties disputed whether the streets had been accepted and opened and whether the owner could claim the rights of the dedicator. As to the streets, the court found that because the town had not opened or maintained most of the streets, dedication could be withdrawn. For one street, though, the town opened the street for two to three years—enough to bar subsequent withdrawal of dedication. Moreover, the trial court found that the particular street was necessary for convenient ingress and egress for other lots. As to the rights of the owner, the original dedicator was a corporation no longer in existence, so the owner had rights to withdraw under G.S. 136-96.

## Janicki v. Lorek, 255 N.C. 53 (1961)

*Dedication; distinguishing subdivision*

An owner developed a large tract of land, including a townsite of small lots and contiguous farms of ten acres each. The purchasers of one farm objected to the withdrawal of dedication of a particular street by a lot owner in the townsite portion. The farm owner argued that he was the owner of property within the subdivision and had the right to keep the street open. The trial court concluded that, although the townsite and farms were depicted together on a common key map, they were intended as distinct subdivisions, not a unified subdivision. As such, the farm owner did not have rights distinct from the general public to bar the lot owner's withdrawal of dedication.

## Cleveland Realty Co. v. Hobbs, 261 N.C. 414 (1964)

*Open space; easement*

The developer recorded a plat showing lots, streets, and a golf course. The golf course property was conveyed to a country club. A neighboring landowner proposed, and the country club agreed, to construct an access road through a portion of the property platted as a golf course. The original developer objected to such use, arguing that it was dedicated for golf course purposes. The court agreed with the developer, finding that when lots are sold or conveyed with reference to a plat, the rights outlined in that plat may not be altered except by agreement or estoppel.

## Wofford v. North Carolina State Highway Commission, 263 N.C. 677, 682, 683 (1965)

*Streets; closing*

Wofford owned a lot on a side street near an arterial road. Most traffic to the lot came from the arterial road, but the lot could also be accessed from the other direction. A highway project to convert the arterial road into an expressway included blocking the side street's access to the arterial road/expressway, turning the side street into a cul-de-sac about one hundred feet from the property owner's lot (the owner could still access the arterial road/expressway by going around the block). The property owner claimed a public and private easement to have the side street open, that blocking the side street damaged his property and amounted to a taking with compensation. The court stated that owners of land abutting a public street have two distinct rights: (1) the public right, common to all citizens, to free use of the street, which may be limited for all by altered routes, cul-de-sacs, or otherwise, and (2) the private right of an easement appurtenant (an easement that applies to a piece of property and not to the owners of that property) for reasonable access to the particular street abutting the property. "In the instant case, no part of plaintiffs' land was taken or physically injured. Their right of reasonable access to [the arterial road] has not been appropriated, limited or interfered with." The reduction of property value from the street closing one hundred feet from the property was not compensable.

Wofford further argued that he had the right to have the street remain open because the lot was sold with reference to a plat showing the streets. The court acknowledged the general right but clarified that "[t]his right of easement is not absolute; it extends only to streets or portions of streets of the subdivision necessary to afford convenient ingress or egress to the lot of the purchaser."

### State v. McBane, 276 N.C. 60 (1969)
*Enforcement*
The county attempted to bring criminal prosecution against the defendant for selling lots from a recorded subdivision that was not approved according to the county subdivision regulations (a misdemeanor under the statute). The court dismissed the case, finding that the warrant for arrest failed to include the proper allegations, namely, that the defendant was the owner of land within the county's subdivision jurisdiction.

### Osborne v. Town of North Wilkesboro, 280 N.C. 696 (1972)
*Dedication; withdrawal of; streets*
Around 1900, land developers surveyed and registered a map showing lots, streets, and alleys for much of what would become the town of North Wilkesboro. Half a century later, the property owner owned three of those lots and operated a sawmill on the lots as well as on adjoining property shown on the map as a street and alley. That particular portion of street and alley were never opened or improved by the municipality. In 1969, the owner filed and recorded a declaration of withdrawal of dedication. The city challenged the withdrawal. The court found that the sale of lots referencing a map showing streets and alleys amounts to an offer to dedicate such streets and alleys. If the municipality improves and opens such streets, acceptance is presumed. However, if the municipality fails to improve and open the streets for fifteen years, the dedicator or successors may withdraw the dedication.

### Marriott Financial Services, Inc. v. Capitol Funds, Inc., 288 N.C. 122 (1975)
*Remedies; enforcement*
The seller sold property that had not been legally subdivided, and the buyer asked the court to rescind the sale. The court found the statutes to be clear: illegal subdivision is a criminal misdemeanor with a penalty set forth by statute. The court also found, however, no legislative intent to invalidate the sale of property that was improperly subdivided. Additional remedies were subsequently added to the statutes.

## Town of Nags Head v. Tillett, 314 N.C. 627 (1985)
*Enforcement*

A property buyer sought a building permit for a lot from an unauthorized subdivision. The town subdivision ordinance prohibited issuance of a building permit for any structure in a subdivision until that subdivision is properly approved. The court, however, found that enforcement of *subdivision* ordinances is limited to criminal proceedings and injunction (G.S. 160A-375). Remedies for *zoning* violations, though, are outlined at G.S. 160A-389 and include "any appropriate action or proceedings" to address the zoning violation. As such, the building permit could be withheld for failure to comply with zoning ordinance requirements, such as minimum lot size. To the extent that the property buyer was prevented from obtaining a building permit and reasonable use of the property for residential purposes, the buyer was entitled to rescission of the sale under the terms of the contract.

Withholding a building permit and other appropriate actions are now authorized for subdivision enforcement as well as zoning enforcement. S.L. 2005-426.

## Batch v. Town of Chapel Hill, 326 N.C. 1 (1990)
*Roads; design*

The landowner sought to develop eleven residential lots on twenty acres. The town's thoroughfare plan, adopted as part of its comprehensive plan, included a future, limited-access two-lane parkway aligned through a portion of the property. The landowner's proposed plat did not include the proposed parkway. The governing board denied the subdivision request for, among other reasons, the development not having streets that coordinate with existing and planned streets and highways. Lower courts found that the denial amounted to an unconstitutional taking. The N.C. Supreme Court disagreed. First, the court found that the trial court improperly made findings of fact. Second, the court found that the governing board had competent, material, and substantial evidence to support that finding. Moreover, the court found that statutes clearly authorize local governments to require a developer to take present and future road development into account when designing a subdivision. Considering future road development in design is not necessarily tantamount to a compulsory dedication.

While the landowner argued (and the N.C. Court of Appeals agreed) that the conditions amounted to an unconstitutional taking under *Nollan v. California Coastal Commission* (483 U.S. 825 (1987)), the N.C. Supreme Court found no taking. The subdivision request was denied, so no exaction ever applied. The subsequent *Koontz v. St. Johns River Water Management District* (133 S. Ct. 2586, 2591 (2013)) decision from the U.S. Supreme Court may require additional analysis in such a case.

## River Birch Associates v. City of Raleigh, 326 N.C. 100 (1990)
*Exactions; open space; enforcement; homeowners association*

A developer sought and obtained preliminary subdivision plat and site plan approval for a 144-unit townhome development, including areas identified on the plat and plan as open space. Subsequently the developer sought plat approval for a 24-unit townhouse development on a three-acre parcel previously identified as open space. Although the overall development met the minimum open space requirements of the zoning ordinance, the city refused to process the application for the three-acre parcel and requested that the developer convey the open space to the homeowners association. The N.C. Supreme Court found that the General Statutes do authorize local ordinances to require conveyance of an open space recreation area to a homeowners association and that when a development creates a need for parks it is reasonable to require the developer to bear that cost. Moreover, the court found that once a developer substantially undertakes a project according to an approved plan, the developer has assented to the conditions of the plan. Failure to comply with those conditions is grounds for revocation. A city may grant a variance to such conditions but is not obligated to do so.

### Homebuilders Association of Charlotte v. City of Charlotte, 336 N.C. 37 (1994)
*Fees; statutory interpretation*
The city imposed a schedule of user fees to cover the cost of regulatory services performed by city departments, including permit reviews, rezoning reviews, subdivision reviews, and others. Opponents challenged the permit fees as unauthorized. The court looked to the interpretive guidance of G.S. 160A-4 and emphasized that the statutes granting local government power *shall* be broadly construed to include any additional and supplementary powers needed to carry out that authority. The court found that reasonable permit fees are reasonably necessary and expedient to the execution of a city's power to regulate land use.

### Three Guys Real Estate v. Harnett County, 345 N.C. 468 (1997)
*Exemptions*
The landowner sought to divide a 231-acre tract into twenty-three lots of ten acres each with no dedicated right-of-way. The county planning department refused to certify that the plat was exempt from subdivision regulations. The trial court found that the private access easements were essentially open for public use and that the proposed division would circumvent the subdivision ordinance's standards for public health and safety. The N.C. Supreme Court found the division of land to be clearly exempt: The private access easements were not dedicated public rights-of-way, and the general standard for public health and safety could not overcome the specific statutory language creating the exemption from subdivision regulation.

### Beechridge Development Co., L.L.C. v. Dahners, 350 N.C. 583 (1999)
*Improvements; easements*
A developer sought a declaratory judgment that a "public easement" noted on the plat of an existing adjacent subdivision could be used for a sanitary sewer line to serve the developer's new subdivision. The N.C. Supreme Court stated that the term "public easement" "encompasses a wide variety of public uses, including a sanitary sewer line."

### Guilford Financial Services, L.L.C. v. City of Brevard, 356 N.C. 655 (2003) (per curiam), *adopting dissent* in 150 N.C. App. 1 (2002)
*Review; quasi-judicial*
The Brevard city council denied the developer's request for preliminary plat approval, citing public health and safety concerns as well as density concerns. The N.C. Supreme Court ruled in favor of the developer, citing the dissenting opinion from the court of appeals. The court

found, among other things, that the nature of a proceeding—legislative or quasi-judicial—is determined by the type of decision to be made, not by the type of notice provided (in this case the proceeding was quasi-judicial, though the city argued it was legislative). When a decision-making board makes a quasi-judicial decision it must have competent, material, and substantial evidence in the record to support that decision. And, when the developer makes a prima facie showing of compliance with the subdivision standards, the developer is entitled to the subdivision plat.

### Jones v. Davis, 163 N.C. App. 628 (2004) *aff'd*, 359 N.C. 314 (2005)

*Definition*

Neighbors contested an approved subdivision in which lots were leased to renters to place mobile homes there. The neighbors argued that the division of land did not meet the definition of subdivision. The N.C. Court of Appeals, citing *State v. Turner* (117 N.C. App. 457 (1994)) (discussed below), found that the phrase " 'for the purpose of sale or building development' includes construction on subdivision lots, which are leased to third parties who place their own improvements on the property."

The neighbors also argued that the mobile home park ordinance, not the subdivision ordinance, should have controlled development. The mobile home park ordinance was not properly before the court for review, so the court did not consider the argument. Even so, the court reviewed the subdivision ordinance and found that it regulates the division of land, not the use of land.

### Lanvale Properties, L.L.C. v. County of Cabarrus, 366 N.C. 142, 169 (2012)

*Fees; schools; statutory interpretation; adequate public facilities*

The county adopted an adequate public facilities ordinance that, in the court's view, required developers to pay a fee for school construction. As with prior school fee cases, the court found that the county lacked authority for a de facto school impact fee, which is not authorized under either the general police power or the zoning power. Moreover, the rules of statutory interpretation of city and county authority do not apply; those rules apply only when the statute is unclear. The court viewed the fee scheme as a "revenue generating mechanism that is disguised as a zoning ordinance."

The court emphasized that zoning and subdivision authority is distinct, even when those elements are combined into a unified development ordinance.

### High Rock Lake Partners, L.L.C. v. NC DOT, 366 N.C. 315 (2012)

*Driveway permits; exactions*

The developer had plans for a sixty-lot residential subdivision on 188 acres. The property is a peninsula jutting into a lake and accessed by State Road 1135, a fourteen-foot-wide gravel road that crosses two sets of railroad tracks a quarter mile before it dead-ends into the property. NCDOT granted a driveway permit with the conditions that the developer widen and pave the railroad crossing, widen and pave the road from the crossing to property (quarter mile), and negotiate with third parties (the N.C. Railroad Co. and Norfolk Southern) to gain their consent for the crossing improvements. The third parties refused such approval, and the developer appealed, arguing that DOT lacked authority for the conditions.

NCDOT argued that the conditions were authorized under its general grant of power to "make rules, regulations and ordinances" for the use of state highways. The court, though, looked to the specific language in the driveway permit statute (G.S. 136-18(29)), under which DOT is authorized to establish policies and rules for driveway connections into any street or highway in the state highway system, including size, location, traffic flow, and construction standards. In addition, DOT may require improvements and dedication of turn lanes, additional lanes, and medians for roads with a traffic volume of at least four thousand cars per day. The court recognized this authority as balancing the public interest in safe highways and the private interest in access. Under the plain language of the statute, however, the court found that NCDOT lacked authority to condition approval of a driveway permit on offsite improvements or to require an applicant seek consent from a third party.

### Town of Midland v. Wayne, No. 458PA13 (N.C. June 11, 2015)
*Vested rights; eminent domain; unity of ownership*
In a condemnation action, unity of ownership may be established when distinct tracts of land are subject to a common development plan and an individual holds significant ownership interests in each tract. Vested rights are part of the calculation of valuation, not a separate compensable property interest.

Wayne owned 90 acres himself. An L.L.C. owned the adjacent 160 acres, and Wayne was the majority owner of the L.L.C. In 1997 Wayne and the L.L.C. obtained a development plan approval for a residential subdivision on the full 250 acres. Wayne and the L.L.C. developed the first two phases on L.L.C. land. Some infrastructure was installed to serve future phases. In 2007 Wayne conveyed his property to his own revocable trust. By 2009 the first two phases were substantially complete; about 40 acres of L.L.C. land and all 90 acres of Wayne's land remained undeveloped.

In 2009 the town of Midland commenced condemnation actions for 3 acres of right-of-way for natural gas and fiber optic lines on the Wayne tracts. When condemnation takes less than the entire tract, compensation is the greater of either the decrease in value of the entire tract or the value of the property taken. G.S. 40A-64(b). The town's condemnation did not consider the vested rights in the property and did include the L.L.C. tracts as part of the calculation. Wayne and the L.L.C. challenged the condemnation action on several issues. They argued that (1) they had vested rights in the 1997 plan for the undeveloped property, (2) Wayne and the L.L.C. had unity of ownership for purposes of determining the impact of the condemnation, and (3) the condemnation damages should include separate compensation for the loss of vested rights. The supreme court found common law vested rights in the 1997 plan for the entire development, the Wayne tracts and L.L.C. tracts. The developer made substantial expenditures in good faith reliance on the 1997 plan. While expenditures were primarily focused on the first two phases of development, those expenditures were part of a unified plan and benefited the entire subdivision. For the compensation calculation under G.S. 40A-67, contiguous tracts that have unity of ownership, unity of use, and physical unity are treated as a single tract. The court found that the Wayne tracts and L.L.C. tracts have such unity. They are contiguous and are being developed according to the same unified 1997 Plan. Notably, despite the differing ownership arrangements for the different tracts (trust v. L.L.C.), the court found that the joint vested rights—in addition to Wayne's central role as trustee of the revocable trust and as controlling owner of the L.L.C.—satisfies unity of ownership. As such, the land should be treated as one tract for purposes of calculating compensation. Wayne argued that the vested right is a separate property interest for which he is owed compensation. The court disagreed. It found development rights to be an important feature in determining property value, not a separate compensable right.

## N.C. Court of Appeals

### Owens v. Taylor, 2 N.C. App. 178 (1968)
*Streets; closing access*

Property owners (lot owners) owned lots that were described with reference to plats that delineated a lane or twenty-foot road. The lot owners claimed that the road was open for use by subdivision residents to access the nearby river. The plaintiff (road-adjacent owner) claimed to own the lane or road as a 20-foot by 150-foot parcel and that the lot owners were trespassing. Evidence showed that lots were sold by reference to a plat showing the road and that NCDOT had accepted and maintained the road. The court found that the lot owners had a right to have the road kept open, and, moreover, that the road-adjacent owner had not established that they held fee title to the road.

### Williamson v. Avant, 21 N.C. App. 211 (1974)
*Definition*

A tract of land was divided into parcels and conveyed for the purpose of dividing the real estate among the heirs of the deceased property owner. The division was never approved by the county commission, as required for subdivisions subject to the subdivision ordinance. The court found that the division of property to settle an estate was not a subdivision as defined by statute—it was not a division of land for immediate or future sales or development—and thus was not subject to local subdivision regulation.

### Sampson v. City of Greensboro, 35 N.C. App. 148, 149 (1978)
*Dedication*

Although the developer's own record plat included a dedication of an easement, the developer claimed that an easement was never properly dedicated and that if property was dedicated, it was for a storm sewer, not a sanitary sewer as the city claimed. The court found that the plat was properly recorded with the developer's signed statement dedicating the easements shown. The court also found that the subdivision ordinance stated that the necessary grants of easements are broad enough for a sanitary sewer. "In one breath, plaintiffs claim all the benefits that are afforded by the defendant's approval of their subdivision and, at the same time, seek to withdraw the burdens on the land that defendant required to be imposed thereon before it would approve the subdivision."

### Springdale Estates Association v. Wake County, 47 N.C. App. 462 (1980)

*Local procedures; quasi-judicial decisions*

A developer of two new subdivisions sought to name them "Springdale Gardens" and "Springdale Woods." Homeowners of the existing and adjacent Springdale Estates subdivision sought to prevent adoption of the similar names. The county commission and superior court permitted the names for the new development, but the court of appeals looked to the ordinance provision requiring that the name of a new subdivision should not duplicate or closely approximate the name of an existing subdivision and found that the proposed names from the developer were too close to the existing name. The court found that the county commission disregarded the county's own ordinance provision regarding names of subdivisions and noted that there was a lack of evidence in the record for certain findings of fact made by the commission.

### Messer v. Town of Chapel Hill, 59 N.C. App. 692 (1982)

*Parks; design; public use*

As a condition of approval of a subdivision plat, the town required that recreation space be moved to a different location and dedicated to the public, in accordance with the ordinance. The developer argued that this request amounted to a taking of private property. The court found statutory authority for the town to set the location of the recreation area and to require dedication for public use, not merely use by residents of the subdivision.

### First American Federal Savings and Loan Association v. Royall, 77 N.C. App. 131, 132 (1985)

*Improvements; enforcement*

The developer agreed to sell a lot in an office park to the purchaser. The conveyance was to be through a general warranty deed providing that "title is marketable and free and clear of all encumbrances." The subdivision approval included a requirement for the developer to install a water line in conformance with city standards that would serve the overall office park. After conveyance, the purchaser could not obtain a certificate of occupancy because the required water infrastructure was not complete (withholding the certificate of occupancy was authorized under G.S. 160A-423). The developer's failure to provide the required water infrastructure was an encumbrance on the property and amounted to a violation of the covenant against encumbrances of the contract and warranty deed.

### Stines v. Willyng, Inc., 81 N.C. App. 98, 99 (1986)

*Parks; easement*

Property was sold in reference to a plat that included two areas marked as "Park Property." Lot purchasers attempted to prevent development of the property designated as parks. One park area lacked boundaries and was not clearly defined. The court found that area to be "patently ambiguous" and ruled that purchasers of lots in that area had no rights to prevent development. The second park area, conversely, was clearly defined. Purchasers of lots sold in the area with a clearly defined park acquired rights to reasonable use of the park area. Such rights cannot be extinguished except by agreement.

## Lyerly v. Malpass, 82 N.C. App. 224, 229 (1986)

*Improvements; enforcement*

Purchasers of lots in a subdivision argued that the contracts, plat, restrictive covenants, and oral representations by the developer indicated that the subdivision would include a boat basin and channel at least six feet deep and a private road built to NCDOT standards. In fact, the developer provided a channel that was impassable at low tide as well as a substandard road. The developer claimed that the purchasers' issues were merely maintenance concerns and were the responsibility of the homeowners association. Asserting that a "developer may not by the use of recorded plats and restrictive covenants create the illusion of a high quality subdivision and then shield itself from responsibility by claiming that it did not promise to construct the amenities implied by the restrictive covenants and that these covenants do not give rise to an affirmative obligation," the court allowed the remedy of specific performance (requiring the developer to perform the necessary improvements).

## Franklin Road Properties v. City of Raleigh, 94 N.C. App. 731 (1989)

*Dedication; variance*

The developer sought approval for a three-building office condominium project, including a special allowance for a setback and a variance to allow parking and a driveway within the setback. The city council approved the site plan and special requests. Subsequently, the inspections department refused to issue permits unless the developer agreed to dedicate and pave an area to widen the existing public road. The developer challenged the demand as beyond statutory authority and unconstitutional. The court found that the developer, having accepted the benefits of the variance, was precluded from attacking the validity of the ordinance. The court also, though, remanded the case for the trial court to apply a rational nexus test to the road-widening requirement.

## Rice v. Randolph, 96 N.C. App. 112 (1989)

*Easements; property disputes*

In a lawsuit to clarify the rights of parties in an easement across several properties, all necessary parties (including all affected lot owners) must be party to the action.

## Town of Atlantic Beach v. Tradewinds Campground, Inc., 97 N.C. App. 655, 657 (1990)

*Dedication; withdrawal of*

A developer platted and sold lots in a subdivision. A subsequent owner of a lot sought to withdraw dedication of a portion of a street (unopened for thirty-two years) under G.S. 136-96. The court, though, found that the statute allows withdrawal of a dedication only by "the dedicator or some one or more of those claiming under him." When an individual owner sells lots by reference to a plat showing streets, the owner retains that fee interest in the streets and the lot purchasers have only an easement interest. In contrast, if a corporation is the dedicator and becomes nonexistent, the lot purchasers may have more than an easement interest. In this case, the dedicators were individuals. The individual owners retained fee interest in the streets and the rights to withdraw. Individual lot owners could not withdraw dedication under G.S. 136-96. Note that adjacent owners may have certain rights if a home-owners association is terminated.

### Shear v. Stevens Building Co., 107 N.C. App. 154, 161–62 (1992)
*Implied easement; open space*

In 1957 a developer recorded a plat for a new development including three hundred lots, streets, a lake, and an undeveloped area around the lake. The deeds for the lots referenced the plat but made no reference to an easement for homeowner access to the lake or to a restriction on the use of the lake. Homeowners claimed there were verbal representations by the developer that the lake was for the use of the residents, who used the lake until NO TRESPASSING signs were erected in the 1980s. After receiving notice that the dam was in disrepair, the developer lowered the water level of the lake and submitted a plat to subdivide and develop an additional twenty-four lots on the undeveloped land. The court of appeals found, in this particular case, an easement by implied dedication for the homeowners to access the lake and surrounding undeveloped property. "[A]n easement may be created by dedication. This dedication may be either a formal or informal transfer and may be either implied or express." The court required the developer to return the lake to its prior level and required the homeowners to maintain the lake and surrounding undeveloped land.

### Dellinger v. City of Charlotte, 114 N.C. App. 146 (1994)
*Exaction; ordinance procedures*

The landowner sought site plan approval for an apartment complex. A proposed thorough-fare right-of-way crossed the property, and because the landowner did not offer to dedicate a right-of-way, the city denied the permit. The court held that the city failed to follow its own ordinance procedures. The ordinance required a finding that the required dedication (1) would not result in deprivation of a reasonable use of the original tract and (2) was either reasonably related to traffic from the development or the impact of the dedication was mitigated by provisions of the ordinance. Because planning staff failed to follow ordinance procedures, there was no evidence presented before the planning commission that could be used to affirm the decision.

### State v. Turner, 117 N.C. App. 457, 458 (1994)
*Streets*

A resident was cited for driving while impaired when he drove his vehicle a short distance on a privately maintained paved road within a privately owned mobile home park. The resident argued that the road was not "any highway, any street, or any public vehicular area within this State" as defined in the statute. The court found that the private road did qualify as a "public vehicular area" under the statutory definition at G.S. 20-4.01(32), which includes private streets used for public vehicular traffic.

### Koontz v. Davidson County Board of Adjustment, 130 N.C. App. 479, 483 (1998)
*Vested rights*

The developer entered into a contract to purchase property for development as a mobile home community. Neighbors had proposed an amendment to the county zoning ordinance to exclude mobile homes from the area. The developer, aware of the proposed zoning amendment, moved forward with development actions in advance of the public hearing for the amendment. The developer obtained subdivision plat approval, recorded the plat, secured zoning and building permits, and constructed a street and landscaping. Shortly thereafter, the county commission adopted the zoning ordinance amendment prohibiting mobile homes in the area. The board of adjustment and the superior court found that the developer had vested rights. The N.C. Court of Appeals, however, found that the developer had knowledge of the proposed zoning amendment. (Efforts and expenditures were made by the developer after learning of the proposed amendment). "Despite this knowledge, developers actively sought and heeded advice on how to avoid or prevent the ordinance from halting their proposed development and unilaterally proceeded with their development activities. Therefore, developers did not exercise good faith reliance on a valid permit, as a matter of law, and thus they do not have a vested right to avoid the enacted zoning changes."

## Harry v. Crescent Resources, Inc., 136 N.C. App. 71 (1999)
*Open space; plats*
A developer subdivided a tract into five residential building lots and four remnant lots. Several purchasers bought the residential lots. One purchaser bought the remnant lots and sought to develop them. The residential lot purchasers claimed a negative easement to require the remnant lots to remain as open space because they appear as open space on the plat (which was referenced in deeds). The court found that the plat did not designate the remnant parcels for any specific purpose (such as street, park, beach, or playground). Also, there was no evidence of representations by the developer that the remnant parcels would remain undeveloped. Moreover, the remnant parcels were not necessary for the residential lot owners to access the nearby lake.

## Buckland v. Town of Haw River, 141 N.C. App. 460 (2000)
*Exactions; streets*
Prior property owners filed a plat and dedicated a U-shaped road within a subdivision to NCDOT. The side portions of the U-shape, connecting to the state highway, were constructed and improved. The bottom of the U-shape was not. Subsequently, the plaintiffs acquired property along the unimproved portion of the road and sought to subdivide. The town conditioned subdivision approval on improvements to the road, and the property owners appealed. The court of appeals, interpreting G.S. 160A-372, found no authority to require off-site road improvements but did note the authority to require fees in lieu of construction for off-site road improvements.

## Nazziola v. Landcraft Properties, Inc., 143 N.C. App. 564 (2001)
*Ministerial decisions*
A developer submitted a preliminary subdivision plat, watershed development plan, and erosion and sedimentation plan, all of which were approved by planning staff. Nearby homeowners challenged the decision as arbitrary and capricious. The court applied the whole-record test and found that the city followed appropriate review to find that the project met the applicable standards. Moreover, the court stated that ministerial decisions are governed

by the literal provisions of the ordinance and may be made without a hearing at all. The subdivision statutes contain no requirement for a hearing or notice to nearby property owners. If an applicant meets the ministerial standards, he or she has a right to the permit.

### Singleton v. Sunset Beach and Twin Lakes, Inc., 147 N.C. App. 736 (2001)
*Plats; easements*

In 1965, the original developer recorded a map subdividing lots and roads of a development. The plat showed, among other things, a sixty-foot-wide North Shore Drive. Subsequent conveyances of land referenced the plat. In 1970, after the area was altered by dredge-and-fill work, the original developer re-subdivided that portion of the development. In 1975, the town took action to realign part of North Shore Drive. In 1976, a purchaser–developer recorded one plat (subdividing the purchased property and showing a sixty-foot-wide drive) and the original developer recorded a separate plat (showing a thirty-foot-wide drive). In 1976, the purchaser–developer recorded yet another plat, once again depicting a sixty-foot-wide drive. In 1999, the original developer recorded a withdrawal of street dedication from the original 1965 plat. The original developer and purchaser–developer disputed whether the town had accepted the 1965 dedication and whether the purchaser–developer had an easement pursuant to a purchase in reference to the 1965 plat.

The court reversed summary judgment, finding genuine issues of material fact. In addition, the court found that the town was a proper party for the declaratory action, even if the town did not dispute the plaintiff's (purchaser–developer) allegations and possibly benefited from the plaintiff's declaratory action.

### Hemphill Nolan v. Town of Weddington, 153 N.C. App. 144 (2002)
*Appeals*

The property owner sought, under prior law, a variance from a subdivision ordinance. The variance was denied, but the owner did not appeal the decision within thirty days. The city argued that the appeal was time-barred. The court of appeals, however, agreed with the owner that G.S. 160A-388, and its thirty-day limit for appeals of variance decisions, applied only to zoning ordinances, not subdivision ordinances.

The variance provisions of G.S. 160A-388 have since been amended to clearly apply to any development regulation ordinance, including subdivision.

### Stephens v. Dortch, 148 N.C. App. 509, 513 (2002)
*Dedication; withdrawal of; easement*

In 1930, owners of two lots in a Charlotte subdivision granted a private easement and public dedication for a roadway. The easement benefited certain other lots in the subdivision. In the 1990s, new owners of a lot burdened by the dedication and easement filed a declaration to withdraw the dedication. The new owners' neighbors sought a declaration that the withdrawal was void and that they were entitled to the easement. The court found the easement to be an easement appurtenant (one that runs with the land, not the owner), noting that the grant included "his heirs and assigns." As such, the neighbors had an easement and more rights than the general public. The court, though, upheld the withdrawal of dedication, as the area was never accepted by a government entity for maintenance or used by the general public.

**William Brewster Co., Inc. v. Town of Huntersville, 161 N.C. App. 132 (2003)**
*Quasi-judicial*

The town denied approval of a sketch subdivision plan as not being consistent with the area or the intent of the zoning requirements for open space. The developer challenged the denial, arguing that it was arbitrary and capricious, erroneous, and not supported by competent, material, and substantial evidence. The court, using a whole record review, found that the developer presented competent, material, and substantial evidence that the project met the requirements of the ordinance; thus, the developer established a prima facie case of entitlement to approval. Because the record did not reflect substantial evidence to overcome the developer's prima facie case, the denial of the sketch plat was arbitrary and capricious.

**Knight v. Town of Knightdale, 164 N.C. App. 766, 766 (2004)**
*Standards; site plan*

A property owner sought permits to construct a modular home on a lot in an existing subdivision, but the town denied the request. The ordinance called for the council to review the site plan to ensure adequate measures to address physical impacts, such as stormwater, parking, and noise. The court, however, found that the council based its decision on impacts to neighboring property values, not physical impacts. Under the ordinance, the town had no authority to consider the site plan's effect on surrounding property values, so the court reversed the town decision and required permits to be issued.

**Sanco of Wilmington Service Corporation v. New Hanover County, 166 N.C. App. 471 (2004)**
*Appeal; ministerial decisions*

The developer obtained preliminary plat approval from the technical review committee to develop a condominium complex pursuant to the objective subdivision standards. A group of citizens opposing the project submitted a petition requesting a public hearing so that their concerns could be heard. The governing board held a public hearing and voted to amend the decision of the technical review committee to allow for less density and address additional conditions. The court agreed with the developer's argument that the ordinance allowed only the applicant to appeal plat decisions to the governing board. A local government is obligated to follow the procedures set forth in the subdivision ordinance. And, when subdivision standards are objective, the decision is ministerial, not quasi-judicial. Once an applicant shows that he or she has met those standards, the applicant has a right to plat approval as a matter of law. G.S. 160A-388, amended after this case was decided, now allows a subdivision ordinance to permit aggrieved parties to appeal administrative approvals.

**Beau Rivage Homeowners Association v. New Hanover County, 167 N.C. App. 370 (2004) (unpublished)**
*Appeal; ministerial decisions*

The developer obtained preliminary site plan approval from the technical review committee. A neighboring homeowners association appealed the decision to the governing board. Referencing the decision in *Sanco of Wilmington Service Corporation v. New Hanover County,* (166 N.C. App. 471 (2004), discussed above), the court found that the ordinance did not give neighbors a right to appeal a ministerial subdivision approval.

## Barton v. White, 173 N.C. App. 717 (2005)

*Plats; easement*

Lots and streets of a subdivision were platted in 1965, and lots were subsequently sold. In 2003, lot owners sought to enforce rights to an easement appurtenant over a sixty-foot-wide grass strip of land adjoining their property. After some years of permissive use of the easement for drainage and a driveway, defendants erected a no trespassing sign and removed the culvert. The lot owners did not claim the easement as necessary for access (their lot fronted on a road) but as arising from the sale of the property in reference to the 1965 plat showing the strip of land. The court, inspecting the plat, found an unmarked sixty-foot-wide strip with no indication that it was intended as a road, public or private. As such, there was no indication that the strip of land was intended as a road and so "remains an undivided part of the original, unsubdivided land owned" by the developer.

## Darbo v. Old Keller Farm Property Owners' Association, Inc., 174 N.C. App. 591 (2005)

*Streets; interpretation*

The purchaser bought a lot served by a right-of-way noted on the plat as a 45-foot private drive. The purchaser proposed to subdivide the one lot into five lots. Neighbors challenged the new subdivision for failing to comply with the county subdivision standards, specifically that the 45-foot private drive was insufficient to serve as a standard county road for use by the new lots (under the ordinance, private driveways were to serve three or fewer lots). The trial court interpreted the original plat and text of the subdivision ordinance to allow upgrades to roads as development progresses, and the court of appeals found that the trial court had sufficient evidence to support its finding.

## Durham Land Owners Association v. County of Durham, 177 N.C. App. 629, *writ denied, review denied,* 360 N.C. 532 (2006)

*Impact fees*

The county adopted a school impact fee ordinance. The court ruled that the fee was not authorized by the general statutory authority for fees under G.S. 153A-102. That provision does not allow for broad-based revenue generation for any county service. Rather, it is a limited authority enabling the collection of fees to cover the cost of the duties of county officers and employees, such as processing a permit or reviewing an application. The court ruled that authority for school impact fees is not a "reasonably expedient" authority necessary under the broad construction of G.S. 153A-4 and ordered repayment of the school impact fees.

## Ocean Hill Joint Venture v. Currituck County Board of Commissioners, 178 N.C. App. 182 (2006)

*Streets*

At the time of platting, streets for a development were not clearly marked as public or private. The developer subsequently conveyed the right-of-way to the homeowners association, which repaired, maintained, and insured the roads. The developer and the homeowners association disputed whether the roads had been public or private in nature. The homeowners association requested and the county assented to withdraw the developer's dedication of the roads under G.S. 153A-241. The county board of commissioners found that closing the roads would not be contrary to the public interest and would not deprive property owners of reasonable ingress and egress. The roads were closed to the general public. The developer appealed the decision, and the jury found that closing the road would *not* be in the public interest.

### Kraft v. Town of Mt. Olive, 183 N.C. App. 415 (2007)
*Dedication; implied acceptance*

A property owner claimed ownership of an alley running alongside his property. The town claimed the property was dedicated to the public by a prior owner. Starting in the 1920s, parcels were sold with reference to the alley, including property that would become the property owner's (plaintiff's) parcel. After the town denied the owner's request to build a courtyard in the alley, the owner filed an action to quiet title to his property (i.e., free it of any claims against it). The court noted that a dedication may be express or implied. The intention to dedicate is the key question, and in this case, the court found an intent to dedicate. The owner argued that the town never accepted the dedication, but the court found that the town did so implicitly. Under the Quiet Title Act, the court found that the town was in open and actual possession of the road by its paving of the alley, maintenance of utilities under the alley, and provision of municipal services to the alley.

### Marriott v. Chatham County, 187 N.C. App. 491 (2007)
*Standing; environmental review*

A developer proposed development of a large tract. The ordinance allowed that the planning board *may* require a subdivider to submit an environmental impact assessment (EIA) pursuant to G.S. 113A. Neighbors opposing the development requested that an EIA be required, but the planning board found an EIA to be unnecessary. Neighbors then sued to make the county, as required by statute, adopt minimum criteria for when an EIA is necessary. The court acknowledged that if a county adopts an EIA ordinance it must include minimum criteria for when an EIA is required but, citing separation of powers, refused to require the county to do so. Because the remedy the neighbors sought (requiring minimum criteria) was unavailable or inappropriate, the neighbors lacked standing to bring the claim. The only remedy, the court held, was to strike the EIA ordinance, but that is not what the neighbors sought.

### Blue Ridge Co., L.L.C. v. Town of Pineville, 188 N.C. App. 466 (2008)
*Standards; schools; roads*

Although the landowner met the objective technical and engineering standards, the town denied the subdivision request based on subjective standards for traffic and school crowding. The subjective standard called for consistency with adopted plans and policies and conformity with the existing community. Regarding school capacity, the court did not find a clearly adopted school crowding policy, nor did the ordinance require a school impact study. So, the court found that denial based on school impact was not supported by the evidence. Regarding the issue of traffic, an engineer provided expert testimony concerning the modesty of traffic impacts, and the opponents rebutted with general perceptions that were not enough to overcome that testimony. Moreover, the court found the conformity standard for the "most advantageous development" to be vague. Finally, the court considered consistency with the adopted land use plan and found that the town lacked sufficient evidence to deny the subdivision on those grounds. The court listed the goals for residential development and substantively matched aspects of the landowner's proposal.

### Town of Pinebluff v. Marts, 195 N.C. App. 659 (2009)
*Enforcement; performance guarantee*

The town's unified development ordinance (UDO) required developers to provide mini-parks and open space for recreational use of their residents. In its application, the developer agreed to install a mini-park and provided draft documents to establish a homeowners association and fees for the maintenance of common areas. The conditional use permit was approved subject to the mini-park being developed before final plat approval of phase three of the development. After completing phase two, the developer sought final plat approval for phase three, and the town approved the plat and accepted an irrevocable letter of credit for $10,000 to ensure completion of the mini-park. A year later, the original developer sold the remainder of the development, informed the town that he did not intend to construct the mini-park, and proposed to place a no trespassing sign on the reserved open space. The town sued the developer, seeking an injunction to comply with the UDO (i.e., build the mini-park). The developer argued that the ordinance was invalid, but the court cited the well-established principle that a defendant who failed to directly challenge the validity of the ordinance at the time of application or approval may not then collaterally attack the validity of the ordinance as a defense to enforcement of it. Although the town allowed the performance guarantee (letter of credit) to expire, that did not preclude other enforcement actions.

The court considered without deciding whether a trial court is required to "balance the equities" before issuing an injunction for ordinance enforcement. Other jurisdictions are split.

### Tonter Investments, Inc. v. Pasquotank County, 199 N.C. App. 579 (2009)
*Exempt subdivisions; relation to zoning*

The landowner attempted to complete an exempt subdivision under the ten-acre exemption. Recent amendments by the county to its zoning ordinance prohibited residential development for a portion of the property and for the remainder of the property required frontage on a public road and public water supply within one thousand feet. The landowner challenged the zoning amendments as an attempt to inappropriately regulate subdivision. The court found that the zoning amendments were within the zoning powers granted by the General Statutes and that the statutory exemptions from subdivision regulation do not provide exemptions from all development regulation. Subsequent adoption of G.S. 153A-340(j) limits the ability of a county to regulate residential structures on lots greater than ten acres.

### Union Land Owners Association v. County of Union, 201 N.C. App. 374, 381 (2009)
*Fees; schools; adequate public facilities*

The county adopted an adequate public facilities ordinance (APFO) to review school capacity for proposed developments. If school capacity was insufficient, the development would be denied or delayed unless the applicant offset the impact through construction or fees in lieu of construction of school facilities. The court did not find authority for the voluntary mitigation payment under general police power, zoning authority, or subdivision authority. A local government "may not use the APFO to obtain indirectly the payment of what amounts to an impact fee given that defendant lacks the authority to impose school impact fees directly."

### Coventry Woods Neighborhood Association, Inc. v. City of Charlotte, 202 N.C. App. 247 (2010)

*Notice; statute of limitations*

Neighbors unsuccessfully challenged a rezoning. Subsequently, the neighbors challenged the subdivision plat approval based on invalid subdivision ordinance provisions (namely, due process violations for failure to provide notice and an opportunity to be heard). The city argued that the claims were time-barred and lacked merit. As to the statute of limitations, the court found that the claims were not time-barred; under G.S. 1-52(5), challenges concerning validity of a subdivision ordinance are subject to the general three-year limit, not the shorter provisions for zoning ordinances. As to the due process claims, the neighbors failed to show a constitutionally protected property interest upon which to base a constitutional claim.

### Amward Homes, Inc. v. Town of Cary, 206 N.C. App. 38 (2010)

*Impact fees*

The town, which adopted an adequate public school facility ordinance, had the custom and practice of developers paying school fees in order to address any lack of school capacity for new residential developments. The court, citing the recent decision in *Union Land Owners Association v. County of Union* (201 N.C. App. 374 (2009), discussed above), again found that the county lacked authority to charge a school impact fee, either through ordinance, custom, or voluntary mitigation. The court also found that the sixty-day statute of limitations applicable to zoning appeals did not apply to this challenge to a subdivision ordinance.

### ExperienceOne Homes, L.L.C. v. Town of Morrisville, 727 S.E.2d 26 (N.C. Ct. App.) (unpublished) *review denied*, 366 N.C. 247 (2012)

*Plat amendment; relation to zoning*

A developer proposed to develop two hundred townhomes. The property was rezoned to residential multi-family conditional use. Conditions included, among other things, that the development would progress in line with the submitted site plan and subdivision plat. After an economic downturn, the developer wanted to amend the conditions to build single-family homes instead of townhomes. Single-family homes required flexible design option approval to alter lot size, setback, and other dimensions. The developer sought administrative approval of the changes, but the town required governing board approval. The governing board denied the requested change, and the developer challenged the necessity and effect of the governing board review. The court found that the proposed changes were not a "minor amendment" and that the town followed its ordinance procedures.

**Synovus Bank v. County of Henderson, 729 S.E.2d 731 (N.C. Ct. App.) (unpublished), *review withdrawn*, 366 N.C. 411 (2012)**

*Performance guarantee*

The developer provided a subdivision improvement guarantee to complete improvements and obtain a performance bond to insure completion. After the developer fell into financial trouble, the county and the surety disputed obligations under the performance bond. The court ruled that the Permit Extension Act of 2009 did not apply to the surety's obligations. The court also ruled that the surety owed the full amount under the bond because the contract identified it as a "penal sum." The court enforced the plain language of the performance bond.

**Waterway Drive Property Owners' Association, Inc. v. Town of Cedar Point, 737 S.E.2d 126 (N.C. Ct. App. 2012)**

*Dedication; withdrawal of*

In 1936, a property owner recorded a subdivision plat that included a fifty-foot right-of-way for Front Street, and it was used for vehicular traffic from the 1950s to the 1970s. After that, neighboring property owners continued to use the street as an access road. Publicly franchised water and cable utilities were installed along the street. The town purported to accept the street in 1989. Meanwhile, the neighboring property owners paved, renamed, and marked the street as private. The court found no acceptance of the dedication, neither express nor implied, so the proper withdrawal of dedication was effective.

**Cox v. Town of Oriental, 759 S.E.2d 388, 390, 391 (N.C. Ct. App. 2014)**

*Road closure; standing*

The town decided to close permanently a public right-of-way and to grant that property to the surrounding landowner in exchange for nearby property. A resident owner of property located three blocks from the vacated right-of-way challenged the closure and exchange (seeking injunctive and declaratory relief for alleged open meeting and public records violations). The town argued that, among other things, the citizen lacked standing for the challenge. G.S. 160A-299(b) provides that "[a]ny person aggrieved by the closing of any street or alley . . . may appeal the . . . order to the General Court of Justice within 30 days after its adoption." The term "person aggrieved" is undefined in the statute, so the court relied on prior judicial definitions of "aggrieved party" from the zoning context: "one who can either show an interest in the property affected, or if the party is a nearby property owner, some special damage, distinct from the rest of the community, amounting to a reduction in the value of his property." The court was unpersuaded by the citizen's argument that he had standing as a taxpaying resident of the town and as a beneficiary of rights in the public rights-of-way from when the town was laid out in 1900. A resident-owned property three blocks away lacks standing to bring action challenging a town's order to close a street.

**Patmore v. Town of Chapel Hill, No. COA13-1049, 2014 WL 1365987 (N.C. Ct. App. April 1, 2014)**

*Zoning enforcement; due process*

The town adopted a zoning ordinance that included a provision to restrict the number of cars that may be parked on a residential lot. Citations for rental properties were issued to landlords rather than tenants. Plaintiff landlords claimed that citing the landlord for a tenant's action violates the landlord's due process rights, but the court of appeals found no merit in the due process claim. The court upheld that zoning violations may be filed against the landlord of rental property.

The landlords claimed that restricting parking is beyond the town's statutory authority, pointing to G.S. 160A-301 concerning "Streets, Traffic and Parking." The court of appeals found that G.S. 160A-301 concerned parking in public vehicular areas, while the zoning ordinance (authorized under the zoning statutes) concerned the number of cars that may be parked on a private lot. The interpretive doctrine of *expressio unius est exclusio alterius* did not apply.

The landlords also argued that under *Lanvale Properties, L.L.C. v. County of Cabarrus* (366 N.C. 142 (2012), discussed above), parking regulation is not authorized under the general zoning power. The court of appeals, though, found that in the *Lanvale* decision the state supreme court determined that the adequate public facilities ordinance at issue was not a zoning regulation; the supreme court did not address local government authority to enact a bona fide zoning ordinance. The court of appeals also found that parking regulation is authorized under the general zoning power.

### Town of Black Mountain v. Lexon Insurance Co., 768 S.E.2d 302 (N.C. Ct. App. 2014), *review denied*, No. 28P15, 2015 WL 1809356 (N.C. Apr. 9, 2015)
*Performance guarantee; standing; statute of limitations*

The county required a performance bond from the developer prior to beginning construction. The developer then obtained four subdivision performance bonds from the insurance company, with the county as the oblige (beneficiary if the bonds were called in). The bonds required that the oblige issue a resolution of developer default before the insurer would pay. Over the course of development, the property was annexed into the town. After the developer companies failed, the county sought the insurer's consent for the county to assign the bonds to the town. The insurer refused, but the county assigned the bonds to the town anyway. The town adopted a resolution of developer default. The insurer refused payment and, at trial, challenged the town's standing and argued that the claims were barred by the statute of limitations.

On standing, the insurer argued that when the town annexed the property, the bonds were extinguished because the county (the contractual obligee) no longer had jurisdiction. The court agreed that the county no longer had standing to enforce its subdivision ordinance or performance bond but also found nothing in the law or the bond agreements to prevent the county from assigning those bond agreement rights to the town. Indeed, the court "believe[s] public policy favors assignability under these facts." If the town could not call in the bond, the insurer "would in effect receive a windfall."

On the statute of limitations, G.S. 1-52(1) sets a three-year limit on claims arising out of contracts. The town asserted the doctrine of *nullum tempus occurrit regi*, which allows governmental bodies to be exempt from statutes of limitation for civil lawsuits. North Carolina case law states that, if the state is not expressly included in the statute of limitation, then the doctrine of *nullum tempus* applies to governmental functions (but not proprietary functions). Citing prior case law, the court found subdivision control—including enforcement of a performance bond—to be a governmental function because it is "a duty owed to the general public, not a specific individual."

### Town of Matthews v. Wright, No. COA14-943 (N.C. Ct. App. April 21, 2015)

*Eminent domain; public use*

The Wrights lived along Home Place, a street with five homes that dead-ends near the Wright home. The street was originally included in the 1984 warranty deed as a thirty-foot street easement. In 1985 the town passed a resolution declaring Home Place a public street. In 1991 the town paved the street. By 2004 a dispute had arisen between the town and the Wrights about whether the street was public or private. Through several rounds of appeals, the court of appeals remanded the case for a determination as to whether Home Place was impliedly dedicated. The trial court determined that the deeds of conveyance did not imply intent to offer a dedication and that there was no implied dedication. The town commenced condemnation of the portion of the street in front of the Wright property. Although taking property for streets is typically a sufficient public use or benefit to justify condemnation, the trial court in this case found no plans for construction, improvement, or alteration to the street.

North Carolina courts review condemnation actions for both *public use* and *public benefit*. In this case, the court found no public benefit. The town argued that it was "opening" the street and that was the public benefit. The court, though, found that the street was not closed in any way to be opened. (It would have been closed, the court says, if the Wrights erected a barricade or if the entire street other than the Wright portion was public.) Moreover, the town was trying merely to open the Wrights' portion of the street; the town was not trying to open other portions of the street for public benefit. Thus any presumed public benefit would be limited to that short section.

The court, as part of its discussion highlights a crucial lesson of public records law: All records created in the course of conducting public business are public records, even a record created on a private machine or email account. The court quoted from the mayor's own email in which he "indicated that he was 'sending this from [his] personal email and not [his] town email in order to protect the privacy of [the] communication.'" Clearly that attempt at privacy did not work.

### China Grove 152, L.L.C. v. Town of China Grove, No. COA14-972, 2015 WL 4082073 (N.C. Ct. App. July 7, 2015)

*Adequate public facilities ordinance; impact fees*

The town of China Grove enacted an adequate public facilities ordinance (APFO) that required payment of fees to cover costs associated with increased needs for public services, including police and fire protection and park space. In 2008 the developer paid over $54,000 in fees pursuant to the fee requirement of the APFO.

In 2012 the supreme court issued the decision in Lanvale Properties, L.L.C. v. County of Cabarrus, 366 N.C. 142, (2012), discussed above), striking down an APFO ordinance that included an unauthorized school fee. Subsequently the developer in China Grove requested reimbursement of the $54,000 fee plus interest. The town sent a check for $54,000 (with no interest) accompanied by a letter stating that acceptance by the developer would be mutual release of all obligations. The developer sought declaratory judgment that the fee was illegal and that the developer was owed interest.

The court of appeals found that the fee was not authorized under N.C. law, and thus illegal. The town argued that its APFO was a subdivision control ordinance authorized under G.S. 160A-372. The court recited a portion of Section 372(c) emphasizing the permissive nature of the language: "[A] subdivision control ordinance 'may provide that a developer may provide funds to the city whereby the city may acquire recreational land' for parks." The court found that this language "does not authorize municipalities to charge fees as a condition precedent to subdivision approval." The court of appeals did not distinguish the Lanvale decision (concerning school fees) from the town's fees (concerning police, fire, and parks).

Notably, the court interprets a narrow provision of Section 372(c). It emphasizes the permissive mays as relegating this authority to a mere option for the developer rather than an ordinance requirement that a municipality may impose. It is challenging to reconcile that interpretation with the statutory sentences that follow. Despite the permissive language that "the city may [use funds to] acquire recreational land . . . ," the next sentence specifies how the funds "shall be used." And the following sentence states the required formula "to determine the amount of funds that are to be provided." This restrictive language contrasts with the permissive mays that precede it and raises more interpretative debate than is reflected in the decision.

The court does not address the authority in Section 372(a). Subsection (a), in contrast to subsection (c), states that "[a] subdivision control ordinance may provide . . . for the dedication or reservation of recreation areas serving residents of the immediate neighborhood within the subdivision or, alternatively, for provision of funds to be used to acquire recreation areas serving residents of the development or subdivision or more than one subdivision or development within the immediate area." Under the plain language of this authority in subsection (a), the local government can require dedication of recreation areas within the subdivision or, in lieu of such dedication, may require funds to acquire recreation areas.

Under G.S. 160A-363, a municipality must repay a tax or fee plus 6 percent interest if that tax or fee is found to have been illegally exacted. Having found that the town's APFO was invalid as a matter of law, the court of appeals ruled that the town owed interest on the reimbursed fee.

The town argued that, based on the letter sent to the developer with the check and the developer cashing the check, there was accord and satisfaction of any obligation for interest. The court found that there was a contract (the letter initialed by the developer and cashing of the check), but the court read the language of the contract narrowly to include release "of all obligations and liabilities under the [APFO]," but not including any obligations of interest payment under the statutes.

## Select Federal Cases on Performance Guarantees

### County of Brunswick v. Lexon Insurance Co., 425 F. App'x 190 (4th Cir. 2011) (unpublished)

*Performance guarantee*

The developer obtained approval for a residential subdivision and executed an improvement guarantee agreement with related performance bonds. After work stalled, a lender foreclosed on the property and the county issued a notice of default to the developer and called in the performance bonds. The surety challenged the obligation to pay the bonds (for procedure and the Permit Extension Act of 2009). The court found that the contractual terms of the bond are controlling. The court also found that the Permit Extension Act did not modify the bond company's obligations to pay the bond. The court required payment of the bonds. The court agreed, though, that the surety did not also owe prejudgment interest to the county.

### Rutherford County v. Bond Safeguard Ins. Co., No. 1:09CV292, 2011 WL 809821 (W.D.N.C. Mar. 2, 2011)

*Performance guarantee*

In conjunction with a large residential subdivision development, the developer provided written performance guarantee agreements and obtained seven surety performance bonds worth approximately $26 million. After the developer failed to complete the agreed to improvements, the county sought to have the bond company either complete the bonded improvements or pay the principal amount of the bonds. The property owners association sought to intervene to represent the interests of the 459 lot owners. The court initially allowed the association to intervene as having interests that were adverse to those of the county based on the association's intent to assert a claim of declaratory relief to ensure that any funds secured from the bonds would be used for infrastructure within the subdivision. However, when the association failed to make that claim, the court granted the defendant's motion to dismiss the association. The court found that the association lacked adversity in interest, lacked standing to sue on behalf of its members, lacked a claim of breach of contract as a third-party beneficiary, and lacked a proper claim of unfair trade practices.

### *In re* Versant Properties, L.L.C., No. 1:10CV98, 2011 WL 1131057 (W.D.N.C. Mar. 25, 2011)

*Performance guarantee*

The developer secured a letter of credit to guarantee completion of subdivision infrastructure. Some infrastructure had been completed before the developer ran into financial troubles. After the town called in the letter of credit, the developer sought to have some of the funds be used to pay contractors for the work that had been completed. The language of the ordinance, though, called for funds "needed to complete the improvements." Moreover, the statutory authority for performance guarantees grants power for *performance* bonds, not *payment* bonds.

**County of Brunswick v. Bond Safeguard Ins. Co., No. 7:12-CV-123-D, 2013 WL 663720 (E.D.N.C. Feb. 22, 2013)**

*Performance guarantee*

Brunswick County sought to recover nearly $12 million from the bond company ensuring several performance bonds for three separate subdivisions. The court found that the developers of the subdivisions were not necessary and indispensable parties.

**Developers Surety and Indemnity Co. v. City of Durham, No. 1:11CV515, 2014 WL 4677181 (M.D.N.C. Sept. 18, 2014)**

*Performance guarantee*

Pursuant to applicable subdivision approvals, the developers were obligated to construct sidewalks and streets and implement stormwater facilities. Pursuant to the ordinance, the developers contracted for three types of surety bonds to ensure completion of the required infrastructure: (1) bonds for street and sidewalk construction, (2) bonds for stormwater facility construction (conversion from sediment and erosion control to permanent facilities), and (3) bonds for stormwater maintenance. The developers failed to complete the required improvements. The city and surety disagreed about the obligation to pay.

In its motion for summary judgment, the city argued that the surety companies had the same obligations as the developer and must pay for all necessary construction for the facilities to meet city standards for acceptance. The surety companies, however, argued that the bonds cover only minimal completion of facilities already constructed. The court, finding that the surety companies had only the obligations specified in the bond language, rejected the city's argument and ruled that the plain reading of the bond language covers only the completion of unfinished sidewalks and the final inch of asphalt for roads (not full construction of un-improved roads). As to the questions of timing for completion and reductions to bonds, the court found that genuine issues of material fact remained, precluding summary judgment.

# Index

Page numbers in *italics* indicate illustrative materials.

www.ingramcontent.com/pod-product-compliance
Lightning Source LLC
Chambersburg PA
CBHW080146170226
39823CB00020B/364